Lotus® 1-2-3®, Release 5 Projects for Windows®

Gary R. Brent
Scottsdale Community College

William J. Belisle

 The Benjamin/Cummings Publishing Company, Inc.
Menlo Park, California • Reading, Massachusetts
New York • Don Mills, Ontario • Harlow, U.K. • Amsterdam
Bonn • Paris • Milan • Madrid • Sydney • Singapore • Tokyo
Seoul • Taipei • Mexico City • San Juan, Puerto Rico

Senior Editor: *Maureen A. Allaire*
Project Editor: *Nancy E. Davis, Kathy G. Yankton*
Assistant Editor: *Heide Chavez*
Executive Editor: *Michael Payne*
Project Manager: *Adam Ray*
Associate Production Editor: *Jennifer Englander*
Marketing Manager: *Melissa Baumwald*
Custom Publishing Operations Specialist: *Michael Smith*
Senior Manufacturing Coordinator: *Janet Weaver*
Composition and Film Manager: *Vivian McDougal*
Copy Editor: *Barbara Conway*
Technical Editor: *Lynda Fox Fields*
Proofreader: *Holly McLean Aldis, Roseann Viano*
Indexer: *Mark Kmetzko*

ISBN 0-8053-1634-5   bundled version
ISBN 0-8053-1630-2   stand alone version

1 2 3 4 5 6 7 8 9 10—DOW—00 99 98 97 96

Ordering from the SELECT System

For more information on ordering and pricing policies for the SELECT System of microcomputer applications texts and their supplements, please contact your Addison-Wesley • Benjamin/Cummings sales representative or call our SELECT Hotline at 800/854-2595.

The Benjamin/Cummings Publishing Company, Inc.
2725 Sand Hill Road
Menlo Park, CA 94025
http://www.aw.com/bc/is
bc.is@aw.com

Getting Started

Welcome to the *SELECT Lab Series*. We invite you to explore how you can take advantage of the newest Windows 95 features of the most popular software applications using this up-to-date learning package.

Greater access to ideas and information is changing the way people work. With Windows 95 applications you have greater integration capabilities and access to Internet resources than ever before. The *SELECT Lab Series* helps you take advantage of these valuable resources with special assignments devoted to the Internet and additional connectivity resources which can be accessed through our web site, **http://www.aw.com/bc/is.**

The key to using software is making the software work for you. The *SELECT Lab Series* will help you learn to use software as a productivity tool by guiding you step-by-step through case-based projects similar to those you will encounter at school, work, or home. When you are finished with this learning package, you will be fully prepared to use the resources this software offers. Your success is our success.

A GUIDED TOUR

To facilitate the learning process, we have developed a consistent organizational structure for each module in the *SELECT Lab Series*.

You begin using the software almost immediately. A brief **Overview** introduces the software package and the basic application functions. **Getting Help** covers the on-line Help feature in each package. **A Note to the Student** explains any special conventions or system configurations observed in a particular module.

Each module contains six to eight **Projects,** an **Operations Reference** of all the operations covered in each module, an extensive **Glossary** of **key terms,** and an **Index.**

The following figures introduce the elements you will encounter as you use each SELECT module.

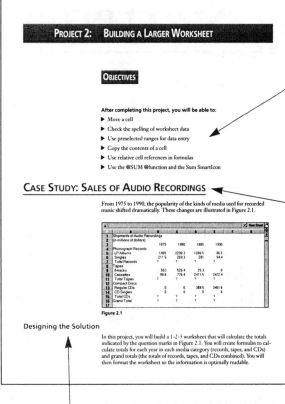

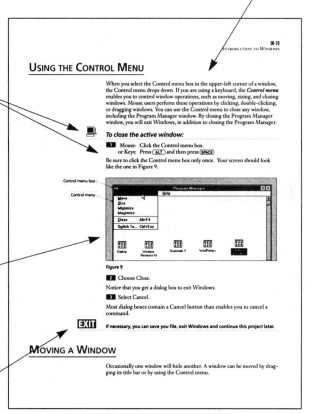

Each project begins with **Learning Objectives** that describe the skills and commands you will master.

Projects revolve around **Case Studies**, which provide real-world scenarios so you can learn an application in a broader context.

Each topic begins with a brief explanation of concepts you will learn and the operations you will perform.

Designing the Solution introduces you to important problem-solving techniques. You will see how to analyze the case study and design a solution before you sit down at the computer.

The **computer icon** provides a cue that you should begin working at the computer, and **Numbered steps** guide you step-by-step through each project, providing detailed instructions on how to perform operations.

Visual cues such as **screen shots** provide examples of what you will see on your own computer screen, reinforce key concepts, and help you check your work.

Exit points identify good places in each project to take a break.

Key Terms are boldfaced and italicized and appear throughout each project.

Margin figures show on-screen tools that are often convenient alternatives to menu commands presented in the numbered steps.

Tips, Reminders, Cautions, and **Quick Fixes** appear throughout each project to highlight important, helpful, or pertinent information about each application.

WRD-12
Word for Windows

Opening a New Document

Word for Windows normally opens with a blank window and is ready to create a new document. If someone was using the computer before you, however, the window may already contain text. In that case, you will need to open a blank window for your new document. (If Word for Windows is not running already, start it by double-clicking the Word for Windows icon on the Windows desktop.)

To open a blank window for a new document:

1 Select New on the File menu or press ALT + F7 and then type n
The New dialog box appears, as shown in Figure 1.1. This dialog box allows you to select from a variety of *templates* and *wizards*. **Templates** are preformatted skeleton documents ranging from memos to newsletters. **Wizards** ask a series of questions about a document format and then use that information to build a document for you to use. Right now, you need the default general-purpose template named Normal.

Figure 1.1

2 If Normal does not appear in the Template box, type Normal

3 Select OK.

Tip You can open a new document with a click of the mouse. Use the New document button on the standard toolbar to open a Normal document with a single click.

The document area of the screen will be blank except for the blinking vertical *insertion point* (I), *the end-of-document mark* (___), and possibly a *paragraph mark* (¶). The **insertion point** marks the position where text will be inserted or deleted when you type at the keyboard. The **end-of-document mark** shows where the document ends; you cannot insert characters after the end-of-document mark. A **paragraph mark** indicates the end of a paragraph and forces the beginning of a new line. The paragraph mark may not show on your screen. If not, you will learn shortly how to make it visible.

Study Questions (Multiple Choice, Short Answer, and For Discussion) may be used as self-tests or homework assignments.

Short Answer
1. What are the two main services offered by My Computer?
2. What objects are considered physical locations in My Computer?
3. Why is a directory structure sometimes called a tree?
4. How do you run a program from My Computer?
5. How do you create a new folder?
6. Will copying a file result in the original being changed in any way?
7. Why should you drag and drop objects using mouse button 2?
8. Will renaming a file cause a second copy of that file to be generated?

For Discussion
1. Why was the ability to create folders for file management on the PC. so important?
2. My Computer will open a new window every time the user double-clicks on a drive or folder of How could this create a problem?
3. Why should you expect there to be some sort of access restrictions on network drives?

Review Exercises

Examining the File System
Use My Computer to examine the root folders of your computer's local hard drive(s). If the computer part of a network, take a look at the network drives as well. Get some practice resizing, moving, and cl the many windows that will be created during this exercise. Draw a tree that shows how information is organized on your system and network—make note of the major folders in the root directories, and lo for other folders within these. You don't have to list the thousands of individual files!

Launching Programs from My Computer
Use My Computer to explore your student data diskette. Without using the Find command, look for i program file AirMail and use My Computer to run the program. After closing AirMail, look on your l hard drive(s) for a folder called Program Files. This is a standard directory on Windows 95 systems, though it may not be present, or may have a different name, on your system. Use My Computer to op the Program Files folder, and examine what's inside. There are probably more folders within Program Files; if an Accessories folder is present, open it and then use My Computer to launch MS Paint or W. Pad.

Assignments

Drag-and-Drop Manipulation of Files and Folders
In this assignment, you will use My Computer to "juggle" files and folders. This will provide extensive practice with window management and using the mouse for drag-and-drop operations.

Open the Temp folder on your student data diskette. Create a folder within it called Reports. Open the Reports folder and create three new text documents called Rain Forest, Desert, and Coral Reef. Using drag-and-drop, *move* the Reports folder (which will include the files you just created) to the Text folder of the student data diskette. Select the two files Rain Forest and Coral Reef and, again using drag-and-drop, *copy* them to the Work subdirectory. Rename the file Desert to Tundra. Finally, delete the Reports folder (which will also delete the files it contains).

Review Exercises present hands-on tasks to help you build on skills acquired in the projects.

Assignments require critical thinking and encourage synthesis and integration of project skills.

Each project ends with **The Next Step** which discusses the concepts from the project and proposes other uses and applications for the skills you have learned, a **Summary,** and a list of **Key Terms and Operations.**

The Next Step

Access has many functions that are part of the You've already seen the Now() function in sev If you're interested in extending your knowle good place to start is the manual.
There are several other Report Wizards we reports have no Detail band. Tabular reports forms. The AutoReport Wizard will attempt that makes the most sense—at least, to the W Word Mail Merge, exports data in a format th Merge feature can read. This is handy for pro Experiment with fonts and print styles, an

SUMMARY AND EXERCISES

Summary
- Access includes ReportWizards for single-column, grouped, and tabular formats, as well as mailing labels. Wizards are also included that generate automatic reports and export data to Microsoft Word's Mail Merge format
- To build a report with fields from two or more tables, you can query by example to create a view first, and then create the report based on that view.
- Grouping lets you create reports with records collated according to the values in one or more fields.
- Grouping also lets you create subtotals for groups as well as a grand total for the report.
- You can display today's date with the Now() function.
- You can change the format in which the date is printed.
- The mailing label ReportWizard handles standard Avery label layouts.
- To insert text characters in a mailing label, you must use the text buttons provided by the ReportWizards.
- The UCase() function is helpful when you want to make sure report output is entirely upper case.

Key Terms and Operations

Key Terms	
group	report footer
group footer	report header
group header	UCase()
inner join	**Operations**
Now()	Create a new report
outer join	Page Preview
page footer	Report Design
page header	Sample Preview

FOLLOWING THE NUMBERED STEPS

To make the application modules easy to use in a lab setting, we have standardized the presentation of hands-on computer instructions as much as possible. The numbered step sections provide detailed, step-by-step instructions to guide you through the practical application of the conceptual material presented. Both keystroke and mouse instructions are used according to which one is more appropriate to complete a task. The instructions in the module assume that you know how to operate the keyboard, monitor, and printer.

> *Tip* When you are using a mouse, unless indicated otherwise, you should assume that you are clicking the left button on the mouse. Several modules provide instructions for both mouse and keyboard users. When separate mouse and keyboard steps are given, be sure to follow one method or the other, but not both.

Each topic begins with a brief explanation of concepts. A computer icon or the ▶ symbol and a description of the task you will perform appear each time you are to begin working on the computer.

To enter the address:

1 Type `123 Elm Street` and press `ENTER`

Notice that the keys you are to press and the text you are to type stand out. The text you will type appears in a special typeface to distinguish it from regular text. The key that you are to press mimics the labels of the keys on your keyboard.

When you are to press two keys or a key and a character simultaneously, the steps show the keys connected either with a plus sign or a bar.

$$\boxed{\text{SHFT}} + \boxed{\text{TAB}}$$
$$\boxed{\text{CTRL}} + \text{C}$$

When you are to press keys sequentially, the keys are not connected and a space separates them.

$$\boxed{\text{CTRL}} \; \boxed{\text{PGDN}}$$
$$\boxed{\text{HOME}} \; \boxed{\text{HOME}} \; \boxed{\uparrow}$$

Be sure to press each key firmly, but quickly, one after the other. Keys begin repeating if you hold them down too long.

In some instances margin figures of single icons or buttons will appear next to the numbered steps. Margin figures provide visual cues to important tools that you can select as an alternative to the menu command in the numbered step.

For typographical conventions and other information unique to the application, please see *A Note to the Student* in the Overview of each module.

THE *SELECT* LAB SERIES—A CONNECTED LEARNING RESOURCE

The *SELECT Lab Series* is a complete learning resource for success in the Information Age. Our application modules are designed to help you learn fast and effectively. Based around projects that reflect your world, each module helps you master key concepts and problem-solving techniques for using the software application you are learning. Through our web site you can access dynamic and current information resources that will help you get up to speed on the Information Highway and keep up with the ever changing world of technology.

Explore our web site **http://www.aw.com/bc/is** to discover:

- **B/C Link Online:** Our on-line newsletter which features the latest news and information on current computer technology and applications.

- **Student Opportunities and Activities:** Benjamin/Cummings' web site connects you to important job opportunities and internships.

- **What's New:** Access the latest news and information topics.

- **Links:** We provide relevant links to other interesting resources and educational sites.

THE TECHSUITE

This module may be part of our new custom bundled system—the **Benjamin/Cummings TechSuite.** Your instructor can choose any combination of concepts texts, applications modules, and software to meet the exact needs of your course. The TechSuite meets your needs by offering you one convenient package at a discount price.

SUPPLEMENTS

Each module has a corresponding Instructor's Manual with a Test Bank and Transparency Masters. For each project in the student text, the Instructor's Manual includes Expanded Student Objectives, Answers to Study Questions, and Additional Assessment Techniques. The Test Bank contains two separate tests (with answers) consisting of multiple choice, true/false, and fill-in questions that are referenced to pages in the student's text. Transparency Masters illustrate 25 to 30 key concepts and screen captures from the text.

The Instructor's Data Disk contains student data files, answers to selected Review Exercises, answers to selected Assignments, and the test files from the Instructor's Manual in ASCII format.

ACKNOWLEDGMENTS

The Benjamin/Cummings Publishing Company would like to thank the following reviewers for their valuable contributions to the *SELECT Lab Series*.

Joseph Aieta
Babson College

Tom Ashby
Oklahoma CC

Bob Barber
Lane CC

Robert Caruso
Santa Rosa Junior College

Robert Chi
California State
Long Beach

Jill Davis
State University of New
York at Stony Brook

Fredia Dillard
Samford University

Peter Drexel
Plymouth State College

Ralph Duffy
North Seattle CC

David Egle
University of Texas,
Pan American

Jonathan Frank
Suffolk University

Patrick Gilbert
University of Hawaii

Maureen Greenbaum
Union County College

Sally Ann Hanson
Mercer County CC

Sunil Hazari
East Carolina University

Bruce Herniter
University of Hartford

Lisa Jackson
Henderson CC

Cynthia Kachik
Santa Fe CC

Bennett Kramer
Massasoit CC

Charles Lake
Faulkner State
Junior College

Ron Leake
Johnson County CC

Randy Marak
Hill College

Charles Mattox, Jr.
St. Mary's University

Jim McCullough
Porter and Chester
Institute

Gail Miles
Lenoir-Rhyne College

Steve Moore
University of
South Florida

Anthony Nowakowski
Buffalo State College

Gloria Oman
Portland State University

John Passafiume
Clemson University

Leonard Presby
William Paterson
College

Louis Pryor
Garland County CC

Michael Reilly
University of Denver

Dick Ricketts
Lane CC

Dennis Santomauro
Kean College of
New Jersey

Pamela Schmidt
Oakton CC

Gary Schubert
Alderson-Broaddus College

T. Michael Smith
Austin CC

Cynthia Thompson
Carl Sandburg College

Marion Tucker
Northern Oklahoma
College

JoAnn Weatherwax
Saddleback College

David Whitney
San Francisco State
University

James Wood
Tri-County
Technical College

Minnie Yen
University of Alaska,
Anchorage

Allen Zilbert
Long Island University

To April, Alice, and my parents.

—GRB

To Liz, B.J., Eric, and my parents.

—WJB

Contents

Overview

Objectives

After completing this overview, you should be able to:

▶ Start Lotus 1-2-3

▶ Identify the major components of the application and worksheet windows

▶ Navigate the worksheet

▶ Identify common pointer shapes

▶ Change the current cell

▶ Select cells and ranges

▶ Use menus and dialog boxes

▶ Use SmartIcons

▶ Access Help

▶ Exit Lotus 1-2-3

Among the many far-reaching developments of the Renaissance was the widespread application, in 14th-century Tuscany, of double-entry bookkeeping. Prior to this, the accounts of bankers and merchants were kept in a haphazard, loosely organized manner. The Tuscan innovation, made possible by the importation of Arabic and Hindu numbers, was to organize accounts into tables with rows and columns, thus making them much easier to maintain.

Now double-entry bookkeeping probably doesn't rank very highly on your list of exciting things, but it contributed to the advent of the commercial and industrial revolution that utterly transformed the Western world.

Until about 1980, most people who created tables of numbers and text worked in much the same way as the Tuscans. Electronic calculators made the job easier, but the use of larger computers was difficult and restricted to major projects.

Accounting tables are called *worksheets* or *spreadsheets,* and if you're creating one the traditional way, you will need some green ledger paper or a lab notebook, a pencil, and a calculator. You'll also need a big eraser, because one of the worst problems with manual worksheets is revision: if one number must change, then it will probably affect dozens of other numbers. The burden of recalculating parts of a traditional worksheet makes it difficult to experiment—to perform "what if" analysis. And if you want to make a chart or graph presenting the information pictorially, you will have to get some help from a graphic artist or do your best with colored pens and a ruler.

The advent of personal computers and electronic spreadsheet programs changed this situation dramatically. An electronic spreadsheet presents the table, with its rows and columns, on a computer screen. It is much easier to make modifications, because recalculation happens automatically in response to changes.

The first electronic spreadsheet programs made the basic tasks of building and modifying a worksheet much easier. Contemporary programs, such as Lotus 1-2-3 Release 4 for Windows, vastly extend these capabilities to include such features as data analysis, charting, and typographic formatting. Erasers and green eye-visors are optional.

DESIGNING WORKSHEETS

An electronic spreadsheet program is not only a tool for accountants. Anyone who wants to organize information in tables can benefit from one. Financial analysts, biologists, engineers, attorneys, marketing specialists, chemists, artists, managers, political analysts, health professionals, and many others routinely use electronic spreadsheets. Apart from being universally useful, spreadsheet programs are fun, because building a worksheet is like creating your own little machine. A worksheet is dynamic; it does things and responds to changes.

If you heard about a car that required you to hoist out the engine to change the oil, you would probably think the machine was poorly designed and difficult to maintain. Because, like machines, worksheets should be functional, you must pay close attention to design principles when creating them. You will want to design worksheets that are efficient, easy to use, easy to change, and easy to understand.

The projects in this module use examples that highlight many common design issues. When you finish the module, you will be able to apply your knowledge of 1-2-3 commands and worksheet-design techniques to your own area of expertise.

A NOTE TO THE STUDENT

As in other programs, there is often more than one way to perform a particular command or action in 1-2-3. You can use the mouse or the keyboard to select commands from 1-2-3 menus, but in general 1-2-3 works best with a mouse. Some powerful features of the program, such as SmartIcons, are accessible *only* with a mouse. This module focuses on using the mouse but gives important keystrokes along the way.

If you want to review how to use the mouse, windows, menus, and dialog boxes, refer to the Introduction to Windows.

STARTING 1-2-3

The standard name of the group window containing the 1-2-3 program icon is Lotus Applications, but on your system the group could have a different name, such as WinApps or 1-2-3.

 To start 1-2-3:

1 Open the group window containing the Lotus 1-2-3 Release 5 icon. Figure 0.1 shows an example of what you will see.

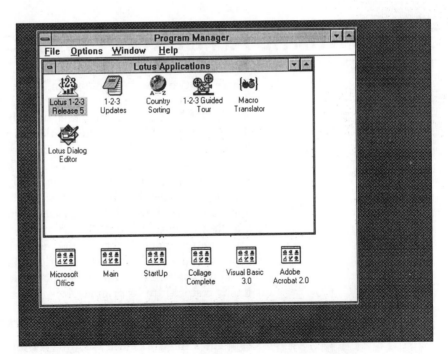

Figure 0.1

2 Double-click the Lotus 1-2-3 Release 5 icon. The screen should now resemble Figure 0.2.

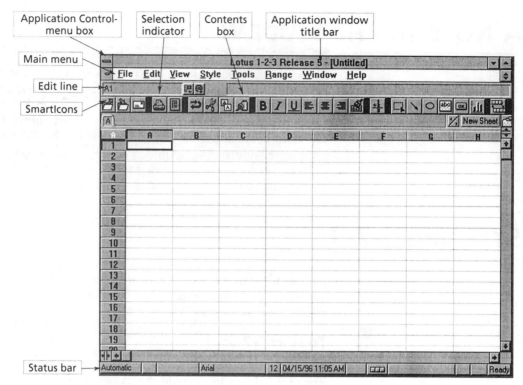

Figure 0.2

EXPLORING THE APPLICATION WINDOW

There are two types of windows in 1-2-3: the ***application window,*** which you can think of as representing the 1-2-3 program itself, and ***worksheet windows,*** which contain individual worksheets that you create using 1-2-3. The application window, whose title bar reads *Lotus 1-2-3 Release 5 - [Untitled]*, is a window that frames one or more worksheet windows. When you start 1-2-3, a single blank worksheet window is displayed full size within the application window. The word *Untitled* within the application title bar indicates that the worksheet does not yet have a name. Both the application window and the worksheet window have Control-menu boxes, and Restore buttons, so it's important not to confuse them.

To better understand the difference between the two windows, you will now use the worksheet Restore button to change the size of the worksheet window. You will then minimize the worksheet window to an icon and finally restore it to its original size.

To minimize and restore the worksheet window:

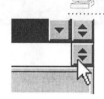

1 Click the worksheet window's Restore button.
The screen should now resemble Figure 0.3. The worksheet window is reduced in size and has its own title bar as well as Minimize and Maximize buttons.

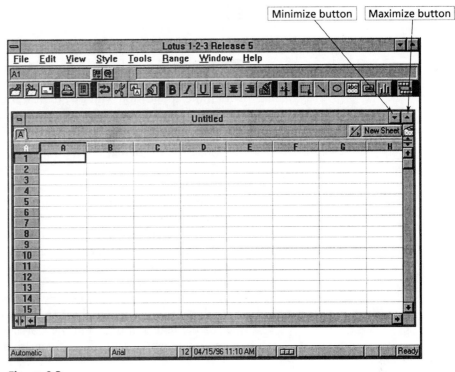

Figure 0.3

2 Click the worksheet window's Minimize button.
The screen should now resemble Figure 0.4. The worksheet window is reduced to an icon, labeled *Untitled*, in the lower-left corner of the application window.

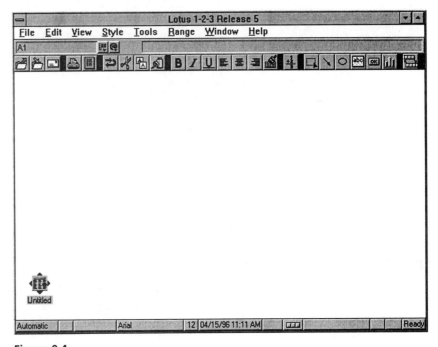

Figure 0.4

3 Double-click the Worksheet icon.

The screen should now resemble Figure 0.3; the worksheet window is again visible within the application window.

4 Click the worksheet window's Maximize button.

The screen should now resemble Figure 0.2, with the worksheet maximized within the application window. Repeat the restore, minimize, restore, and maximize procedures, if necessary, to clearly distinguish between the application and worksheet windows.

Lotus 1-2-3 commands are grouped on the ***main menu*** displayed across the top of the application window. You can select the options on the main menu by clicking them with the mouse or by pressing (ALT) in combination with the underlined letter in the option.

Beneath the main menu is the ***edit line,*** which contains the ***selection indicator*** and the ***contents box.*** This section of the application window becomes active when you type information into a worksheet.

Below the edit line is a set of ***SmartIcons,*** which allow you to perform many tasks quickly within 1-2-3, such as saving and printing a worksheet. The SmartIcons are accessible only with the mouse.

At the bottom of the application window is the ***status bar,*** which shows the current date and time and the worksheet status, and also allows you to determine which set of SmartIcons to display.

NAVIGATING THE WORKSHEET WINDOW

A 1-2-3 worksheet is composed of ***columns*** and ***rows.*** As shown in Figure 0.5, columns are labeled with the letters of the alphabet, starting with A and continuing through Z, followed by AA, AB, and so forth, to IV, for a maximum of 256 columns. Rows are labeled with numbers from 1 to 8192. The worksheets you will build won't use nearly so large an area; the average worksheet size for this module is about 10 columns by 20 rows.

The basic building block of a worksheet, the intersection of a column and row, is called a ***cell,*** and it is identified by its column letter and row number. For example, the ***cell reference*** C15 refers to the cell at the intersection of column C and row 15. The term ***cell address*** means the same thing as cell reference.

Worksheets are stored on disk in a ***file,*** which allows you to save your work and retrieve it at a later time. A single 1-2-3 file can contain one or more worksheets, each of which is identified by a letter of the alphabet. When a file contains more than one worksheet, you must specify the worksheet name along with the cell reference. For example, the cell reference B:C15 refers to cell C15 in worksheet B. In later projects, you will use multiple worksheets within a single file and learn how to select a specific worksheet for modification.

Scrolling the Worksheet Window

Think of the worksheet window as a frame through which you can see only part of the total worksheet area. To view a different area, you can shift the frame using the scroll bars and the arrow keys.

Tip Even if you plan primarily to use a mouse, in the steps that follow you should experiment with both the mouse and keyboard actions.

To scroll the worksheet window:

1 Mouse: Click the down scroll arrow (at the bottom of the vertical scroll bar). Press and hold down the mouse button on the scroll arrow to repeat the scrolling action.

  or Keys: Press and hold down (↓) until the window begins to move. The window shifts down row by row. You can use the other scroll arrows (and the other arrow keys, (←) (→) (↑)) to move by single columns or rows in other directions. Experiment with the other scroll arrows or arrow keys.

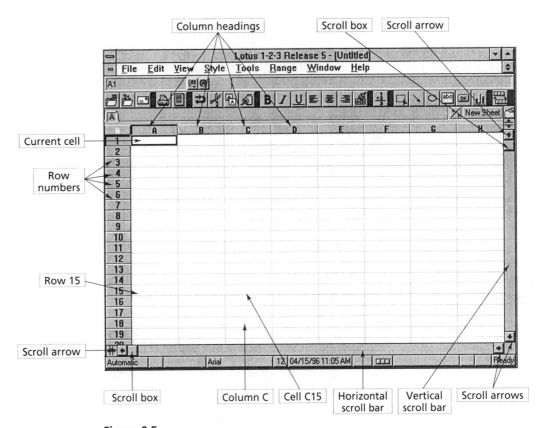

Figure 0.5

2 Press (HOME) to return to the upper-left corner of the worksheet, cell A1.

3 Mouse: Click in the middle of the vertical scroll bar. Notice that the vertical scroll box moves toward the bottom of the vertical scroll bar. You can click above the scroll box to shift the window up, or click below the scroll box to shift the window down.

  or Keys: Press (PGDN) to shift the window down by one window's length to show a different portion of the worksheet. Press (PGUP) to shift the window farther up; press (PGDN) to shift the window farther down. Experiment with (PGDN) and (PGUP).

4 Press (HOME) to return to the upper-left corner of the worksheet, cell A1.

5 Mouse: Click within the middle of the horizontal scroll bar to move the horizontal scroll box toward the right edge of the horizontal scroll bar.

or Keys: Press (CTRL)+(→) to shift the window right by one window's width to show a different portion of the worksheet. Press (CTRL)+(→) to shift farther to the right and (CTRL)+(←) to shift to the left.

6 Press (HOME) to return to the upper-left corner of the worksheet, cell A1.

Positioning the Current Cell

The cell appearing with a heavy border indicates the *active cell*. The active cell (also called the selected cell, current cell, or cell pointer) is where the action will take place if you type data or perform a command. When you first open a new, empty worksheet, A1 is the current cell.

> *Caution*   Don't confuse the term *cell pointer*, which refers to the current cell, with the term *mouse pointer*, which refers to the symbol representing the position of the mouse on the screen. In this module, when the term *pointer* is used by itself, it refers to the mouse pointer.

To position the current cell:

1 Mouse: Move the pointer to cell C3 and click the mouse button.
or Keys: Use the arrow keys to move the current cell to C3.
Notice that the cell reference of the current cell is displayed in the selection indicator.

2 Try scrolling the window (by clicking one of the scroll arrows). Notice that scrolling with the mouse does *not* change the current cell.

Changing Mouse Pointer Shapes

The shape of the mouse pointer changes depending on where the pointer is positioned on-screen. In the steps that follow, you will carefully move the pointer to the locations described and observe the changes in its appearance. Notice that pointer shapes change in response to specific mouse movements and screen locations.

To change pointer shapes:

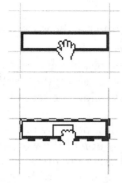

1 Position the pointer so that it just touches any side of the current cell. The pointer appears as an open hand. This is used when you copy and move cells.

2 With the pointer displayed as an open hand, press the mouse button. The hand closes into a fist, allowing you to drag a dashed outline of the cell anywhere within the worksheet. You can use this pointer to move the contents of a cell or a group of cells from one place to another.

3 Release the mouse button.

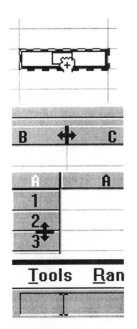

4 Press and hold down (CTRL) and, with the pointer positioned just touching any side of the current cell, press the mouse button.
The pointer changes to a fist with a plus sign. You can use this pointer to copy the contents of a cell or a group of cells.

5 Release the (CTRL) key and the mouse button.

6 Position the pointer on a line separating two column letters.
You will use this double arrow in later projects to change the width of a column.

7 Position the pointer on the line separating any two row numbers. This double arrow is similar to the column-width pointer and is used to change the height of a row.

8 Position the pointer in the middle of the contents box. The pointer shape changes to an insertion symbol, called an *I-beam.* You can use the I-beam to edit text within the contents box.

9 Position the pointer over the small black rectangle at the top of the vertical scroll bar. This area is called the *horizontal splitter,* and you can use it to split a window into two sections. A vertical splitter bar is at the left of the horizontal scroll bar.

MAKING SELECTIONS

As you use 1-2-3, you will occasionally want to perform an action that affects an entire worksheet, but most of the time you will want to change only a portion of a worksheet. You will first indicate your *selection,* the part of the worksheet you want to change. Many 1-2-3 commands operate on a selection. You can select a single cell, a *range* (a rectangular block of cells), or a group of ranges (called a *collection*). After you make a selection, you can choose a command to affect that selection.

Selecting a Single Cell

You can select a single cell by positioning the cell pointer. You can select a cell that is not currently visible by first scrolling the window and then clicking on the cell to make a selection.

 To select cell B5:

1 Mouse: Position the pointer on cell B5 and click the left mouse button.
   or Keys: Use the arrow keys to position the cell pointer in cell B5.

2 Scroll until cell J35 is visible and then select it.

Selecting a Range of Cells

A *range* is a rectangular block of cells referred to by its upper-left and lower-right diagonal corner cells. For example, the range whose upper-left corner is cell B2 and whose lower-right corner is C5 would be referred to as B2..C5. A range can be as small as a single cell or as large as the entire worksheet.

To select a range, you first select any corner cell and then use the mouse or keyboard keys to extend the selection to cover the entire range. Suppose you want to select the range B2..C5.

To select the range B2..C5:

1 Make B2 the current cell.

2 Mouse: Position the mouse pointer at the center of cell B2. Hold down the left mouse button, drag the pointer down to row 5 and across to column C to select the range, and then release the mouse button.

or Keys: Hold down the (SHFT) key, press ⊕ several times to move down to row 5, press ⊖ to move across to column C, and then release the (SHFT) key.

The screen should be similar to Figure 0.6. You can also extend the selection right first and then down; the order doesn't matter. Practice selecting other ranges. Notice that when you make a new selection, the previous selection markings disappear.

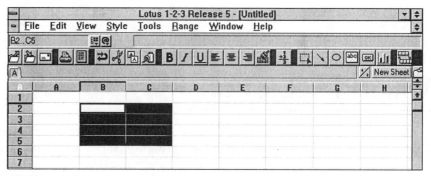

Figure 0.6

> *Tip* If you need to select a large range and don't want to hold down the mouse button for a long time, select a cell that is any corner of the range, move the pointer (without holding the mouse button down) to the cell that will be a diagonally opposite corner, hold down (SHFT), and click.

Selecting an Entire Column or Row

A complete column or row is just a large range. Selecting an entire column or row is easy: you click the column letter or row number.

To select an entire column or row:

1 Click the column heading (letter) G.

This selects all of column G (the range G1..G8192). Your screen should resemble Figure 0.7.

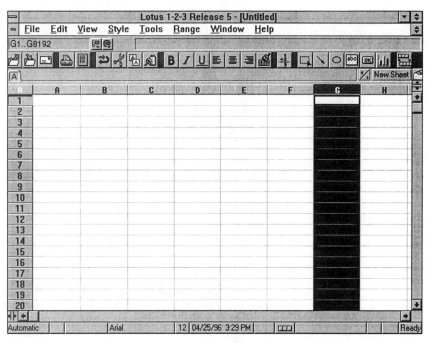

Figure 0.7

2 Click the row heading (number) 7.
This selects all of row 7 (the range A7..IV7).
Practice selecting other columns and rows.

Selecting Adjacent Columns or Rows

To select a group of adjacent columns or rows, you will first select one column or row and then extend the selection through the other columns or rows.

 To select an adjacent group of columns or rows:

1 Select column C.

2 Hold down the left mouse button, drag to column F, and release the mouse button.
This extends the selection across columns D, E, and F. The selected range is C1..F8192.

3 Select row 7.
The previous selection is canceled.

4 Extend the selection down through row 10.
Practice with other column-and-row group selections.

Making Nonadjacent Selections

You will sometimes want to affect an area of the worksheet that is not rectangular and that cannot be selected as a single range. Lotus 1-2-3 allows you to compose a more complicated selection, called a ***collection***, from a group of ranges.

You have noticed that if you move away from a selection and make another cell active, the selection is no longer marked. If you want to make a composite selection out of a group of separate ranges, columns, or rows, you hold down (CTRL) while making your selections with the mouse.

To select a collection of ranges:

1 Select the range B3..D8 and then release the mouse button.

2 Position the mouse pointer on cell G10.

3 Press and hold down (CTRL) and then press and hold down the mouse button.

4 Drag to select the range G10..H15.

The screen should resemble Figure 0.8. Using this method, select other collections of ranges.

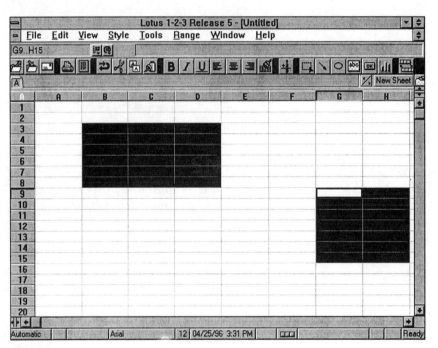

Figure 0.8

Selecting the Entire Worksheet

You can click the worksheet letter button (the A button above the heading for row 1 and to the left of the heading for column A) to select the entire worksheet.

To select the entire worksheet:

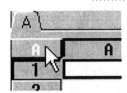

1 Click the worksheet letter button.
The entire worksheet is selected, as shown in Figure 0.9.

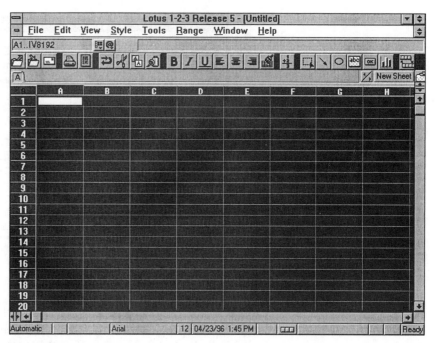

Figure 0.9

2 To cancel the selection, click an individual cell or reposition the current cell using the arrow keys.

GETTING ON-SCREEN HELP

The Help system in Lotus 1-2-3 conforms to the standard Help conventions of Microsoft Windows, which may be familiar to you if you have used other Windows applications. In the steps that follow, you will use the Search option from the Help menu to get information on cell addresses. In the Search dialog box, you can type a word naming a topic that you're interested in, and 1-2-3 will search its alphabetical list of topic areas for that word. The first few characters of the word are often sufficient for 1-2-3 to do its search.

To access the Help system:

1 Choose Search from the Help menu.
The Search dialog box appears on-screen.

2 Type **cel** in the text box to get help on cell addresses.
As shown in Figure 0.10, several topic areas beginning with the word *cell* are displayed, including *Cell addresses. Cell addresses* is also the selected topic area because it is the first one in the list.

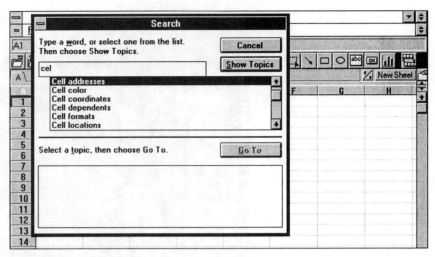

Figure 0.10

3 Select Show Topics.
The specific topics concerning cell addresses for which 1-2-3 can provide help are displayed. The list offers three topics. The first item, *cell address, defined*, is currently selected.

4 Select Go To.
The definition of a cell address is displayed.

5 Select Contents.
A table of contents for Help appears. If you want to read about one of the listed topics, you can click it with the mouse or use TAB to activate your choice and then press ENTER

6 Choose Exit from the File menu. (Do not choose Exit from the application window.)

> **Tip** If you want to return to your worksheet but wish to leave the Help window displayed for your reference, choose Always On Top from the Help menu within the Help window. You can resize the Help window if necessary and then click within the worksheet to resume your work.

Getting Help within a Dialog Box

The upper-right corner of each 1-2-3 dialog box contains a question mark, which you can select to obtain help about each item within the dialog box.

 To display Help from the Open File dialog box:

1 Choose Open from the File menu.
The Open File dialog box appears. The screen should look similar to Figure 0.11.

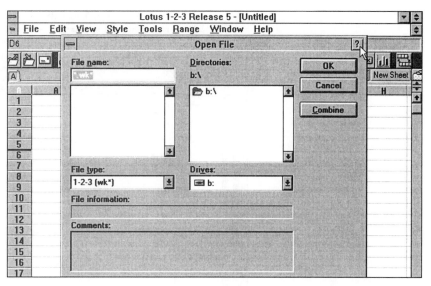

Figure 0.11

2 Select the question mark in the upper-right corner of the Open File dialog box.

A Help window appears, giving detailed information about opening files. You can scroll the Help window up or down using the scroll bar or arrow keys.

3 Close the Help window.

4 Select Cancel from the Open File dialog box.

WORKING WITH SMARTICONS

As previously mentioned, SmartIcons provide a quick method for performing many 1-2-3 tasks. The SmartIcons you see on your screen are only a fraction of the total available. Different sets of SmartIcons can be displayed, allowing you to display only those SmartIcons most applicable to the type of work being performed on the worksheet. You will now select different sets of SmartIcons and display Help about SmartIcons.

To select different sets of SmartIcons:

1 With the mouse pointer positioned over the SmartIcons selector in the status bar, as shown in Figure 0.12, click the left mouse button.

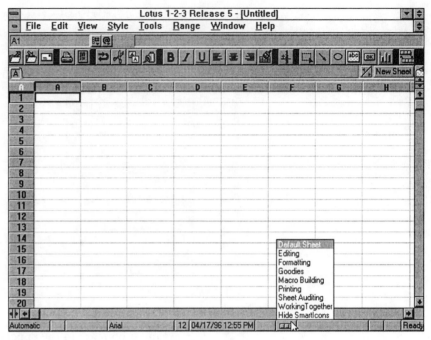

Figure 0.12

2 Select Formatting from the list of SmartIcon sets.
A different set of SmartIcons is displayed. The Formatting set is most useful for changing the appearance of a worksheet.

3 Select Default Sheet from the SmartIcons selector to return to the default SmartIcons used in 1-2-3.

EXITING LOTUS 1-2-3

You will now exit the 1-2-3 program. It is not necessary to save this empty worksheet (although if you happened to have made changes to it, 1-2-3 will give you the opportunity to save it before exiting). You can use one of several methods to exit the program.

To exit Lotus 1-2-3:

1 Choose Exit from the File menu, or double-click the Control-menu box.

> *Reminder* A smaller Control-menu box belongs to the current worksheet window. Double-clicking this box closes only the worksheet window, not the 1-2-3 program.

2 Because you do not need to save this worksheet, select No in the Save Changes dialog box if it appears.

THE NEXT STEP

Now that you are acquainted with the 1-2-3 application and worksheet windows, you are ready to enter information into a worksheet and to use commands to affect the information. The next project, Building a Small Worksheet, will illustrate many of the basic aspects of 1-2-3 worksheets.

SUMMARY AND EXERCISES

Summary

- Lotus 1-2-3 builds worksheets (spreadsheets) consisting of tables of information presented in rows and columns. Beyond its basic ability to perform arithmetic, 1-2-3 offers powerful formatting, data analysis, and charting features.
- The top portion of the 1-2-3 application window contains a main menu, an edit line consisting of a selection indicator and a contents box, and a set of SmartIcons.
- A 1-2-3 worksheet is composed of columns (labeled A, B, C,...,Z; AA, AB,...,IV) and rows (labeled 1 through 8192).
- The intersection of a row and a column is called a cell, which is the basic building block of a worksheet. You refer to a cell by its row and column (for example, the cell at the intersection of column C and row 15 is called cell C15).
- If a worksheet file contains more than one worksheet, cell references are preceded by the sheet name (for example, B:C15 refers to cell C15 in worksheet B).
- The current cell is where the action takes place in a worksheet. The current cell appears with a thick outline.
- The mouse pointer can take a variety of shapes, depending on precisely where it is positioned on the screen.
- A range is a rectangular block of cells. You can select a range of cells by holding down the left mouse button and dragging the mouse and pointer through the cells that you want to select. Keyboard users can hold down (SHFT) while pressing arrow keys to make a selection.
- A standard Windows Help system is available to explain 1-2-3 commands and features. You can search for topics of interest using the Search command from the Help menu.
- SmartIcons provide shortcuts for many 1-2-3 tasks.

Key Terms and Operations

Key Terms

active cell	range
application window	row
cell	selection
cell address	selection indicator
cell reference	SmartIcon
collection	spreadsheet
column	status bar
contents box	worksheet
edit line	worksheet window
file	
horizontal splitter	**Operations**
I-beam	Exit
main menu	Help

Study Questions

Multiple Choice

1. In 1-2-3, the intersection of a column and a row is called a
   a. block.
   b. selection.
   c. cell.
   d. range.
   e. formula.

2. How deep (how many rows) is a 1-2-3 worksheet?
   a. 64
   b. 256
   c. 1024
   d. 2048
   e. 8192

3. To select the upper-left corner of the worksheet (cell A1), press
   a. CTRL + PGUP
   b. PGUP
   c. HOME
   d. CTRL + HOME
   e. ALT + PGUP

4. What two kinds of windows are displayable in 1-2-3?
   a. spreadsheet and worksheet
   b. worksheet and workbook
   c. application and worksheet
   d. application and navigation
   e. navigation and command

5. A rectangular block of cells is called a
   a. data block.
   b. paragraph.
   c. data segment.
   d. code segment.
   e. range.

6. How do you use the mouse to select an entire column in 1-2-3?
   a. Click any cell in the column.
   b. Click the column heading letter.
   c. Click the top cell and drag to the bottom of the screen.
   d. Click the Column Select tool on the Toolbar.
   e. Click the top cell of the column and press F8.

7. How do you use the keyboard to open a menu in the main menu?
   a. Press (ALT) and the menu's first letter.
   b. Press (CTRL) and the menu's underlined letter.
   c. Press (ALT) and the menu's underlined letter.
   d. Press (ALT) + (CTRL) and the menu's first letter.
   e. Press (SHFT) and the menu's underlined letter.

Short Answer

1. The intersection of column C and row 5 is referred to as what?

2. The rectangular block of cells whose upper-left corner is B3 and whose lower-right corner is E8 is referred to as what?

3. The location where the "action" takes place in the worksheet is called what?

4. How can a collection of ranges be selected using the mouse in 1-2-3?

For Discussion

1. Who, other than accountants, might benefit from Lotus 1-2-3?

2. How might you use 1-2-3 in your own work or specialty?

3. What were some of the problems of spreadsheets before spreadsheet computer programs were available? What distinguishes electronic spreadsheets from their manual predecessors?

4. What distinguishes 1-2-3 from the first generation of electronic spreadsheets?

Objectives

After completing this project, you should be able to:

▶ Enter text and numeric constants

▶ Change column widths

▶ Build simple formulas

▶ Recalculate a worksheet

▶ Use and identify arithmetic operators

▶ Automatically format a worksheet

▶ Save, close, and open a worksheet

▶ Edit cell entries

▶ Open a new worksheet

CASE STUDY: CALCULATING NET PAY

In this project, you will build a small worksheet that calculates a person's net pay. You will use each of the three basic kinds of cell entries common to all 1-2-3 worksheets: *labels*, *numbers*, and *formulas*. You will enter text titles, numbers that will serve as the basic data manipulated in the worksheet, and a formula that refers to the numbers and computes a result. You will then format the worksheet to improve its appearance. Finally, you will save the worksheet to the disk so that the worksheet can be used later.

Designing the Solution

This first worksheet will calculate a person's net pay by subtracting taxes withheld from gross pay. A rough version of what the worksheet will look like follows:

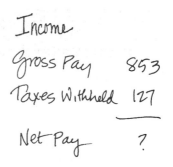

The question mark is a reminder that you will design the 1-2-3 worksheet to compute the net pay.

ENTERING CONSTANTS

A cell can contain three basic kinds of data: *text constants*, *numeric constants*, and *formulas*. **Text constants,** called **labels** in 1-2-3, consist of comments, titles, and other nonmathematical information. ***Numeric constants,*** simply referred to as **numbers,** are mathematical values that can be used in calculations. Labels and numbers are constants, which do not change after you type them into a cell.

Formulas compute a result, usually by performing arithmetic on information obtained from other cells. The value (result) of a formula can change if any of the cells it refers to change. Formulas do the work of a worksheet, and well-designed formulas are the key to building a worksheet that is flexible and powerful. In 1-2-3, the term *value* refers both to the result of a formula as well as to a number constant.

You will start by entering the labels of this worksheet. Labels are usually words that identify the different parts of a worksheet to make it easier to understand.

To enter labels:

1 Start 1-2-3.

2 Make cell A1 the active cell.

3 Type **Income**

The screen should look similar to Figure 1.1. Notice that the text appears in the contents box as well as in the cell.

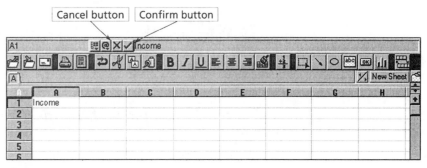

Figure 1.1

4 Select the Confirm button or press (ENTER) or press any arrow key to finish entering the text into cell A1.

5 Move the active cell to A2, and enter **Gross Pay**

6 Move the active cell to A3, and enter **Taxes Withheld**

7 Enter **Net Pay** in cell A4.

Tip To cancel an entry before it is complete, you can select the Cancel button or press (ESC).

Changing the Width of a Column

The label *Taxes Withheld* in cell A3 appears to spill over into column B. However, the entire text is stored in cell A3. In this section, you will see how to adjust the width of a column manually so that it accommodates long entries.

You can adjust the width of the column by first positioning the pointer on the right edge of a column heading and then dragging the mouse, or by using the Column Width command from the Style menu. If, instead of dragging the mouse, you double-click the mouse button, the width will automatically be set to fit the widest entry in that column. This is called Best Fit.

To change the width of column A:

1 Move the pointer to the right edge of the heading for column A (to the boundary line between the headings for columns A and B). The pointer should change to a double arrow.

2 Hold down the left mouse button. Notice that the current column width is displayed in the selection indicator.

3 Drag the column width so it is somewhat wider than the longest text entry (*Taxes Withheld*), and then release the mouse button. The screen should look like Figure 1.2.

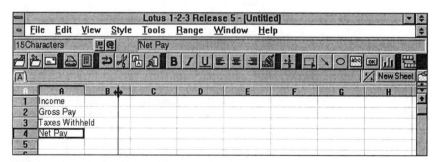

Figure 1.2

To set the column width to fit the widest entry:

1 Position the pointer on the right edge of the heading for column A (so that the pointer forms a double arrow).

2 Double-click the mouse button to set Best Fit.

> *Tip* Sometimes the Best Fit option will actually be too narrow, and you will need to manually increase a column's width. A column is too narrow when numeric entries appear as lines of asterisks (∗).

Entering Numeric Constants

In general, when you type numbers in 1-2-3, you should leave out extra punctuation such as dollar signs and commas. Although 1-2-3 will preserve this punctuation in your entry, it is best to assign a consistent appearance to a group of cells by using 1-2-3's extensive formatting commands.

Include a decimal point only if the number has a fractional part. If you type a percent sign after a number, the number will be divided by 100 and displayed with a percent sign.

This worksheet contains two numeric constants: gross pay and taxes withheld.

To enter the numeric constants:

1 Select cell B2.

2 Enter the sample gross pay amount **853** in cell B2.

3 Enter the sample taxes withheld amount **127** in cell B3.

Notice that 1-2-3 aligns a number against the right edge of its cell and aligns text against the left edge. Later you will learn how to adjust the alignment of cell contents.

ENTERING FORMULAS

There are several ways to create a formula in 1-2-3. The simplest and least prone to error is to use *point mode*. In **point mode,** you use the mouse or arrow keys to point to the various cells that are to be included in the formula, and 1-2-3 figures out what the actual cell references are. When you use point mode, you don't have to worry about figuring out cell addresses yourself.

> *Riddle*
> Q. How can you tell when people aren't using point mode in 1-2-3?
> A. They are trying to figure out cell references by holding a ruler or piece of paper against the computer screen to line up the rows and columns.

In the following steps, you will use a formula to calculate net pay. The formula will refer to the gross pay amount and subtract the taxes withheld from that amount. Note that all formulas begin with a plus sign.

To enter the formula to calculate net pay:

1 Make cell B4 the active cell.

This cell, to the right of the label *Net Pay*, will contain the formula to calculate net pay.

2 Type +

The screen should look similar to Figure 1.3.

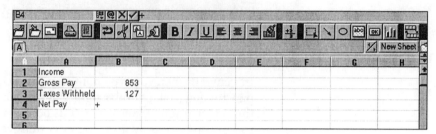

Figure 1.3

3 Point to the gross pay amount that you entered in cell B2 by either selecting that cell or using the arrow keys to move to the cell.
The screen should resemble Figure 1.4. Notice that 1-2-3 is building the formula for you both in the contents box and in cell B4.

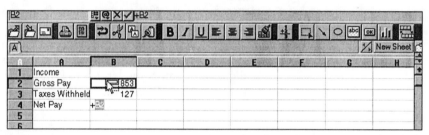

Figure 1.4

The formula is supposed to subtract from the gross pay amount.
4 Type - as shown in Figure 1.5.

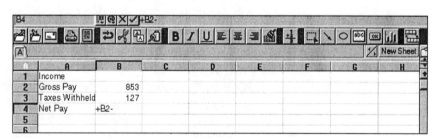

Figure 1.5

5 Point to the taxes withheld amount by either selecting cell B3 or using the arrow keys.
The screen should look like Figure 1.6.

Figure 1.6

6 As shown in Figure 1.7, finish the formula by selecting the Confirm button or by pressing (ENTER)

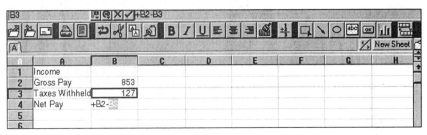

Figure 1.7

Notice that 1-2-3 has built the formula $+B2-B3$, as shown in the contents box of Figure 1.8. Cell B4 contains the result of this formula, which is currently 726.

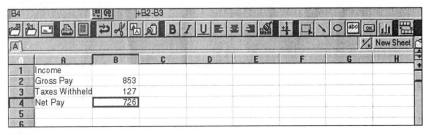

Figure 1.8

Reminders Here are some reminders about formulas and the pointing method:

- All formulas start with a plus sign.
- You use the mouse or arrow keys to select the cells that the formula refers to.
- You press (ENTER) (or select the Confirm button on the edit line) only once, when you have completed the entire formula.

Recalculating a Worksheet

The foremost advantage of an electronic spreadsheet is that its formulas can *recalculate* and show new results if there are changes in the cells to which the formulas refer. For example, suppose that taxes withheld changed from 127 to 179.

To change and recalculate the worksheet:

1 Select cell B3, where you entered 127 as the current taxes withheld.

2 Change the taxes withheld to 179 by typing **179** and pressing (ENTER)

As shown in Figure 1.9, the new entry replaces the previous one, and the result of the net pay formula adjusts automatically. Experiment with other changes to gross pay and taxes withheld.

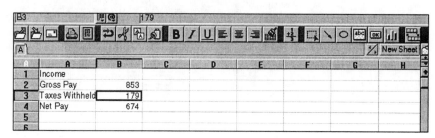

Figure 1.9

Arithmetic Operators

The formula you just created uses the subtraction operator. Lotus 1-2-3 has several major operators, which are listed in Table 1.1 in *precedence* order. The precedences of the various operators in a formula determine the order in which 1-2-3 performs the operators' actions. Operators with lower precedence numbers have higher priority and are performed first. For example, because multiplication and division are operations with lower precedence numbers (higher priority) than addition and subtraction, $+8-3*2$ is calculated with implied parentheses; $+8-(3*2)$, which results in 2, not 10. You can use parentheses to override the standard precedence: $+(8-3)*2$ is 10.

Table 1.1

Precedence Number	Symbol	Operator	Function	Example Formula	Example Result
1	∧	Exponentiation	Raises a number to a power	$+3\wedge2$	9
2	−	Negative	Identifies number as negative	$+3*-2$	−6
	+	Positive	Identifies number as positive	$+3++3$ ($+3+3$)	6
3	*	Multiplication	Multiplies two numbers	$+4*2$	8
	/	Division	Divides one number by another	$+12/3$	4
4	+	Addition	Adds two numbers	$+3+2$	5
	−	Subtraction	Subtracts one number from another	$+7-4$	3
5	=	Equal to	1 if a = b, 0 otherwise	$+5=3$	0
	<>	Not equal to	1 if a<>b, 0 otherwise	$+6<>7$	1
	<	Less than	1 if a<b, 0 otherwise	$+6<7$	1
	>	Greater than	1 if a>b, 0 otherwise	$+2>3$	0
	<=	Less than or equal to	1 if a<=b, 0 otherwise	$+17<=17$	1
	>=	Greater than or equal to	1 if a>=b, 0 otherwise	$+16>=17$	0
6	#NOT#	Logical NOT	1 if a is 0, 0 otherwise	#NOT#1	0
7	#AND#	Logical AND	1 if a and b are 1, 0 otherwise	1#AND#1	1
	#OR#	Logical OR	1 if a or b (but not both) are 0, 0 otherwise	!#OR#0	1
	&	Text concatenation	Connects two strings	+"Uh"&"Oh"	UhOh

Tip When you need to type /, *, −, or +, use the keys on the numeric keypad at the right of the keyboard. This will save you the trouble of using (SHFT).

FORMATTING CELLS

The *style,* or format, of a cell indicates how the information in the cell should appear on-screen or in a printout. The many attributes of a cell style include number punctuation (such as dollar signs and commas), alignment, borders, and font.

In the following steps, you will use the Gallery template command to have 1-2-3 automatically assign styles to the cells in your worksheet. In later projects, you will learn more about cell styles. A template is a predefined group of cell styles.

To apply Gallery templates to the worksheet:

1 Select the range A1..B4 by selecting cell A1, holding down the left mouse button, dragging to cell B4, and then releasing the mouse button.

2 Choose Gallery from the Style menu.
The Gallery dialog box appears.

3 Examine available samples of the Gallery templates by selecting a template name in the list box using the mouse or arrow keys.

4 Select B&W1 from the list, and then select OK, as shown in Figure 1.10.

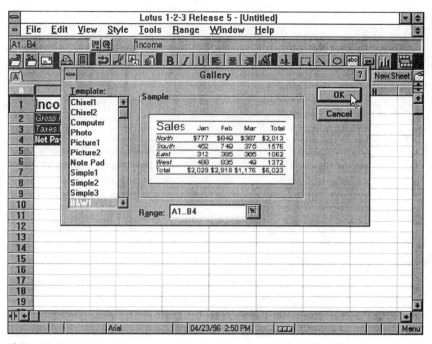

Figure 1.10

5 Click the left mouse button on any cell to unselect the range.

6 If necessary, adjust the width of column A to show all of the contents of cell A3.

The screen should now resemble Figure 1.11.

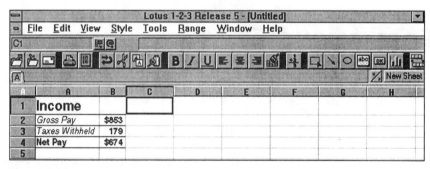

Figure 1.11

The Gallery template assigns customized styles to the worksheet. Notice some of the appearance attributes affected by the template:

- The title *Income* is displayed in a larger-size bold type.
- The gross pay and net pay amounts (that is, the first and third rows of numeric values in the worksheet) appear with leading dollar signs.
- The labels *Gross Pay* and *Taxes Withheld* are in italics.
- Each row of the worksheet has a thin border line at the top and bottom of each cell.

SAVING, CLOSING, AND UPDATING WORKSHEETS

The worksheet you have built exists only in the computer's *random access memory* (RAM). If the computer were to be turned off or the power interrupted at this point, you would lose your work.

> *Tip* Save your work often, perhaps every five or ten minutes. A rule of thumb is that it is time to save when (1) it would be troublesome to re-create the work you've done since you last saved, (2) you are about to make a major change or addition to the worksheet, or (3) you are about to use a command that has unpredictable or extensive effects.

Saving a Worksheet

You will now use the Save command to save a copy of the worksheet to disk. Because this is a new file, 1-2-3 will display the Save As dialog box, in which you can choose the disk drive where you would like to store the file and type the name you would like to give the file.

To save the worksheet:

1 Choose Save from the File menu or click the SmartIcon. The Save As dialog box appears, and 1-2-3 proposes the name FILE0001.WK4.

2 Choose the disk drive on which to save the file from the Drives list box, and then choose a directory using the Directories list box.

3 Press (ALT) + **N** to activate the File Name text box.

4 Type **PAY1** in the File Name text box, and then select OK, as shown in Figure 1.12.

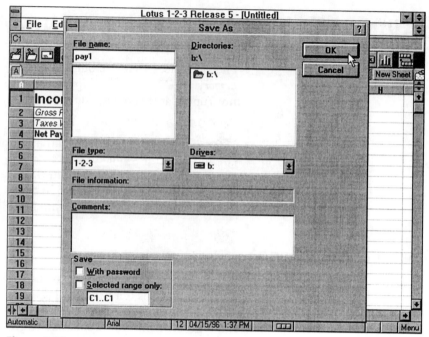

Figure 1.12

The Save command does not close the worksheet window, so your worksheet remains visible. Notice that the name you just assigned to your file, PAY1.WK4, now appears in the title bar. Lotus 1-2-3 automatically assigned the file extension .WK4. Because the worksheet now has a file name, subsequent uses of the Save command will be quicker; you will not be prompted to type in a name.

> **Tip** If you want to save a worksheet with a name different from the one already assigned to it, choose the Save As command from the File menu. With this command, the original file is preserved and a second file, with the new name, is created.

Closing a Worksheet

Closing a worksheet removes that worksheet from the screen. To close a worksheet, you can either choose Close from the File menu or double-click the *worksheet* Control-menu box (which is under the 1-2-3 application window Control-menu box). If you made any changes to the worksheet since you last saved it, the Close dialog box will appear, asking whether you want to save the updated version of the worksheet.

To close the worksheet:

1 Choose Close from the File menu, or double-click the worksheet Control-menu box.

2 Select Yes from the Close dialog box.

 If necessary, you can quit 1-2-3 now and continue this project later.

Opening a Worksheet

Opening the PAY1 worksheet file loads a copy of the worksheet from disk into memory, where you can modify the worksheet. The original copy of the file remains unchanged on the disk until you save the updated worksheet over it.

To open a worksheet file:

1 Choose Open from the File menu, or select the SmartIcon to open a file.
The Open File dialog box appears.

2 Change disk drives and directories, if necessary, by using the Drives and Directories list boxes.

3 Choose the file PAY1.WK4 from the alphabetical file list.

4 Select OK.

> *Tip* If you save your worksheets frequently, you can return to a recently saved version if you "mess up" the worksheet currently on-screen. You can choose the Close command from the File menu to clear the messed-up worksheet from the screen (without saving), and then choose the Open command to retrieve the earlier version from disk.

Editing Cell Entries

One way to change the contents of a cell is to type a new entry to replace an old one, as you did when you changed the value of taxes withheld earlier in this project. However, there will be times when you need to change only part of a long entry—perhaps you will need to make a small correction to a long title or formula. In such cases, editing the cell entry can save you some typing. Lotus 1-2-3 provides several ways of editing the contents of a cell.

Before you can edit a cell entry, you must position the insertion point by clicking with the mouse or by using the arrow keys. Then you can press (BKSP) to erase characters to the left of the insertion point or (DEL) to erase characters to the right.

Suppose that you wanted to change the label *Taxes Withheld* to *Tax Withheld*.

To edit a cell entry:

1 Select cell A3, which contains the label *Taxes Withheld*.

2 Double-click cell A3, or press (F2)
The cell entry appears with the insertion point at the end of the last word in the cell.

3 Using the mouse or the arrow keys, position the insertion point just after the *s* in *Taxes*.

4 Press (BKSP) twice (don't press (ENTER) yet).
The screen should resemble Figure 1.13.

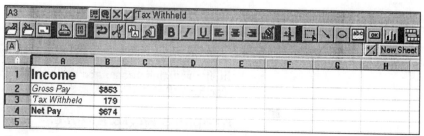

Figure 1.13

Notice that, as you type, the text in the contents box changes as well. The contents box displays none of the text formatting applied to the cell (the text is not in italics, for example). The contents box always displays the "raw" contents of the active cell—that is, with no text formatting.

The fact that the text in cell A3 is in italics can make it difficult to position the insertion point for editing. In such cases, you can use the contents box to edit a cell.

To edit a cell entry using the contents box:

1 Select the Cancel button or press (ESC) twice to cancel the editing changes made in the previous steps.

2 Position the pointer within the contents box.
Notice that the pointer changes to an insertion point, or I-beam.

3 With the insertion point positioned just after the *s* in *Taxes*, click the left mouse button.

4 Press (BKSP) twice.
The screen should resemble Figure 1.14.

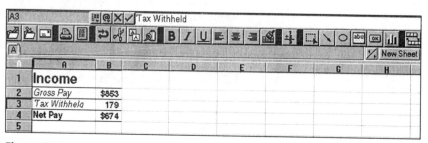

Figure 1.14

5 To enter the revised text, select the Confirm button or press (ENTER)

6 Select OK.

Creating a New Worksheet

When you first start the program, 1-2-3 presents you with an empty worksheet. If at any later time during your 1-2-3 session you want to begin working on a new, blank worksheet, you can choose the New command from the File menu.

Tip You can have many different worksheets open at once. If you have finished working with one worksheet and want to begin a new one, you can reduce the clutter on-screen by closing the first worksheet. If you need to switch between (or simultaneously view) the worksheets, keep them both open.

To open a new worksheet:

1 Choose New from the File menu. If the New File dialogue box appears choose *create a plain worksheet*.
A new worksheet appears.

2 Type **Test Worksheet** in cell A1, and press (ENTER)

Switching Among Open Worksheets

Currently, there are two open worksheets: the PAY1 worksheet you were previously editing and a new worksheet (automatically assigned the name FILE0001.WK4) that you just opened. Although you can't see the PAY1 worksheet at the moment, you can select the worksheet to be displayed by choosing the worksheet name from the Window menu.

To display different worksheets:

1 Choose PAY1.WK4 from the Window menu.
The PAY1 worksheet is now displayed on-screen, hiding the FILE0001.WK4 worksheet.

2 Choose Tile from the Window menu.
The screen should now resemble Figure 1.15.

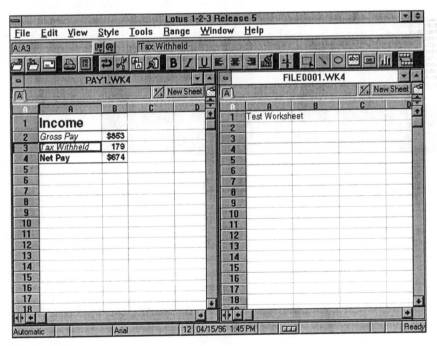

Figure 1.15

You can size each worksheet manually using the mouse. You may want to experiment with the Cascade option from the Window menu as well.

Exiting 1-2-3

You will now exit the 1-2-3 program. Because you modified both the PAY1 worksheet and the FILE0001 worksheet, 1-2-3 will ask whether to save the updated versions. You will save the PAY1 worksheet and not save the FILE0001 worksheet.

To exit 1-2-3:

1 Choose Exit from the File menu.
The Exit dialog box is displayed, asking whether to save the PAY1.WK4 worksheet.

2 Select Yes.
Another Exit dialog box is displayed, asking whether to save the FILE0001.WK4 worksheet.

3 Select No.

> **Tip** Selecting Cancel in the Exit dialog box will cancel the Exit command and return you to the current 1-2-3 worksheet.

THE NEXT STEP

Now that you have seen some examples of basic cell entries common to most worksheets, you are ready to create them in a larger worksheet. In the next project, you will build more sophisticated formulas and learn how to copy and move cell contents. You will see how Gallery templates perform in a more complicated context, and you will begin to take more control over the appearance of the worksheet.

SUMMARY AND EXERCISES

Summary

- A cell can contain a label, a number, or a formula.
- Numbers should be entered without extra punctuation.
- A formula's result is called its value.
- You can change the width of a column in a worksheet.
- Formulas do the work in a worksheet. Formulas are built most easily with the pointing method.
- When a formula in one cell depends on the data in another cell, the formula will automatically recalculate if the contents of that other cell change.
- The precedence of arithmetic operators determines the order in which operations are performed in a formula.

- You can quickly improve the appearance of simple worksheets by using Gallery templates.
- Worksheets should be saved frequently.
- You can edit a cell entry rather than having to retype it.
- The Open command in the File menu is used to open a worksheet that was saved to a disk; the New command is used to open a new, blank worksheet.

Key Terms and Operations

Key Terms	Operations
formula	Cascade
label	Close
number	Exit
numeric constant	Gallery
point mode	New
precedence	Open
recalculate	Save
style	Save As
text constant	Tile
value	

Study Questions

Multiple Choice

1. What determines the order in which arithmetic operations are performed in a 1-2-3 formula?
    a. The order is strictly left to right.
    b. The order is strictly right to left.
    c. The order is determined by the precedence of the operators used.
    d. The order doesn't matter.
    e. The order is determined by the settings you specify in the Operator Precedence menu.

2. The two types of constants are
    a. text and number.
    b. formula and value.
    c. label and text.
    d. relative and absolute.
    e. formula and number.

3. If you change a cell entry upon which a formula depends (which a formula refers to), what will happen?
    a. The formula will display an error message.
    b. The formula will automatically recalculate to reflect the changed data.
    c. You will need to rebuild the formula before it will display a new result.
    d. You will need to copy the formula upon itself.
    e. Nothing will happen.

4. How many times do you press (ENTER) (or select the Confirm button) when building a 1-2-3 formula?
   a. once
   b. twice
   c. as many times as there are cell references in the formula
   d. as many times as there are arithmetic operators in the formula
   e. never

5. In 1-2-3, what is the result of $+3+2*5+4$?
   a. 29
   b. 72
   c. 26
   d. 17
   e. none of the above

6. In 1-2-3, what is the result of $+3+(4-2)*3$?
   a. 15
   b. 1
   c. 3
   d. 9
   e. none of the above

7. The way information appears in a cell (such as its alignment, font, or numeric punctuation) is referred to as the cell's
   a. style.
   b. attributes.
   c. display mode.
   d. format.
   e. Gallery.

8. You should save your work in 1-2-3
   a. when you are about to make a major modification to the worksheet.
   b. every five or ten minutes.
   c. when it would be time-consuming to recreate the work you've done since you last saved.
   d. when you are about to experiment with an unfamiliar 1-2-3 command.
   e. All of the above.

9. What happens when you close a worksheet in 1-2-3?
   a. The worksheet is automatically saved.
   b. You will automatically exit 1-2-3.
   c. You will automatically lose all changes made since you last saved the worksheet.
   d. A new, empty worksheet will automatically appear.
   e. All of the above.

10. How do you begin to edit a cell entry?
    a. Make the cell active, and then select the contents box.
    b. Make the cell active, and then press (F2)
    c. Double-click in the cell.
    d. All of the above.
    e. None of the above.

Short Answer

1. What is the result of a formula called?

2. What kind of information is usually represented with labels?

3. If you enter a label that is larger than a cell's width, what does 1-2-3 do?

4. When you enter a number, should you include punctuation (dollar signs, commas, and so on)? Why or why not?

5. In general, what is the best method to use when building formulas that refer to other cells? Why?

6. What determines the order in which arithmetic operations are performed in 1-2-3 formulas?

7. What determines the way information in a cell will appear?

8. What command is used to format a range automatically?

9. What command is used to open a new, blank worksheet?

10. What steps are required to edit an existing cell entry?

For Discussion

1. What aspects of a cell's appearance does a Gallery template affect?

2. What is the most beneficial feature of electronic spreadsheets?

3. Describe the pointing method for building formulas.

Review Exercises

Simple Income Statement

Build and format a worksheet based on the information shown in Figure 1.16. Income is calculated by subtracting cost of goods sold from sales. Choose any of the B&W templates when you use the Gallery command. Save the worksheet as INCOME1.

	A	B	C	D	E	F	G
1	Income Statement						
2	Sales	$57,189					
3	Cost of Goods Sold	33202					
4	Income	?					
5							
6							
7							

Figure 1.16

Population Report

Build and format a worksheet similar to Figure 1.17. Use an addition formula to compute the total population of the United States, Canada, and Mexico combined. If the column containing the numbers is too narrow, 1-2-3 will display the number in scientific notation. If the column is very narrow, 1-2-3 will display the number as a series of asterisks (*). Once you apply a Gallery template or manually widen the columns, the numbers themselves will appear. Choose any of the B&W templates from the Gallery dialog box. Save the worksheet as POPREP1.

	A	B	C	D	E	F	G
1	**Country**	**Population**					
2	United States	248710000					
3	Mexico	900007000					
4	Canada	26835500					
5	Total	?					

Figure 1.17

Assignments

Detailed Income Statement

Build a worksheet based on Figure 1.18. Gross income is sales minus cost of goods sold. Net income is gross income minus expenses. Choose the B&W2 template in the Gallery dialog box. Save the file as INCOME2.

	A	B	C	D	E	F	G	H
1	**Income Statement**							
2	Sales	93126						
3	Cost of Goods Sold	32117						
4	Gross Income	?						
5	Expenses	16909						
6	Net Income	?						
7								

Figure 1.18

Population Density

Build a worksheet based on Figure 1.19. The population density is the number of people per square mile; calculate it by dividing the population of a city by the city's area. Use the Gallery dialog box to apply the Simple3 template. Experiment with the width of column D. Notice that the number of digits that display to the right of the decimal point varies with the width of the column. Save the file as DENSITY1.

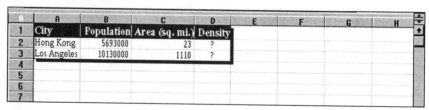

	A	B	C	D	E	F	G	H
1	City	Population	Area (sq. mi.)	Density				
2	Hong Kong	5693000	23	?				
3	Los Angeles	10130000	1110	?				
4								
5								
6								
7								

Figure 1.19

Coffee House Income

Figure 1.20 shows cost and price information for the top selling coffee at Clem's Coffee Clutch. Enter the data as shown in Figure 1.20. The formula that calculates income will subtract the cost from the selling price and multiply the result by the number sold. You will need to use parentheses in the formula. Adjust column widths as necessary, but do not format the worksheet; it will be used for an exercise in a later project. Save the worksheet as COFFEE1.

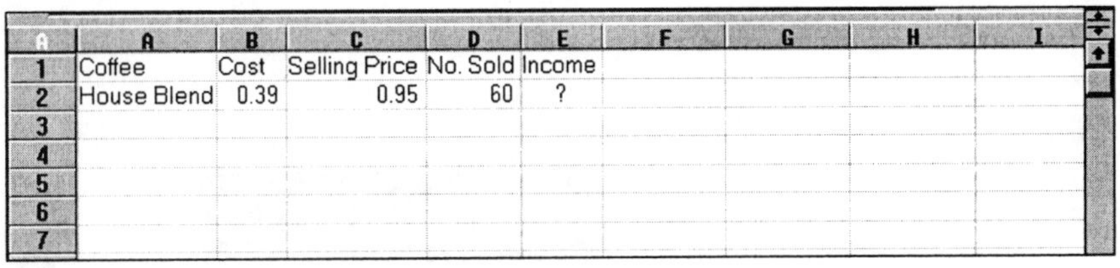

	A	B	C	D	E	F	G	H	I
1	Coffee	Cost	Selling Price	No. Sold	Income				
2	House Blend	0.39	0.95	60	?				
3									
4									
5									
6									
7									

Figure 1.20

PROJECT 2: BUILDING A LARGER WORKSHEET

Objectives

After completing this project, you should be able to:

- Move a cell
- Check the spelling of worksheet data
- Use preselected ranges for data entry
- Copy the contents of a cell
- Use relative cell references in formulas
- Use the @SUM function and the Sum SmartIcon

CASE STUDY: SALES OF AUDIO RECORDINGS

From 1975 to 1990, the popularity of the kinds of media used for recorded music shifted dramatically. These changes are illustrated in Figure 2.1. In this project, you will build this 1-2-3 worksheet and add formulas to calculate the totals (indicated by question marks in the figure).

A	A	B	C	D	E	F	G
1	Shipments of Audio Recordings						
2	(in millions of dollars)						
3		1975	1980	1985	1990		
4	Phonograph Records						
5	LP Albums	1485	2290.3	1280.5	86.5		
6	Singles	211.5	269.3	281	94.4		
7	Total Records	?	?	?	?		
8	Tapes						
9	8-tracks	583	526.4	25.3	0		
10	Cassettes	98.8	776.4	2411.5	3472.4		
11	Total Tapes	?	?	?	?		
12	Compact Discs						
13	Regular CDs	0	0	389.5	3451.6		
14	CD Singles	0	0	0	6		
15	Total CDs	?	?	?	?		
16	Grand Total	?	?	?	?		
17							

Figure 2.1

Designing the Solution

The formulas you will create for this worksheet will calculate totals for each year in each media category (records, tapes, and CDs) and grand totals (the totals of records, tapes, and CDs combined). You will then format the worksheet so the information is more readable.

In the steps that follow, as important new concepts and features are introduced, you can refer to Figure 2.1 to orient yourself in the worksheet. Although you might be tempted to jump ahead and type everything in immediately, please follow the steps carefully.

BUILDING THE SKELETON OF A WORKSHEET

When you create a worksheet, it is often easiest to enter the static (unchanging) information first. To establish an overall skeleton or shape for the worksheet, you will enter the row and column titles before you enter the numbers and formulas. You will find it easier to wait until the worksheet is complete and functioning correctly before doing detailed formatting.

 ### *To enter the main titles:*

1 Start 1-2-3.

2 Make cell A1 active and enter the text **Shipments of Audio Recordings**

3 Enter **(in millions of dollars)** in cell A2.

After entering the text *(in millions of dollars)*, you may be surprised to see that 1-2-3 displays "ERR" in cell A2, and the text you typed displays in uppercase in the contents box. Clearly, 1-2-3 is interpreting the text that was entered as something other than a label—but why? The answer is that 1-2-3 tries to determine the type of cell entry (value or label) based on the first character entered in the cell. If the first character of a cell is a + (plus sign), − (minus sign), = (equal sign), ((left parenthesis), @ ("at" sign), . (period), or # (pound sign), then 1-2-3 assumes the entry is a value (or formula). In this case, the first character entered was a left parenthesis, so 1-2-3 presumed that the entry was a value.

Lotus 1-2-3 provides four *label prefix characters* that remove any ambiguity about the contents of a cell. A label prefix character signals 1-2-3 that the information you are entering is a label. The particular label prefix character you use depends on how the label should be aligned within the cell (see Table 2.1).

Table 2.1

Label Prefix Character	Alignment
'	Left alignment
"	Right alignment
^	Centered
\	Repeats label

In general, any time you want to enter a label that contains numbers or any of the symbols previously mentioned, you should enter a label prefix character first.

To enter a label with a label prefix character:

1 If necessary, make cell A2 the active cell.

2 Type `'(in millions of dollars)`
Be sure to enter the single apostrophe as the first character.

> **Tip** The status bar mode indicator displays "Value" or "Label" when you are entering data into a cell. Use the mode indicator to quickly determine whether 1-2-3 is interpreting your entry as a value or a label.

Moving Cells

In the following steps, you will enter the first row title, *Phonograph Records*, in the wrong cell. Then, rather than retyping the title, you will move the cell contents to the correct cell. In 1-2-3, to *move* means to pick up an object from one location (in this case, the original cell) and place the object in another location. When the mouse pointer changes to a closed fist, you can drag the cell anywhere within the spreadsheet and then drop that cell on any other cell. Appropriately enough, this feature is known as ***drag and drop***.

To move a cell:

1 Enter **Phonograph Records** in cell A3.
The sample worksheet in Figure 2.1 shows the first row title, *Phonograph Records*, in row 4, one row *below* the row containing the years. Rather than retyping the information you just entered, you can move it to the correct cell, cell A4.

2 Select cell A3, which now contains the label *Phonograph Records*.

3 Position the pointer to touch any edge of the active-cell rectangle.
The pointer becomes an open hand.

4 Hold down the left mouse button.
The hand will close into a fist.

5 Drag the dashed-line cell outline to cell A4, and then release the mouse button.
The text that was in cell A3, *Phonograph Records*, is now in the new location.

Entering Row Titles

Notice that the row subtitles are slightly indented to create an outline format. One simple way to accomplish this in 1-2-3 is to precede each text entry with two space characters.

To enter the row titles:

1 Make cell A5 the active cell.

2 Press (SPACE) twice, and then enter **LP Albums**

3 Move to cell A6, press (SPACE) twice, and then enter **Singles**

4 Move to cell A7, press (SPACE) twice, and enter **Total Records**

5 Referring back to Figure 2.1, enter all the remaining row titles. Remember to indent where indicated in the figure.

Reminder If you discover that you have made an incorrect entry in a cell, you can edit the cell by:

- Double-clicking in the cell
- Making the cell active and then pressing (F2)
- Clicking in the contents box

As shown in Project 1, you then will be able to type new information or use the editing keys to correct your mistake.

Checking the Spelling in a Worksheet

Once you have entered all the labels into a worksheet, you can use 1-2-3 to check your spelling.

To check the spelling in the worksheet:

1 Choose Spell Check from the Tools menu.
The Spell dialog box appears.

2 Select Entire file, and then select OK.

The spelling checker will pause on any word in the worksheet that it does not find in the spelling dictionary. The Spell Check dialog box will suggest replacements for the possibly misspelled word. If the original word you typed is spelled correctly, you can select Skip All in the dialog box; the spelling checker then skips over all subsequent occurrences of that word. (Choosing Skip causes only the current occurrence to be ignored.) If the spelling needs to be corrected, you can choose from the list of suggestions, or type a new spelling and then select Replace.

As illustrated in Figure 2.2, the spelling checker pauses on *8tracks*. It also will pause on any other words that you may have misspelled when typing the text.

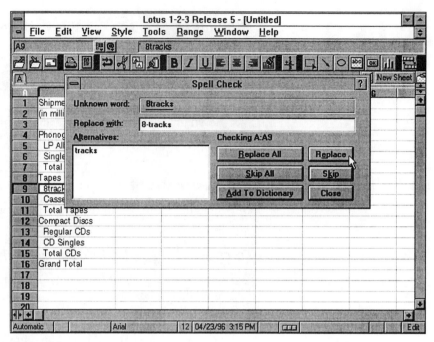

Figure 2.2

Entering the Column Titles

The years 1975, 1980, 1985, and 1990 need to be entered as column titles. In the steps that follow, you will learn several methods for entering data.

To enter the column titles:

1 To make the worksheet easier to read as you enter data, make column A slightly wider than *Phonograph Records*, the longest row title.

2 Select cell B3. Type **1975** and then press (ENTER)

3 Select cell C3. Type **1980** and then press ⊖

4 Enter **1985** and **1990** in the appropriate cells.

> *Tip* Pressing an arrow key after you type in data will automatically enter the data and move the cell pointer one cell in the direction of whichever arrow key you pressed.

Using Selection to Speed Data Entry

You need to enter the various sales figures in the main section of the worksheet. Although you could enter the sales figures without the use of a preselected range, the steps that follow demonstrate how you can make repetitive entry more convenient by preselecting a data entry range.

To use selection to speed data entry:

1 Select the range B5..E6.
The screen should look like Figure 2.3. This is the range where you will place sales amounts for LP albums and singles.

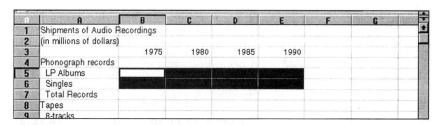

Figure 2.3

2 Experiment with pressing (ENTER) to move down or to the right and
(SHFT) + (ENTER) to move up or left within a selection.
At the lower-right corner of a selection, pressing (ENTER) moves to the upper
left; at the upper-left of a selection, pressing (SHFT) + (ENTER) moves to the
lower right. You can use these keys to change which cell is active within
the selected range.

3 Use (ENTER) to make cell B5 the active cell in the selected range.

4 Type **1485**
The screen should look like Figure 2.4.

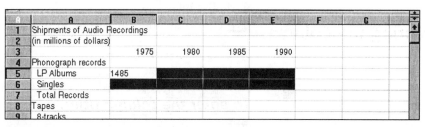

Figure 2.4

5 Press (ENTER)
Pressing (ENTER) makes your entry of multiple columns of numbers somewhat
more convenient, because as you complete the last entry in a column, the
active cell will wrap around, or continue, to the next column automatically.

6 Enter the remaining figures for phonograph record sales in the appropriate cells.

7 Enter the sales figures for tapes and compact discs. As you enter the
data, remember that some cells are kept blank for now.

SAVING THE WORKSHEET

In the following steps, you will save the worksheet to disk, giving it the
name AUDIO1.

To save the worksheet:

1 Choose Save from the File menu, or click the SmartIcon to save a file.
The Save As dialog box appears.

2 Choose the appropriate disk drive and directory.

3 Type **AUDIO1** for the file name, and then select OK.

EXIT If necessary, you can quit 1-2-3 now and continue this project later.

Constructing Formulas and @Functions

In the steps that follow, you will use point mode to build a formula that calculates total sales of LP albums and singles for 1975.

To enter the formula for total record sales:

1 Select cell B7.

2 Type + to indicate the entry of a formula.

3 Use the mouse or arrow keys to point to cell B5, which contains sales of LP albums for 1975.

4 Type +

5 Use the mouse or arrow keys to point to cell B6, which contains sales of singles for 1975.

6 Click the Confirm button, or press (ENTER)

	A	B	C	D	E	F	G
1	Shipments of Audio Recordings						
2	(in millions of dollars)						
3		1975	1980	1985	1990		
4	Phonograph records						
5	LP Albums	1485	2290.3	1280.5	86.5		
6	Singles	211.5	269.3	281	94.4		
7	Total Records	1696.5					
8	Tapes						
9	8-tracks	583	526.4	25.3	0		
10	Cassettes	98.8	776.4	2411.5	3472.4		
11	Total Tapes						
12	Compact Discs						
13	Regular CDs	0	0	389.5	3451.6		
14	CD Singles	0	0	0	6		
15	Total CDs						
16	Grand Total						
17							

Figure 2.5

Compare the screen with Figure 2.5. A formula's result is called its *value*. The value of this formula is 1696.5, which appears in cell B7. If you look in the contents box, you will see the formula itself: +B5+B6.

Copying Formulas

In 1-2-3, any type of cell entry—label, number, or formula—can be duplicated in other cells. But duplication of formulas is most important. Worksheets tend to have repeating patterns; total record sales for 1980, 1985, and 1990 are all calculated in a manner similar to the calculation of total record sales for 1975. Copying allows you to create a formula once and then have its operation duplicated in other cells that require the same computation.

You will now copy the formula to the cells in the range C7..E7 so that you also can calculate total record sales for 1980, 1985, and 1990.

 ### To copy a formula:

1 Select cell B7, which contains the total records formula.

2 Touch any edge of the active-cell rectangle with the pointer so the pointer becomes an open hand.

3 Press and hold down (CTRL), and then press the left mouse button. The hand will close into a fist containing a plus sign.

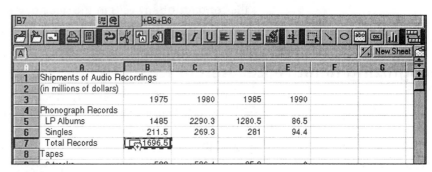

Figure 2.6

4 Drag the dashed-line cell outline to cell C7. Release the mouse button first and then release (CTRL)
The formula should now appear in cell C7, as shown in Figure 2.7.

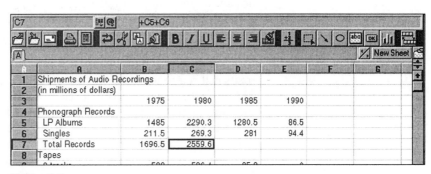

Figure 2.7

It would be tedious to copy each of the formulas a single cell at a time. The steps that follow show a method of copying a single cell to a number of adjacent cells. Even if you already have copied the formula in the preceding steps, you can try this method; it will harmlessly copy over the existing formula in cell C7.

To copy a formula using the Copy Right command:

1 Select cell B7, which contains the formula for calculating total records.

2 Select the range B7..E7.

3 Choose Copy Right from the Edit menu.
Be sure to choose Copy Right, not Copy.

The Copy Right command makes a copy of the leftmost cell in a range and places that copy in all of the other cells designated in the range. In a similar manner, Copy Down copies the topmost cell in a range to those below it.

> ***Caution*** Use the Copy Right and Copy Down commands with care: the contents of any cells in the selected range will be overwritten with the cell being copied.

Recognizing Relative Cell References

What was copied when you performed the previous steps? It wasn't the value 1696.5, because different numbers appear in each of the cells showing totals. To see what is actually in a cell, you can select that cell and then look in the contents box.

 To examine the relative cell references:

1 Select cell B7, which contains the original formula for total record sales for 1975.

2 Examine the contents box. The formula is +B5+B6.

3 Select cell C7, which contains the formula for 1980.
The formula in this cell is a copy of the original formula, but the contents box shows that this formula reads +C5+C6.

4 Examine the formulas for 1985 and 1990. You will discover that they read +D5+D6 and +E5+E6, respectively.

The formula +B5+B6 was not literally copied. In a formula, 1-2-3 treats cell references as being *relative* to the cell containing the formula. Although the original formula reads +B5+B6, 1-2-3 actually interprets the formula to mean "Take what is two cells above [the formula] and add to it what is one cell above." 1-2-3 will interpret cell references in formulas as being *relative* to the location of the formula; this is called ***relative cell referencing***. When the formula in cell B7 is duplicated in cell C7, 1-2-3 shifts all the addressing one cell to the right, so the formula reads +C5+C6.

Relative cell referencing is why the duplicated formulas each read differently from the original. This adjustment of a copied formula to reflect a new location is most often what you will want 1-2-3 to do. For example, the formula that calculates total record sales for 1990 *should* read +E5+E6, not +B5+B6.

Using 1-2-3 @Functions

The total sales for tapes and compact discs also need to be calculated. You could use an addition formula identical to that used to calculate total record sales, but instead you will now try another approach: you will build a formula that contains a 1-2-3 @*function*.

An @***function*** is an operation whose use simplifies formula building. @Functions are similar to the keys on an electronic calculator that perform specialized calculations. Lotus 1-2-3 has more than 200 @functions, including mathematical, financial, engineering, statistical, date, and text @functions. Each @function has an identifying name, such as @SUM, @AVG, and @TIME.

All @functions in 1-2-3 begin with @ (an "at" sign). For most @functions, you also must provide additional items of information inside parentheses. These additional items, called ***arguments*** to the @function, give the @function the data it needs to complete its task and compute a *result*. If you are adding multiple arguments, you should separate them with commas. Table 2.2 lists several basic 1-2-3 @functions and provides examples based on the figure in the margin.

	H	B
1	1000	100
2	2000	Hello
3	3000	500

Table 2.2

@Function	Syntax	Description	Example Formula	Example Result
@SUM	@SUM(*range*)	Totals a range	@SUM(A1..B3)	6600
@AVG	@AVG(*range*)	Averages a range	@AVG(A1..A3)	2000
@MIN	@MIN(*range*)	Gets smallest value in a range	@MIN(A1..B3)	0
@MAX	@MAX(*range*)	Gets largest value in a range	@MAX(A1..B3)	3000
@COUNT	@COUNT(*range*)	Counts values in a range	@COUNT(A1..B3)	6
@IF	@IF(*test, result if true, result if false*)	Performs test; result of function depends on whether test is true or false.	@IF(A1<60,A3,B2)	Hello

The @SUM function, in its basic form, is designed to total the values in a range of cells. The argument you provide to the @function indicates the range the @function is to sum. For example, @SUM(H1..H12) totals all the values in the range H1..H12. The much longer addition formula $+H1+H2+H3+H4+H5+H6+H7+H8+H9+H10+H11+H12$ arrives at the same result as @SUM(H1..H12), but using the @SUM function is a more efficient way to create the formula.

In the steps that follow, you will use point mode to build an @SUM function formula that calculates total tape sales for 1975. You will begin the formula with @, followed by SUM and an open parenthesis. Then, using pointing techniques, you will select the range to be summed, and finally you will end the formula with a close parenthesis.

 To enter the @SUM function to calculate total tape sales for 1975:

1 Select cell B11.

2 Type + `@SUM(`

Although the word *SUM* can be upper- or lowercase letters, there must not be spaces between any of the characters. The screen should now resemble Figure 2.8.

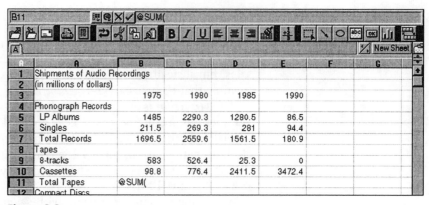

Figure 2.8

3 Select cassette sales for 1975 in cell B10 and drag up to 8-track sales for 1975 in cell B9. Once the range B9..B10 is selected, release the mouse button.

The screen should look similar to Figure 2.9. Notice that 1-2-3 builds the formula as you select the range.

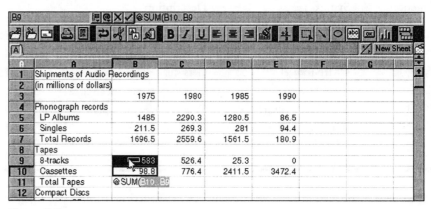

Figure 2.9

4 Type **)** and press (ENTER) to complete the formula.

The completed formula reads @SUM(B10..B9), as shown in Figure 2.10.

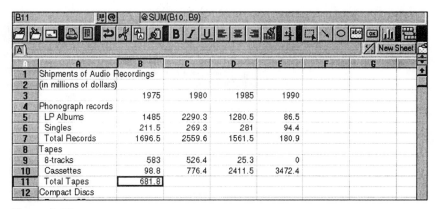

Figure 2.10

For totaling such a small range, the @SUM function might appear to have little advantage over a regular addition formula. But @functions are more flexible than regular formulas. For example, if you inserted a new row between 8-track and cassette sales—say, a row for sales of cassette singles—the range reference in the @SUM function would automatically expand to include the new information. A simple addition formula would not change to include this new row.

The formula @SUM(B10..B9) uses relative cell references; the formula means "sum the two-cell range immediately above the formula." Because it uses relative addresses, the formula will work correctly if copied to another cell. You will now learn about a shortcut method of building @SUM formulas before you copy the @SUM formula to other cells.

Using the SmartIcon Sum Tool

You can always write an @SUM formula manually, but a SmartIcon is included in 1-2-3 that writes an @SUM formula for you. The SmartIcons are located just below the edit line.

When you choose the Sum SmartIcon, it looks at the cells surrounding the active cell and makes a guess about what range you want to total.

To use the Sum SmartIcon:

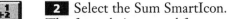

1 Select cell C11, which is to contain total tape sales for 1980.
2 Select the Sum SmartIcon.
The formula is entered for you. As shown in Figure 2.11, the formula @SUM(C9..C10) appears in the contents box. After examining the contents of cells neighboring cell C11, the SmartIcon concludes that the range you probably want to sum is C9..C10, which is correct.

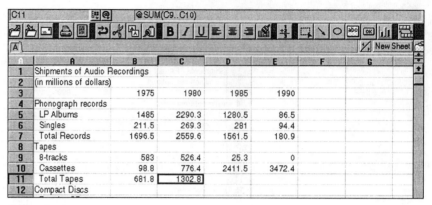

Figure 2.11

3 Copy the formula for 1980 total tape sales to the cells designated for total tapes (for the years 1985 and 1990).

4 Build a formula containing an @SUM function to calculate total CD sales for 1975. You can either construct the formula manually or use the SmartIcon. The formula should read @SUM(B13..B14).

5 Copy the formula for total CDs sold in 1975 to the cells designated for the 1980, 1985, and 1990 totals.
The screen now should resemble Figure 2.12.

	A	B	C	D	E	F	G
1	Shipments of Audio Recordings						
2	(in millions of dollars)						
3		1975	1980	1985	1990		
4	Phonograph Records						
5	LP Albums	1485	2290.3	1280.5	86.5		
6	Singles	211.5	269.3	281	94.4		
7	Total Records	1696.5	2559.6	1561.5	180.9		
8	Tapes						
9	8-tracks	583	526.4	25.3	0		
10	Cassettes	98.8	776.4	2411.5	3472.4		
11	Total Tapes	681.8	1302.8	2436.8	3472.4		
12	Compact Discs						
13	Regular CDs	0	0	389.5	3451.6		
14	CD Singles	0	0	0	6		
15	Total CDs	0	0	389.5	3457.6		
16	Grand Total						
17							

Figure 2.12

Calculating Grand Totals

You can compute the grand total for a year by adding together total records, total tapes, and total CDs. This total cannot be calculated using a simple @SUM function, because you need to add the values of three nonadjacent cells.

To build the grand total formula:

1 Select cell B16, which will contain the grand total for 1975.

2 Use point mode to build the formula +B7+B11+B15.

3 Copy this formula in the correct cells across the row to calculate the grand totals for the other years.

The screen should resemble Figure 2.13.

	A	B	C	D	E	F	G
1	Shipments of Audio Recordings						
2	(in millions of dollars)						
3		1975	1980	1985	1990		
4	Phonograph Records						
5	LP Albums	1485	2290.3	1280.5	86.5		
6	Singles	211.5	269.3	281	94.4		
7	Total Records	1696.5	2559.6	1561.5	180.9		
8	Tapes						
9	8-tracks	583	526.4	25.3	0		
10	Cassettes	98.8	776.4	2411.5	3472.4		
11	Total Tapes	681.8	1302.8	2436.8	3472.4		
12	Compact Discs						
13	Regular CDs	0	0	389.5	3451.6		
14	CD Singles	0	0	0	6		
15	Total CDs	0	0	389.5	3457.6		
16	Grand Total	2378.3	3862.4	4387.8	7110.9		
17							

Figure 2.13

4 Save the file.

THE NEXT STEP

In this project, you built the functional parts of a worksheet. In the next project, your primary concern will be the appearance of the worksheet—its format. You will retrieve the worksheet, modify it, format it, print it, and learn more about several different formatting techniques.

SUMMARY AND EXERCISES

Summary

- The first step in building a large worksheet is to enter the row and column titles, followed by any other constant information. You can then construct formulas. You should complete the worksheet before doing detailed formatting.
- You can copy a cell's contents easily with the mouse. You can change a cell entry by double-clicking in the cell, making the cell active and pressing (F2), or clicking the contents box.
- You can copy a cell using the drag-and-drop method. When a formula containing relative cell references is copied, those cell references will change relative to the new cell.
- Lotus 1-2-3 can check the spelling of worksheet data.
- You can use preselection of a range to speed the entry of large amounts of data.

- An @function is a built-in mathematical procedure that can be used in a formula. The @SUM function, which totals a range of cells, can be typed in or entered using the Sum SmartIcon.

Key Terms and Operations

Key Terms	Operations
argument	Copy Right
drag and drop	Copy Down
@function	Spell Check
label prefix character	
relative cell reference	

Study Questions

Multiple Choice

1. What should usually be done first when building a large worksheet?
   a. formatting
   b. entry of labels and numbers
   c. entry of formulas
   d. saving
   e. column-width adjustment

2. What best describes what happens when you move a single cell?
   a. The cell's contents are duplicated in another location and you have to erase the contents from the original cell.
   b. The cell's contents are removed from their original location and placed in a new cell.
   c. The active cell is repositioned in a new location.
   d. The current selection is extended so the selection is larger than a single cell.
   e. None of the above.

3. What key can be used to move within a preselected data-entry range?
   a. ⬇
   b. ENTER
   c. F1
   d. ➔
   e. all of the above

4. What kinds of cell entries can be copied?
   a. formulas
   b. labels
   c. numbers
   d. all of the above
   e. none of the above

5. Items of information provided to an @function are called
   a. values.
   b. formulas.
   c. variables.
   d. parameters.
   e. arguments.

6. What is a shorter way of computing $+C1+C2+C3+C4+C5+C6+C7+C8$?
   a. @ADD(C1:C8)
   b. @TOTAL(C1..C8)
   c. @SUM(C1..C8)
   d. @SUMMATION(C1..C8)
   e. @C1..C8

7. What tool can be used to quickly create @SUM formulas?
   a. Summation
   b. @SUM
   c. Sum SmartIcon
   d. Sum-O-Matic
   e. Sum from the Formula menu

8. To have 1-2-3 skip all occurrences of a word that isn't in the 1-2-3 dictionary, what should you select in the Spelling dialog box?
   a. Skip
   b. Skip All
   c. Replace
   d. Replace All
   e. Close

9. When you use the mouse to copy a cell, the mouse pointer will change to a(n):
   a. hand.
   b. double arrow.
   c. hand with a plus sign.
   d. insertion symbol.
   e. hollow arrow.

10. Suppose the formula @SUM(A1..A5) was entered in cell A6. What best describes the meaning of the formula?
    a. Total the cells A1 and A5.
    b. Total the five-cell range immediately above the cell containing the formula.
    c. Count the number of entries in the range A1 through A5.
    d. Total the cells A1, A2, A3, and A4.
    e. None of the above.

Short Answer

1. What is an efficient way to compute $+E7+E8+E9+E10+E11+E12+E13$? What are the reasons to use this other method?

2. Does moving a cell create two copies of the cell (the original and the duplicate)?

3. If the spelling checker pauses on a word in the worksheet, does this mean that the word is misspelled? If so, what can be done?

4. What technique can be used to speed the entry of a block of data in a worksheet?

5. When a formula is copied from one cell to another cell, will the original and the copy necessarily display the same value?

6. What does the Sum SmartIcon do?

7. Approximately how many built-in @functions does 1-2-3 have?

8. If the formula @SUM(B2..B5) was entered into cell B6, how would the formula change when copied to cell C6?

9. What is a simple way to indent text entries?

10. What are label prefix characters? When are they used?

For Discussion

1. Describe the general steps you should follow when building a worksheet.

2. Describe how to move a cell.

3. Describe how to copy a cell.

4. Describe relative cell referencing and how it affects the way formulas are copied.

5. Describe @functions and their components. Use the example of the @SUM function.

Review Exercises

Municipal Waste Trends

The Environmental Protection Agency (EPA) reports the information shown in Figure 2.14 about the composition of municipal waste and how it has changed over time (the figures reflect pounds per day per person). Build a worksheet to present this data and calculate the various totals. Use the @SUM function to compute the required totals. Save an unformatted version of this worksheet to disk, under the name EPA1, for use in a review exercise in Project 3. After you save the worksheet, experiment with different Gallery templates, but do not save the formatted version.

	A	B	C	D	E	F	G	H
1	Municipal Waste							
2		1960	1970	1980	1990			
3	Nonfood Wastes							
4	Paper	0.91	1.19	1.32	1.6			
5	Glass	0.2	0.34	0.36	0.28			
6	Plastics	0.01	0.08	0.19	0.32			
7	Total Nonfood	?	?	?	?			
8	Other							
9	Food	0.37	0.34	0.32	0.29			
10	Yard	0.61	0.62	0.66	0.7			
11	Total Other	?	?	?	?			
12	Grand Total	?	?	?	?			
13								

Figure 2.14

Winter Olympic Medals

Figure 2.15 shows the number of medals won by selected countries during the 1992 Winter Olympic Games. Create a worksheet that presents this information and calculates the required totals. Note that row and column totals are both computed. Save an unformatted version of the worksheet on your disk, using the name OLYMPIC1. Experiment with Gallery templates if you wish.

	A	B	C	D	E	F	G	H
1	1992 Winter Olympiad							
2								
3	Country	Gold	Silver	Bronze	Total			
4	Germany	10	10	6	?			
5	Unified Team	9	6	8	?			
6	Austria	6	7	8	?			
7	Norway	9	6	5	?			
8	Total	?	?	?	?			
9								

Figure 2.15

Assignments

Coffee-House Income

Open the file COFFEE1 that you created in an assignment at the end of Project 1. Modify the worksheet, as shown in Figure 2.16, to show sales figures for other kinds of coffee. Note that the original formula for income uses relative addresses and can be copied down to compute income for the other coffee flavors. Create @SUM formulas that compute totals for the number sold and for income. Do not format the worksheet. Choose the Save As command in the File menu to save the updated worksheet under a new name, COFFEE2.

	A	B	C	D	E	F	G	H	I
1	Coffee	Cost	Selling Price	No. Sold	Income				
2	House Blend	0.39	0.95	60	?				
3	Espresso	0.61	1.25	12	?				
4	Cappuccino	0.74	1.5	22	?				
5	Cafe Mocha	0.55	1.45	35	?				
6	Total			?	?				
7									

Figure 2.16

Personal Budget

Build a personal budget that describes your income and expenses for a typical month. Begin with income items, such as salary, tips, interest earned, grouped and indented under the heading *Income*. Build a formula that calculates a total of the income items. Similarly, group expense items, such as food, rent, electricity, and insurance, and calculate their total. Finally, build a formula to calculate the difference between total income and total expenses. Do not format the worksheet, but save it to disk under the name BUDGET1 for use in another project.

Space Payloads

Figure 2.17 documents the number of payloads (objects carried into space) launched by various countries for the years 1988 through 1991. Construct a worksheet to present this data and compute the totals. You can use the @SUM function to calculate column totals; you can calculate the average for each country by dividing its row total by 4 or by using the @AVG function. You can use the @SUM function to calculate row totals. Do not format the worksheet; save it to disk under the name SPACE1. You will use this worksheet in an assignment in Project 3.

	A	B	C	D	E	F	G	H
1	Space Payloads							
2								
3		1988	1989	1990	1991	Average		
4	USSR	107	95	96	101	?		
5	United States	15	22	31	30	?		
6	Japan	2	4	7	2	?		
7	Total	?	?	?	?	?		
8								

Figure 2.17

After completing this project, you should be able to:

► Identify and analyze formulas in a worksheet

► Insert blank cells into a worksheet

► Recognize and correct circular references

► Clear cells

► Center titles across columns

► Change row height

► Change formatting applied by a template

► Print the worksheet

► Apply number formats

► Change the width of multiple columns

CASE STUDY: SALES OF AUDIO RECORDINGS

In this project, you will continue to work with the audio-recordings worksheet you created in Project 2. You will add the following numbers for sales of cassette singles to the worksheet. The new data will appear between the rows labeled Cassettes and Total Tapes.

	1975	1980	1985	1990
Cassette singles	0	0	0	87.4

Once this information is added, some formulas in the worksheet will need to be adjusted to reflect the new information. In the final phase of the project, you will learn about formatting, or changing the appearance of the worksheet.

Designing the Solution

First you will need to make room for the new information on sales of cassette singles. You could move the lower half of the worksheet (A11..E16) down one row to create the needed space, but for this exercise you will use the Insert command. This procedure is easier because it does not require you to select a large range.

MODIFYING A WORKSHEET

When you modify a worksheet, you must consider how the change will affect other parts of the worksheet. You need to analyze carefully the way formulas depend on other cells. Usually formulas adjust automatically as you'd like them to, but in some cases they do not. Consider the consequences of inserting a new row: the area where you want to place extra cells might be quite small, but if you choose to insert an entire row, a new blank row will extend across the entire worksheet, perhaps inserting blank space through the middle of some other portion of the worksheet that you do not want to affect. Deleting an entire row or column is even more sensitive, because information is removed from across the worksheet.

> *Reminder* You should save a worksheet before executing a command that might significantly affect the worksheet. You should also consider the possible side effects of using the command. If, when the command is performed, the worksheet is adversely affected, you can close the damaged worksheet without saving it, return to your previously saved copy, and then try again.

Identifying Formula Precedents and Dependents

Lotus 1-2-3 has several features that make it easier for you to understand the formulas in a worksheet. If you select a cell containing a formula and then choose Audit from the Tools menu, the Audit dialog box will be displayed. Selecting Formula Precedents will cause 1-2-3 to select the cells the formula depends on for its data. These cells are called *precedents*. The Audit dialog box also allows you to select *cell dependents*, which are cells that contain formulas that refer to a particular cell.

In the following steps, you will use the Audit command to review how the formulas work in the audio-recordings worksheet. In most cases, the purpose of selecting formula precedents or cell dependents is to distinguish them visually.

To open and prepare the AUDIO1 worksheet:

1 Open the AUDIO1.WK4 worksheet file you saved in Project 2.

To select formula precedents:

1 Select cell B11.
This cell contains the formula that calculates total tape sales for 1975.

2 Choose Audit from the Tools menu.

3 Select Formula Precedents, and then select OK.

Lotus 1-2-3 selects the range B9..B10, because the formula in B11 depends on these cells.

4 Select cell B16.

5 Choose Audit from the Tools menu, select Formula Precedents, and then select OK.

All the cells that the grand total depends on are selected. Remember that one cell in a selection or collection will not be darkened though it is still a part of the selection.

To select cell dependents:

1 Select cell B7, total record sales for 1975.

2 Choose Audit from the Tools menu, select Cell Dependents, and then select OK.

Only one formula, the grand total for 1975 in cell B16, depends on cell B7.

Bearing in mind the modification planned for this worksheet, you will want to make sure that the data for sales of cassette singles, once entered into the worksheet, are also included in the total tape sales formula. You will not have to worry about the grand total formula in this case, because it depends on the total tape sales formula.

Inserting Cells in a Worksheet

A range of blank cells needs to be inserted directly above the total tapes row. Lotus 1-2-3 lets you insert either a range of cells or an entire column or row. It is often safest to insert a range, because the effect doesn't stretch as far across the worksheet as it does when an entire column or row is inserted.

To insert blank cells:

1 Select cell A11, the total tapes cell, and then select the range A11..E11

2 Choose Insert from the Edit menu.

The Insert dialog box appears. Because the selected range is wider than it is deep, 1-2-3 presumes that you want to insert a row, which is correct.

3 Select Insert Selection.

The screen should look like Figure 3.1. Choosing Insert Selection causes 1-2-3 to shift the cells below the range down one row. If you did not select Insert Selection, an entire row would be inserted.

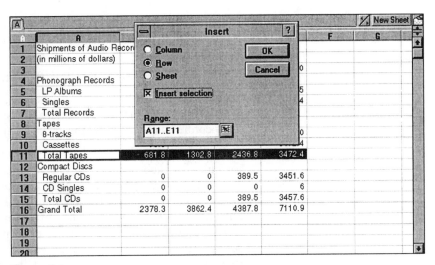

Figure 3.1

4 Select OK.

A new range of blank cells is now available.

To enter the new information:

1 Select cell A11.

2 Press (SPACE) twice and enter **Cassette Singles**

3 Enter **0** in cells B11, C11, and D11.

4 Enter **87.4** in cell E11.

Your worksheet should now resemble Figure 3.2.

A	B	C	D	E	F	G
1 Shipments of Audio Recordings						
2 (in millions of dollars)						
3	1975	1980	1985	1990		
4 Phonograph Records						
5 LP Albums	1485	2290.3	1280.5	86.5		
6 Singles	211.5	269.3	281	94.4		
7 Total Records	1696.5	2559.6	1561.5	180.9		
8 Tapes						
9 8-tracks	583	526.4	25.3	0		
10 Cassettes	98.8	776.4	2411.5	3472.4		
11 Cassette Singles	0	0	0	87.4		
12 Total Tapes	681.8	1302.8	2436.8	3472.4		
13 Compact Discs						
14 Regular CDs	0	0	389.5	3451.6		
15 CD Singles	0	0	0	6		
16 Total CDs	0	0	389.5	3457.6		
17 Grand Total	2378.3	3862.4	4387.8	7110.9		
18						

Figure 3.2

Assessing the Effects of a Command

Now that you have entered the data for sales of cassette singles, you can determine whether adjustments are required to accommodate the new information. The sales of cassette singles should be included in the computation of total tapes, so you should examine the formulas in the *Total Tapes* row.

To examine the total tapes formulas:

1 Select cell E12.

The formula reads @SUM(E9..E10), so the range being summed does not include the new information in cell E11.

2 Display the formula precedents of cell E12.

This confirms visually that the range being totaled is not correct.

Because the total tape sales formula depends upon the result of the formulas for each of the subtotals, it should also be clear that total tape sales is no longer being correctly computed.

Since cassette singles had no sales for 1975 through 1985, you might conclude that the only formula that you need to fix is the one for 1990. But leaving the other total tape sales formulas unchanged would be a serious design mistake; it would create an inconsistency in the worksheet that could later prove troublesome. What if the worksheet were reused and different years' data (all with nonzero sales of cassette singles) was entered over the older data?

You may wonder why the range referred to in the @SUM function did not automatically adjust. Lotus 1-2-3 will automatically adjust a range reference within a formula if the newly inserted row is *within* the existing top and bottom rows of the range, but not if the inserted row lies *outside* the existing range. Had the row for cassette singles been inserted between the 8-track and cassette rows, 1-2-3 would have adjusted the range reference in the formula.

In the steps that follow, you will build a new @SUM formula for total tape sales for 1975 and copy it to the other total tape cells. Please follow the steps carefully, because the steps will purposefully instruct you to make a common mistake that you will then learn how to correct. *Do not use the Sum SmartIcon for these steps.*

 To build a self-referential @SUM formula:

1 Select cell B12, where the formula for total tape sales for 1975 resides.

2 Type @SUM(

3 Click on cell B9, 8-track tape sales for 1975.

4 Drag the selection down through cell B12 to highlight the range B9..B12.

5 Type) and press ENTER

The word *Circ* is displayed in the status bar.

6 Display the formula precedents of cell B12. Notice that B12 is dependent on itself.

Understanding Circular References

A ***circular reference*** occurs when a formula refers, either directly or indirectly, to itself. This kind of formula usually doesn't make any sense, so it is considered an error. The erroneous formula you just entered is an example of one of the more common places where circular references can occur. When using the mouse or arrow keys to select a range within a formula, you should drag or select *away* from the formula: this will reduce the chance of inadvertently including the formula's own cell within the selected range.

In the following steps, you will rebuild the formula. Although you need not clear the old formulas first, you will do so in order to learn about the Clear command.

> *Tip* Clicking on the word *Circ* in the status bar (or selecting Circular References from the Audit dialog box) will position the cell pointer on the formula containing the circular reference.

To clear a range of cells:

1 Select the total tapes formulas in the range B12..E12.

2 Choose Clear from the Edit menu.
The Clear dialog box appears. The Cell Contents Only button is currently selected, which is correct.

3 Select OK.
The formulas in the range B12..E12 should now be erased.

Clearing cells is not the same as deleting them. When cells are cleared, their contents are erased but the cells themselves remain. Deleting cells removes the cells from the worksheet and shifts neighboring cells to take up the space.

You will now create the correct formula, copy it to the Total Tapes cells, and save the worksheet.

To build the correct Total Tapes formula:

1 Select cell B12, the cell that will display total tape sales for 1975.

2 Type +@SUM(

3 Select cell B11, cassette-single sales for 1975.

4 Select the range B11..B9.
Note that the range B11..B9 is the same as B9..B11.

5 Type) and press (ENTER)
The correct formula is @SUM(B11..B9)

6 Copy the formula to the range C12..E12 so that the total tape sales for 1980, 1985, and 1990 will also be calculated.
The screen should look like Figure 3.3.

	A	B	C	D	E	F	G
1	Shipments of Audio Recordings						
2	(in millions of dollars)						
3		1975	1980	1985	1990		
4	Phonograph Records						
5	LP Albums	1485	2290.3	1280.5	86.5		
6	Singles	211.5	269.3	281	94.4		
7	Total Records	1696.5	2559.6	1561.5	180.9		
8	Tapes						
9	8-tracks	583	526.4	25.3	0		
10	Cassettes	98.8	776.4	2411.5	3472.4		
11	Cassette Singles	0	0	0	87.4		
12	Total Tapes	681.8	1302.8	2436.8	3559.8		
13	Compact Discs						
14	Regular CDs	0	0	389.5	3451.6		
15	CD Singles	0	0	0	6		
16	Total CDs	0	0	389.5	3457.6		
17	Grand Total	2378.3	3862.4	4387.8	7198.3		
18							

Figure 3.3

7 Check the formula precedents of the newly copied formulas to confirm that they are correct.

8 Save the worksheet using the Save command in the File menu or the Save SmartIcon.

FORMATTING THE WORKSHEET

As in Project 1, you will use a Gallery template to format the worksheet. Templates work best on worksheets that have a relatively simple and consistent structure. This worksheet will require several manual adjustments after you use the Gallery template.

To apply a template to the worksheet:

1 Select the range A1..E17

2 Choose Gallery from the Style menu.
The Gallery dialog box appears.

3 Select the B&W3 template, and then select OK.
Notice that the template made column A too wide. It based its decision on the length of the worksheet's main title, *Shipments of Audio Recordings*. You will center this title across the columns of the worksheet in the next step, so column A does not need to be this wide.

4 Adjust the width of column A to about 18, so that it is slightly wider than the label *Phonograph Records*, as shown in Figure 3.4.

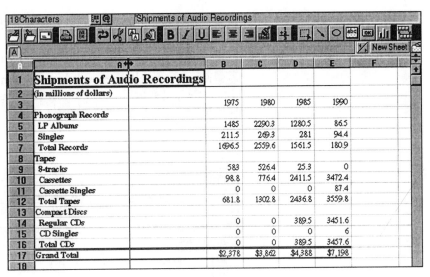

Figure 3.4

Centering Text Across Columns

The main title, *Shipments of Audio Recordings*, and the subtitle, *(in millions of dollars)*, would look better centered over the worksheet. You can center the contents of one cell over a selected group of columns by selecting Across Columns in the Alignment dialog box. Centering text across columns requires that you select a range whose leftmost cell contains the text you want to center; the selected range should extend across the columns within which you want the text centered.

To center text across columns:

1 Select cell A1, which contains the title *Shipments of Audio Recordings*.

2 Extend the selection to include the subtitle row (row 2) and the column for 1990 (column E), as shown in Figure 3.5.

	A	B	C	D	E	F	G	H
1	**Shipments of Audio Recordings**							
2	(in millions of dollars)							
3		1975	1980	1985	1990			
4	**Phonograph Records**							
5	LP Albums	1485	2290.3	1280.5	86.5			
6	Singles	211.5	269.3	281	94.4			
7	**Total Records**	1696.5	2559.6	1561.5	180.9			
8	**Tapes**							
9	8-tracks	583	526.4	25.3	0			
10	Cassettes	98.8	776.4	2411.5	3472.4			
11	Cassette Singles	0	0	0	87.4			
12	**Total Tapes**	681.8	1302.8	2436.8	3559.8			
13	**Compact Discs**							
14	Regular CDs	0	0	389.5	3451.6			
15	CD Singles	0	0	0	6			
16	**Total CDs**	0	0	389.5	3457.6			
17	**Grand Total**	$2,378	$3,862	$4,388	$7,198			
18								

Figure 3.5

3 Select Alignment from the Style menu.
The Alignment dialog box appears.

4 Select Center, select Across Columns, and then select OK.

5 Click any cell to cancel the selection.
The title and subtitle should now be centered above the worksheet, as shown in Figure 3.6. *Note that the text for these titles is still stored in cells A1 and A2.*

	A	B	C	D	E	F	G	H
1	Shipments	of Audio Recordings						
2		(in millions of dollars)						
3		1975	1980	1985	1990			
4	Phonograph Records							
5	LP Albums	1485	2290.3	1280.5	86.5			
6	Singles	211.5	269.3	281	94.4			
7	Total Records	1696.5	2559.6	1561.5	180.9			
8	Tapes							
9	8-tracks	583	526.4	25.3	0			
10	Cassettes	98.8	776.4	2411.5	3472.4			
11	Cassette Singles	0	0	0	87.4			
12	Total Tapes	681.8	1302.8	2436.8	3559.8			
13	Compact Discs							
14	Regular CDs	0	0	389.5	3451.6			
15	CD Singles	0	0	0	6			
16	Total CDs	0	0	389.5	3457.6			
17	Grand Total	$2,378	$3,862	$4,388	$7,198			
18								

Figure 3.6

Changing Row Height

The worksheet might look better if there were more vertical space between the titles and the years. To create this extra space, you could insert a new row. However, you will have more precise control over the spacing if instead you change the height of the years' row. This process is very similar to that of changing the width of a column.

Whereas the width of a column is measured in characters, the height of a row is measured in **points,** a traditional type-measurement unit employed by printers and typographers. A point, abbreviated as *pt.*, is equal to 1/72 inch.

To change row height:

1 Position the pointer so that it is over the *lower* edge of the heading for row 3 (on the line separating rows 3 and 4).
The pointer should change to a vertical double arrow.

2 Hold down the left mouse button and drag downward slightly to extend the lower edge of row 3.
The selection indicator shows the height.

3 Drag to set the height anywhere between 23 and 28 points, and then release the mouse button.

Saving the Worksheet Under a Different Name

The worksheet has once again changed significantly. In the steps that follow, you will save the worksheet before you print it. You will save this worksheet with a different name.

To save the worksheet with a different name:

1 Choose Save As from the File menu.
The Save As dialog box appears.

2 Type AUDIO2 for the file name, and then select OK.

EXIT If necessary, you can quit 1-2-3 now and continue this project later.

PRINTING THE WORKSHEET

Before you print a worksheet, you should quickly check your printer to make sure that it is turned on, has paper, and is online (communicating with your computer). If it is a dot-matrix printer, you should check that the paper is properly lined up.

To print the worksheet:

1 Make sure your printer is ready.

2 Choose Print from the File menu.
The Print dialog box appears.

3 Select OK.

Adding Cell Grid Lines

Your printout should look something like Figure 3.7. Notice that the printout does not show the cell grid lines. Although worksheets that have been formatted with border lines usually look better (and are less confusing to use) if the cell grid lines are turned off, you will occasionally want to print a worksheet with the cell grid lines displayed.

Shipments of Audio Recordings
(in millions of dollars)

	1975	1980	1985	1990
Phonograph Records				
LP Albums	1485	2290.3	1280.5	86.5
Singles	211.5	269.3	281	94.4
Total Records	1696.5	2559.6	1561.5	180.9
Tapes				
8-tracks	583	526.4	25.3	0
Cassettes	98.8	776.4	2411.5	3472.4
Cassette Singles	0	0	0	87.4
Total Tapes	681.8	1302.8	2436.8	3559.8
Compact Discs				
Regular CDs	0	0	389.5	3451.6
CD Singles	0	0	0	6
Total CDs	0	0	389.5	3457.6
Grand Total	$2,378	$3,862	$4,388	$7,198

Figure 3.7

To add cell grid lines:

1 Choose Page Setup from the File menu.
The Page Setup dialog box appears.

2 Select Grid Lines, as shown in Figure 3.8, and then select OK.

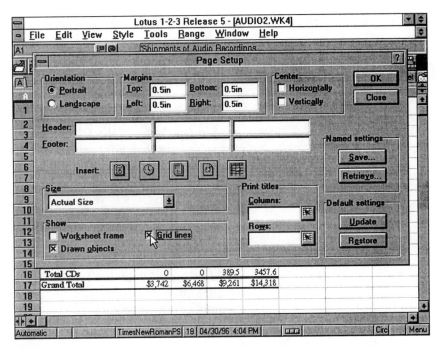

Figure 3.8

3 Print the file again.

Your printout should look similar to Figure 3.9.

Shipments of Audio Recordings			
(in millions of dollars)			
	1975	1980	1985	1990
Phonograph Records				
LP Albums	1485	2290.3	1280.5	86.5
Singles	211.5	269.3	281	94.4
Total Records	1696.5	2559.6	1561.5	180.9
Tapes				
8-tracks	583	526.4	25.3	0
Cassettes	98.8	776.4	2411.5	3472.4
Cassette Singles	0	0	0	87.4
Total Tapes	681.8	1302.8	2436.8	3559.8
Compact Discs				
Regular CDs	0	0	389.5	3451.6
CD Singles	0	0	0	6
Total CDs	0	0	389.5	3457.6
Grand Total	$2,378	$3,862	$4,388	$7,198

Figure 3.9

4 Save the AUDIO2 worksheet.

CHANGING NUMBER FORMATS

The Gallery template previously applied to the worksheet changed not only the type styles of the cells but also the way numbers within certain cells were displayed. For example, the last row of the worksheet (row 17) displays dollar signs in front of each number. Each cell also has a comma in the thousands place and is displayed with no decimal places. The Gallery template changed the *number format* of the cells. Number formats are used to punctuate numbers and to indicate any special units of measurement that apply to numbers in a worksheet. For example, dollar amounts are most clearly displayed with a dollar sign in front of the number, but the worksheet would be confusing if the year 1990 was displayed as $1,990. While a variety of number formats are available to punctuate numbers, it is important to note that the number itself remains unchanged, regardless of the number format applied. You will now alter the number formats of several cells to make the worksheet easier to read and to improve its appearance.

To change the number format of a cell:

1 Select cell B5, which contains the dollar amount 1485.

2 Select Number Format from the Style Menu.
The Number Format dialog box appears.

3 Scroll through the list of number formats available, and select Currency. When you select the Currency format, a Decimal Places text box appears, allowing you to select the number of decimal places that will be displayed.

4 Select 2 in the Decimal Places text box (if necessary), and then select OK.
Your screen should now resemble Figure 3.10.

	A	B	C	D	E	F	G	H
1	Shipments of Audio Recordings							
2	(in millions of dollars)							
3		1975	1980	1985	1990			
4	Phonograph Records							
5	LP Albums	$1,485.00	2290.3	1280.5	86.5			
6	Singles	211.5	269.3	281	94.4			
7	Total Records	1696.5	2559.6	1561.5	180.9			
8	Tapes							
9	8-tracks	583	526.4	25.3	0			
10	Cassettes	98.8	776.4	2411.5	3472.4			
11	Cassette Singles	0	0	0	87.4			
12	Total Tapes	681.8	1302.8	2436.8	3559.8			
13	Compact Discs							
14	Regular CDs	0	0	389.5	3451.6			
15	CD Singles	0	0	0	6			
16	Total CDs	0	0	389.5	3457.6			
17	Grand Total	$2,378	$3,862	$4,388	$7,198			
18								

Figure 3.10

Tip On some systems, the column width may be too narrow to display the formatted number, and a line of asterisks will be displayed instead. If this happens, make the column wider. In later steps, you will learn how to adjust the width of several columns at once.

Applying Number Formats to a Range

You can apply number formats to a range of cells in the same manner as you apply a format to a single cell. In the steps that follow, you will apply a currency format to the remaining dollar amounts in the worksheet. Although you could use the Number Format dialog box, you will instead use a shortcut method.

To change the number format of a range of cells:

1 Select the range B5..E17

2 Select the leftmost box on the status bar.
As shown in Figure 3.11, a list of format choices is displayed.

	A	B	C	D	E	F	G	H
1	**Shipments of Audio Recordings**							
Automatic		(in millions of dollars)						
Fixed								
Scientific		1975	1980	1985	1990			
, Comma								
General	raph records							
Percent	bums	$1,485.00	2290.3	1280.5	86.5			
Text	s	211.5	269.3	281	94.4			
Hidden								
Label	Records	1696.5	2559.6	1561.5	180.9			
British Pound								
Canadian Dollar	cs	583	526.4	25.3	0			
Japanese Yen	tes	98.8	776.4	2411.5	3472.4			
Mexican Peso	te Singles	0	0	0	87.4			
US Dollar	Tapes	681.8	1302.8	2436.8	3559.8			
31-Dec-93	ct Discs							
31-Dec	ar CDs	0	0	389.5	3451.6			
Dec-93								
12/31/93	ngles	0	0	0	6			
12/31	CDs	0	0	389.5	3457.6			
11:59:59 AM	Total		$2,378	$3,862	$4,388	$7,198		
11:59 AM								
23:59:59								
23:59								

Figure 3.11

3 Select U.S. Dollar from the list.
The range B5..E17 is displayed using U.S. Dollar format.

Notice that the number 2 now appears immediately to the right of the box on the status bar you used to select the U.S. Dollar number format. When you select the U.S. Dollar number format, 1-2-3 assumes that you want to display two decimal places to the right of the decimal point. You can click on the 2 to display a list from which you can select the number of decimal places to display.

Figure 3.12 shows some of the other tools that appear on the status bar.

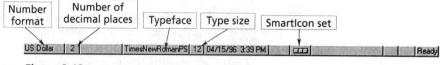

Figure 3.12

Adjusting the Width of Multiple Columns

The U.S. Dollar number formatting added several characters to each of the dollar amounts in the worksheet, leaving little separation between numbers in columns B through E. In some cases, applying a U.S. Dollar number format will add enough characters to the cell that the column is no longer wide enough to display the entire cell contents. When the column width is too narrow to display all of the characters within a cell, a row of asterisks is displayed instead of the value of the cell.

While the widths of columns B through E could be adjusted individually, you will adjust the width of a group of columns by selecting the group and then adjusting the width of any column in the group.

To adjust the width of a group of columns:

1 Select columns B through E by dragging the mouse pointer across the column headings B through E and then releasing the mouse button.

2 Position the mouse pointer on the *right* edge of any selected column heading. Using the information provided in the selection indicator, drag to select a new width of about nine characters, as shown in Figure 3.13.

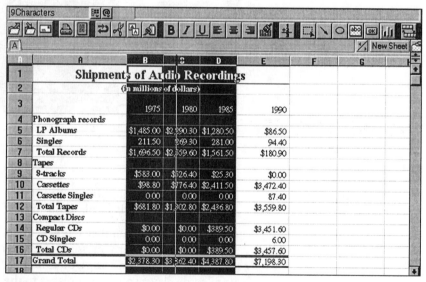

Figure 3.13

Using the Comma Number Format

The worksheet might look better if only the first and last rows within each category were displayed with a leading dollar sign. Comma format displays numbers in much the same way as U.S. Dollar format but without the leading dollar sign. In the steps that follow, you will apply Comma format to several cell ranges.

To change cells to display in Comma format:

1 Select the range B6..E6.

2 Select Comma format from the number formats menu on the status bar.

The dollar signs in the range are no longer displayed.

3 In a manner similar to steps 1 and 2, apply the Comma format to the range B10..E11 and then to B15..E15.

Your worksheet should now resemble Figure 3.14.

	A	B	C	D	E	F	G
1	Shipments of Audio Recordings						
2	(in millions of dollars)						
3		1975	1980	1985	1990		
4	Phonograph Records						
5	LP Albums	$1,485.00	$2,290.30	$1,280.50	$86.50		
6	Singles	211.50	269.30	281.00	94.40		
7	Total Records	$1,696.50	$2,559.60	$1,561.50	$180.90		
8	Tapes						
9	8-tracks	$583.00	$526.40	$25.30	$0.00		
10	Cassettes	98.80	776.40	2,411.50	3,472.40		
11	Cassette Singles	0.00	0.00	0.00	87.40		
12	Total Tapes	$681.80	$1,302.80	$2,436.80	$3,559.80		
13	Compact Discs						
14	Regular CDs	$0.00	$0.00	$389.50	$3,451.60		
15	CD Singles	0.00	0.00	0.00	6.00		
16	Total CDs	$0.00	$0.00	$389.50	$3,457.60		
17	Grand Total	$2,378.30	$3,862.40	$4,387.80	$7,198.30		
18							

Figure 3.14

4 Click the mouse button to cancel the range selection.

5 Save the worksheet.

6 Print the worksheet.

THE NEXT STEP

You are now ready to build a larger and more powerful worksheet. With the insight you have gained about formatting, you will be able to begin taking more control over formatting your worksheets, because, as you have seen, Gallery templates won't always do what you want them to.

In the next project, you will build and format a worksheet on energy conservation that estimates the electricity used by a household and allows you to identify high-energy-cost appliances.

SUMMARY AND EXERCISES

Summary

- When you make major additions or changes to a worksheet, you must consider the effect those changes might have on existing parts of the worksheet—especially formulas.
- Formula precedents are those cells on which the formula depends.
- Cell dependents are other cells that refer to that cell.
- You can insert blank cells into a worksheet, shifting existing cells away to make room. Formulas do not always automatically adjust the way you might want them to.
- A circular-reference error occurs when a cell either directly or indirectly refers to itself.
- Clearing a range of cells erases the contents of the cells but does not remove the cells from the worksheet.
- You can center cell entries across multiple columns; this is especially useful for worksheet titles.
- Row height can be changed in a manner similar to that for changing column width.
- Number formats affect the way numbers are displayed in the worksheet, and help differentiate and give meaning to different types of numbers.
- The format applied to a number does not change the underlying number stored in the cell.
- The width of several columns can be changed at the same time by first selecting the columns and then adjusting the width of one of the selected columns.
- Tools on the status bar can be used to select several types of number formats and type characteristics.

Key Terms and Operations

Key Terms	Operations
circular reference	Alignment
cell dependent	Audit
precedent	Clear
number format	Insert
point	Number Format
	Page Setup
	Print

Study Questions

Multiple Choice

1. Cells containing formulas that refer directly or indirectly to another cell are called cell
   - a. descendants.
   - b. ancestors.
   - c. lineage.
   - d. dependents.
   - e. precedents.

2. Cells (containing formulas) that refer either directly or indirectly to a particular cell are called cell
   a. referents.
   b. dependents.
   c. terminal nodes.
   d. signs.
   e. descendants.

3. Which statement about the Edit Insert command is correct?
   a. Any information present in the insert area is automatically cleared before the inserted text is added.
   b. The command will prompt you to type the text or numeric constants to be inserted.
   c. The command works on cells containing formulas.
   d. Existing cells in the insertion range will be shifted to accommodate the inserted, blank cells.
   e. None of the above.

4. The formula @SUM(B3..E3) is stored in cell E3. What (if anything) is the problem with the formula?
   a. It contains a circular reference and should be @SUM(B3..D3).
   b. It should be @SUM(B3 + C3 + D3 + E3).
   c. It contains a circular reference and should be @SUM(E3..B3).
   d. It should be + B3 + C3 + D3 + E3.
   e. Nothing is wrong with the formula.

5. When a label in cell A1 is centered across columns A through D, in what cell is the label stored?
   a. cell A1
   b. cell B1
   c. cell C1
   d. cell D1
   e. Between cells B1 and C1

6. A line of asterisks in a cell usually indicates that
   a. you entered asterisks in that cell.
   b. the column is too narrow to fit the formula in that cell.
   c. the column is too narrow to fit the label in that cell.
   d. the column is too narrow to fit the number in that cell.
   e. All of the above.

7. A Gallery template affects what characteristics of the selected cells?
   a. type style
   b. number format
   c. cell borders
   d. cell height
   e. all of the above

8. The status bar can be used to change quickly what aspect(s) of a selected cell (or range of cells)?
   a. type style
   b. number of displayed decimal places
   c. number format
   d. type size
   e. all of the above

9. What number format is used to display a number with a leading dollar sign?
   a. Comma
   b. Dollar
   c. Font
   d. Automatic
   e. Regular

10. What command should be used to save a file under a new name?
    a. New on the File menu
    b. Save on the File menu
    c. Rename on the File menu
    d. Save As on the File menu
    e. Save As on the Edit menu

Short Answer

1. The formula +A1-A2+A3 is stored in cell A2. What (if anything) is wrong with it?

2. What mouse action or command is used to find the precedents of the currently selected cell?

3. Will centering text across columns change the cells where the text is stored? Will it break up the text and distribute the pieces to be stored in various cells?

4. List the formatting settings that can be changed using the status bar.

5. Is inserting a blank row the best way to increase the space between rows of information in a worksheet? If not, what is a better way?

6. What is the easiest way to change the width of several columns at once?

7. What is the advantage of using a number format over entering cell contents with dollar signs, commas, and decimals?

8. When would you use a Gallery template instead of formatting individual cells?

9. Under what circumstances will a formula fail to refer to the correct cells after inserting a row?

10. What is the easiest way to locate a circular reference?

For Discussion

1. Why should you be careful when making major changes to a worksheet? What things should you do before you make a change? What should you check after the change?

2. What is a circular reference? Give an example.

3. Describe what happens when a Gallery template is applied to a worksheet. How does this affect the type style and number formatting?

Review Exercises

Municipal Waste Trends

In the first review exercise in Project 2, you built a worksheet about municipal waste and saved it under the name EPA1. If you haven't already created that worksheet, refer to Project 2 to build it. Then proceed to add the new information shown in Figure 3.15 for metals in the nonfood category.

	A	B	C	D	E	F	G	H
1	Municipal Waste							
2		1960	1970	1980	1990			
3	Nonfood Wastes							
4	Paper	0.91	1.19	1.32	1.6			
5	Glass	0.2	0.34	0.36	0.28			
6	Plastics	0.01	0.08	0.19	0.32			
7	Metals	0.32	0.38	0.35	0.34			
8	Total Nonfood	1.44	1.99	2.22	2.54			
9	Other							
10	Food	0.37	0.34	0.32	0.29			
11	Yard	0.61	0.62	0.66	0.7			
12	Total Other	0.98	0.96	0.98	0.99			
13	Grand Total	2.42	2.95	3.2	3.53			
14								

Figure 3.15

Use the Insert command to create a blank row for this new information; it should be between the rows labeled *Plastics* and *Total Nonfood*. Check, adjust, and copy formulas as necessary and save it under the name EPA2 for use in Project 4 before proceeding. Now, format the worksheet using a Gallery template. Save the worksheet under the name EPA3.

Winter Olympic Medals

In the second review exercise of Project 2, you built and saved OLYMPIC1, a worksheet that tabulates medals won by selected countries during the 1992 Winter Olympics. If you haven't already created that worksheet, refer to Project 2 to build it.

Use the information shown in Figure 3.16 to add Italy to the worksheet.

	A	B	C	D	E	F	G	H
1	1992 Winter Olympiad							
2								
3	Country	Gold	Silver	Bronze	Total			
4	Germany	10	10	6	26			
5	Unified Team	9	6	8	23			
6	Austria	6	7	8	21			
7	Norway	9	6	5	20			
8	Italy	4	6	4	?			
9	Total	34	29	27	90			
10								

Figure 3.16

Use the Insert command to create a blank row for this new information; it should be the last country in the list. Check, adjust, and copy formulas as necessary. Format the worksheet using a Gallery template. Save the worksheet under the name OLYMPIC2.

Assignments

Space Payloads

In the third assignment in Project 2, you built and saved SPACE1, a worksheet that tabulates rocket payloads put into space by selected countries. If you haven't already created that worksheet, refer to Project 2 to build it.

Add the information for the European Space Agency (ESA) as shown in Figure 3.17. Adjust and copy formulas as necessary, format the worksheet using a Gallery template, and save the worksheet under the name SPACE2.

A	A	B	C	D	E	F	G	H
1	Space Payloads							
2								
3		1988	1989	1990	1991	Average		
4	USSR	107	95	96	101	99.75		
5	United States	15	22	31	30	24.5		
6	ESA	2	2	1	4	?		
7	Japan	2	4	7	2	3.75		
8	Total	126	123	135	137	130.25		
9								

Figure 3.17

Coffee House Income

Starting with the third assignment in Project 1 and continuing in the first assignment in Project 2, you built and saved COFFEE2, a spreadsheet that calculates the income derived from sales of various coffees at Clem's Coffee Clutch. If you haven't already created that worksheet, refer to Projects 1 and 2 to build it.

Add information for Cafe Royale, as shown in Figure 3.18. Adjust and copy formulas as necessary.

A	A	B	C	D	E	F	G	H	I
1	Coffee	Cost	Selling Price	No. Sold	Income				
2	House Blend	0.39	0.95	60	33.6				
3	Espresso	0.61	1.25	12	7.68				
4	Cappuccino	0.74	1.5	22	16.72				
5	Cafe Mocha	0.55	1.45	35	31.5				
6	Cafe Royale	0.68	1.85	55	?				
7	Total			184	89.5				
8									

Figure 3.18

Important   Save a copy of the worksheet under the name COFFEX for use in Project 4 before proceeding. Format the worksheet using a Gallery template and save the worksheet under the name COFFEE3.

Additions to AUDIO2

Modify the AUDIO2 worksheet to include data for 1991, as well as figures for shipments of music videos, as shown in Figure 3.19.

	A	B	C	D	E	F
1	Shipments of Audio Recordings					
2	(in millions of dollars)					
3		1975	1980	1985	1990	1991
4	Phonograph Records					
5	LP Albums	$1,485.00	$2,290.30	$1,280.50	$86.50	$4.80
6	Singles	211.50	269.30	281.00	94.40	22.00
7	Total Records	$1,696.50	$2,559.60	$1,561.50	$180.90	$26.80
8	Tapes					
9	8-tracks	$583.00	$526.40	$25.30	$0.00	$0.00
10	Cassettes	98.80	776.40	2,411.50	3,472.40	360.10
11	Cassette Singles	0.00	0.00	0.00	87.40	69.00
12	Total Tapes	$681.80	$1,302.80	$2,436.80	$3,559.80	$429.10
13	Compact Discs					
14	Regular CDs	$0.00	$0.00	$389.50	$3,451.60	$333.30
15	CD Singles	0.00	0.00	0.00	6.00	5.70
16	Total CDs	0.00	0.00	389.50	3,457.60	339.00
17	Music Videos	$0.00	$0.00	$0.00	$9.20	$6.10
18	Grand Total	$2,378.30	$3,862.40	$4,387.80	$7,207.50	$801.00
19						

Figure 3.19

After inserting the new information, adjust and copy formulas as necessary, reformat the worksheet, and save it under the name AUDIO3.

Objectives

After completing this project, you should be able to:

▶ Magnify or reduce your view of a worksheet

▶ Change the default worksheet font

▶ Change the alignment of cell entries

▶ Apply number formats

▶ Recognize and use absolute cell references

▶ Change the font attribute and font size of a cell entry

▶ Add borders to the worksheet

▶ Define and use named ranges

CASE STUDY: HOME ENERGY USAGE

One way to decide how to save on home-electric bills—and reduce electricity consumption and related power-plant pollution—is to determine how each electrical appliance in your home or apartment contributes to your total monthly bill. Along with your personal electricity-usage patterns, many other factors, such as season, climate, and the availability of less expensive gas heating, will influence the total bill. Lotus 1-2-3 is the ideal tool for making sense of these variables and simplifying the task of estimating electricity consumption.

Designing the Solution

In this project, you will build a worksheet that lists various electrical appliances and estimates their monthly consumption of electricity. The worksheet will describe a basic, all-electric home during a mild winter month in a moderate climate. Constructing this worksheet will involve calculating the monthly energy used by each appliance, a calculation based on each appliance's energy-consumption rate and the amount of time it is used during a month.

There are several ways you could design a worksheet to implement the calculation described above. You could construct one giant formula to perform all calculations on all variables, but the worksheet will be easier to understand and modify if you break the process into smaller steps comprising a series of simpler formulas. You will take the latter approach in this project.

Figure 4.1 shows the completed worksheet. Separate columns designate each of the major variables involved in the calculation. The flexibility of this electronic worksheet will make possible easy experimentation and adaptation with variables such as different appliances, different electricity-usage habits, and so on.

Residential Electricity Usage

Cost per kilowatt-hour: $0.08

Appliance	Wattage	Mon	Tue	Wed	Thu	Fri	Sat	Sun	Operating Hours per Month	Kilowatt-hours per month	Estimated Cost per Month
					Hours Cycled-On						
Heating/Cooling											
Heat pump (3 ton)	4,800	4.00	4.00	4.00	4.00	4.00	6.00	6.00	128	614	$49.15
Portable heater	1,500	1.00	1.00	1.00	1.00	1.00	2.00	2.00	36	54	4.32
Water heater	4,100	2.00	2.00	2.00	2.00	2.00	4.00	4.00	72	295	23.62
Kitchen											
Frost-free refrigerator	460	15.00	15.00	15.00	15.00	15.00	15.00	15.00	420	193	15.46
Convection oven	3,000	0.00	0.00	0.00	0.00	0.00	3.00	3.00	24	72	5.76
Microwave oven	1,500	0.25	0.25	0.25	0.25	0.25	0.50	1.00	11	17	1.32
Dishwasher	1,200	1.00	0.00	1.00	0.00	1.00	1.00	1.00	20	24	1.92
Laundry											
Washing machine	510	0.00	0.00	0.00	0.00	0.00	3.00	3.00	24	12	0.98
Clothes dryer	4,850	0.00	0.00	0.00	0.00	0.00	3.00	3.00	24	116	9.31
Lighting											
Incandescent	150	5.00	5.00	5.00	5.00	5.00	5.00	5.00	140	21	1.68
Fluorescent (twin)	96	5.00	5.00	5.00	5.00	5.00	5.00	5.00	140	13	1.08
Fluorescent (compact)	18	5.00	5.00	5.00	5.00	5.00	5.00	5.00	140	3	0.20
Electronics											
Color television	145	2.00	2.00	2.00	2.00	4.00	6.00	7.00	100	15	1.16
Personal computer	160	1.00	1.00	1.00	1.00	1.00	2.00	3.00	40	6	0.51
Total											$116.46

Figure 4.1

ENTERING THE WORKSHEET CONSTANTS

You will first enter some of the worksheet titles and number constants. You will do some formatting early in the project, to make subsequent data entry and formula construction easier to follow. You can refer to Figure 4.2 to see a partial, unformatted version of the worksheet. As in the previous project, the more intricate formatting steps will be completed in the final phase of worksheet construction.

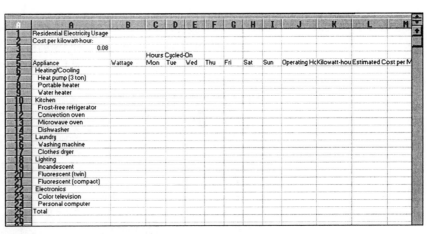

Figure 4.2

To enter the main title and first subtitle:

1 Enter `Residential Electricity Usage` in cell A1.

2 Enter `Cost per kilowatt-hour:` in cell A2.

3 Enter `0.08` in cell A3.

4 Widen column A so that it contains all of *Residential Electricity Usage*.

Magnifying and Reducing a Worksheet Window

At normal magnification, a worksheet is rarely visible in its entirety; the screen and the worksheet window restrict your view. Lotus 1-2-3 lets you *zoom out* (reduce) or *zoom in* (magnify) your view of the worksheet to let you see more or less of the worksheet. Zoom Out reduces the size of the worksheet by 10 percent, while Zoom In magnifies the worksheet by 10 percent. Occasionally, you will zoom in for a closer look, but more often you will zoom out to see more of the worksheet at once. A disadvantage of zooming out is that, because you see more of the worksheet in a reduced size, it is more difficult to position your cursor correctly on specific cells.

In the steps that follow, you will experiment with the Zoom commands in the View menu. From now on, you should use the Zoom commands whenever you want to change your view of a worksheet.

To magnify a worksheet:

1 Choose Zoom In from the View menu.
Each worksheet cell appears much larger, but you can't see as many cells.

2 Choose Custom—87% from the View menu.
The worksheet returns to its original size. The standard magnification of a 1-2-3 worksheet is 87 percent.

To reduce a worksheet:

1 Choose Zoom Out from the View menu.
You can see many more cells on the worksheet, but individual cells become more difficult to read. This is especially true when Windows is running with standard VGA video (rather than with SuperVGA).

To set a custom magnification:

1 Choose Set View Preferences from the View menu.

The Set View Preferences dialog box appears.

2 Using the up and down arrows on the Custom Zoom % text box, change the magnification to 60 percent, as shown in Figure 4.3.

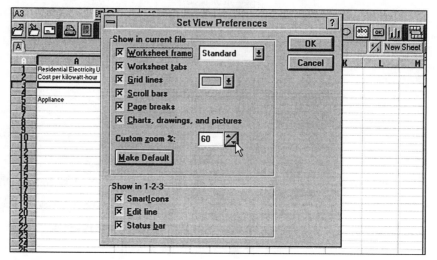

Figure 4.3

3 Select OK.
The worksheet is reduced in size.

4 Click the View menu.
Notice that the menu item for Custom Zoom now reads *Custom—60*. The magnification setting of 60 is saved with the worksheet, so that the next time the worksheet is retrieved, the Custom zoom magnification will remain at 60 percent. Other worksheets, however, will always use the standard 87 percent magnification until you change them.

To return to standard magnification:

1 Choose Set View Preferences from the View menu.

2 Type **87** in the Custom Zoom % text box, and then select OK.

Changing the Default Worksheet Font

The worksheet in this project will be created and modified using a reduced magnification. On many systems, the worksheet will be easy to read if you use a TrueType font. A *font,* or typeface, is the form or design of letters. The TrueType font technology is built directly into Microsoft Windows. The default font in 1-2-3, called Arial, is a TrueType font. In this section, you will learn how to change the worksheet default font setting.

To change the worksheet default font:

1 Select Worksheet Defaults from the Style menu.
The Worksheet Defaults dialog box appears.

2 Choose Arial from the Font face list, as shown in Figure 4.4.

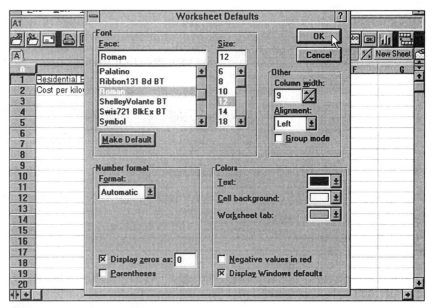

Figure 4.4

3 Select OK.

Because the worksheet default has been changed, the contents of all the cells appear in the Roman font. Notice that the status bar font indicator now displays Roman instead of Arial.

4 Choose Undo from the edit menu.

Using the Fill by Example Command

In the sections that follow, you will enter and partially format the column titles. To make it easier to see what you are typing, you will first reduce the magnification of the worksheet by setting a custom zoom percent. As you work, you can refer to Figure 4.5.

You could manually enter the days of the week as the column headings in C5..I5, but 1-2-3 provides a shortcut called Fill by Example that you can use when entering the days of the week or names of the months. When you select a range that represents part of a standard sequence or series, 1-2-3 automatically fills in the other members of the series. For example, if you select a range that contains the text *Feb* in the leftmost cell and three blank cells to the right, the Fill by Example command will enter *Mar*, *Apr*, and *May* in the blank cells.

Figure 4.5

To enter the column titles:

1 Set a custom zoom percent of 60 to reduce magnification of the worksheet.

2 Enter `Appliance` in cell A5.

3 Enter `Wattage` in cell B5.

4 Enter `Mon` in cell C5.

5 Select the range C5..I5.

6 Select Fill by Example from the Range menu.

The range now contains abbreviations for the days of the week, as shown in Figure 4.5.

7 Change the width of columns C through I to 4 characters.

> **Reminder** To change the width of multiple columns, you can select the columns by dragging the pointer across the column headings. Then you can position the pointer on the right edge of any selected column heading, so that the pointer becomes a double-ended arrow, and then drag to select a new width.

8 In cell C4, *above* the column title *Mon*, enter `Hours Cycled-On`

9 In cell J5, enter `Operating Hours per Month`

This column will be used to estimate how many hours per month an appliance is used. Do not be concerned if a column title or other cell entry appears to spill over into a neighboring cell or to be cut off by a neighboring cell.

10 In cell K5, enter `Kilowatt-hours per Month`

Later you will construct a formula to calculate the number of kilowatt-hours used each month.

11 In cell L5, enter `Estimated Cost per Month`

This column will contain a formula that computes the electricity cost. Your worksheet should resemble Figure 4.6.

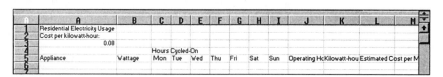

Figure 4.6

Changing the Alignment of Cell Entries

A text entry is automatically aligned against the left edge of its cell and a number entry against the right edge, but you can change these default alignments. Text titles appearing above numeric entries will look better if they are aligned at the center or to the right.

Notice that Figure 4.1 shows the long column titles, such as Operating Hours per Month, *wrapping* in their cells. Wrapping means to continue a long entry onto a separate line.

In the steps that follow, you will center the column titles Wattage through Estimated Cost per Month and specify that long entries be wrapped.

To center and wrap selected column titles:

1 Select B5..L5, the range of text entries to be aligned.

2 Choose Alignment from the Style menu.
The Alignment dialog box appears.

3 Select the Center option under Horizontal.

4 Select the Wrap Text checkbox.
Your screen should resemble Figure 4.7.

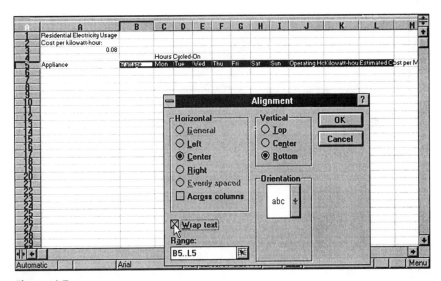

Figure 4.7

5 Select OK to complete the alignment.
The column headings should now be centered and where necessary wrap within their cells. Notice that wrapping automatically adjusts the height of row 5.

6 Increase the width of columns J, K, and L to 10 characters to make the worksheet look less cramped.

Entering the Remaining Text Constants

In the following steps, you will enter the text constants for the row titles. Note that two levels of indentation are used for the row titles to visually outline the list of appliances. Section titles such as Heating/Cooling are indented two spaces, and individual appliance names, such as Water heater, are indented four spaces. You can use Figure 4.8 as a reference.

To enter the row titles:

1 Select cell A6. Press (SPACE) twice, type **Heating/Cooling** and then press (ENTER)

2 Select cell A7. Press (SPACE) four times, type **Heat pump (3 ton)** and then press (ENTER)

3 Enter the remaining row titles, referring to Figure 4.8.
Note that *Total* is not indented; *Kitchen*, *Laundry*, *Lighting*, and *Electronics* are indented by preceding the text with two spaces, and the remaining titles are indented four spaces.

4 Choose Spell Check from the Tools menu, and check the spelling of the worksheet.

5 Save the worksheet under the name ENERGY1. Your worksheet should resemble Figure 4.8.

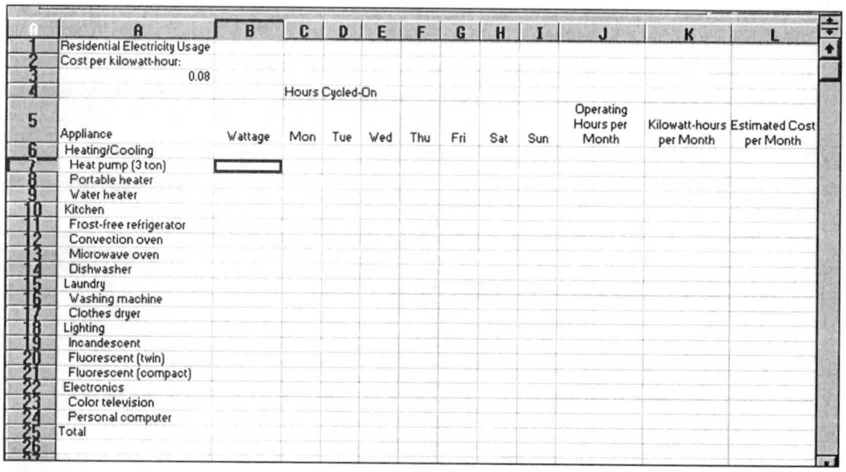

Figure 4.8

> *Tip* If you are building a worksheet that requires several levels of indentation, you can use separate columns for each indentation level, rather than using spaces. Although this approach slightly increases the complexity of the worksheet, adjusting (by means of column width changes) the indentation for each level is much easier.

Entering the Number Constants

You will now enter the number constants for wattage and hours cycled-on. Note that the values in the Hours Cycled-On section are ordinary decimal numbers: an hour-and-a-half is written as 1.50, not 1:30. In the following steps, you will also learn a data-entry shortcut that lets you fill a large selection of cells easily with a single entry.

The first step in calculating the energy used by an appliance over the course of a month is to determine the appliance's power consumption, or the rate at which it uses up energy. The amount of electrical power an appliance consumes is measured in *watts*. A typical light bulb uses 100 watts; a typical microwave oven uses 1500 watts.

If you need to know how many watts an appliance uses, check the appliance's operating manual or look for the information on the appliance itself. If watts are not listed on the appliance, volts (V) and amps (A) generally are. You can multiply volts by amps to calculate watts. Note that sometimes the appliance's power supply will list the maximum rated power consumption, not what the appliance actually uses under normal operating conditions.

To enter the appliance-wattage constants:

1 Enter **4800** in cell B7.

This is the wattage of the 3-ton heat pump.

2 Enter carefully the remaining number constants for the Wattage column only, referring to Figures 4.1 or 4.9.

Because all punctuation is added through formatting, do not type commas in any of the numbers.

Appliance	Wattage	Mon	Tue	Wed	Thu	Fri	Sat	Sun	Operating Hours per Month	Kilowatt-hours per Month	Estimated Cost per Month
Residential Electricity Usage											
Cost per kilowatt-hour:											
0.08											
			Hours Cycled-On								
Heating/Cooling											
Heat pump (3 ton)	4800	4	4	4	4	4	6	6			
Portable heater	1500	1	1	1	1	1	2	2			
Water heater	4100	2	2	2	2	2	4	4			
Kitchen											
Frost-free refrigerator	460	15	15	15	15	15	15	15			
Convection oven	3000	0	0	0	0	0	3	3			
Microwave oven	1500	0.25	0.25	0.25	0.25	0.25	0.5	1			
Dishwasher	1200	1	0	1	0	1	1	1			
Laundry											
Washing machine	510	0	0	0	0	0	3	3			
Clothes dryer	4850	0	0	0	0	0	3	3			
Lighting											
Incandescent	150	5	5	5	5	5	5	5			
Fluorescent (twin)	96	5	5	5	5	5	5	5			
Fluorescent (compact)	18	5	5	5	5	5	5	5			
Electronics											
Color television	145	2	2	2	2	4	6	7			
Personal computer	160	1	1	1	1	1	2	3			
Total											

Figure 4.9

Your next step is to estimate how many hours per month the appliance is used. With many appliances, you can estimate how many hours the appliance runs each day of the week, total these times, and then approximate a month's worth of use by multiplying the total by four (there are an average of about four weeks in a month).

Notice that in Figure 4.9 all three types of lighting are estimated to run at five hours per day, every day of the week. Rather than using the Copy command or typing 5 in each of the 21 cells, you will use an alternative for this type of repetitive entry.

To quickly enter the usage times for lighting:

1 Select the range encompassing hours used for each of the lighting types for all the days, C19..I21.

2 Choose Fill from the Range menu.

The Fill dialog box appears.

3 In the Start text box, type **5**

4 In the Increment text box, type **0**

Your screen should resemble Figure 4.10.

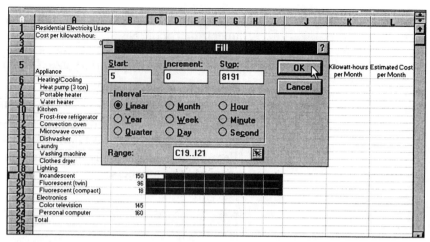

Figure 4.10

The Fill command lets you fill a range with numbers, starting with a specified number and incrementing by a certain amount, in each cell in the range. For example, to fill a range with even numbers beginning with 4, you would enter 4 as the starting number, with an increment of 2. If the increment is zero, 1-2-3 will fill the selected range with whatever the starting number was; in this case, 5.

5 Select OK.
The number 5 should be entered in all the cells of the selected range.

Other appliances vary in their consumption of electricity. For example, an air conditioner or an oven consumes significant amounts of electricity but only when actually in use. When calculating the hours cycled-on in your own home, you may need to refer to published approximations of typical running times for certain appliances.

To enter the remaining usage times:

1 Enter the remaining numbers for hours cycled-on. Use the various shortcut methods you've learned so far to do this quickly and easily.

2 Save the worksheet.
Your worksheet should now resemble Figure 4.9.

Entering the Worksheet Formulas

Electric bills are based on the number of hours each appliance runs, and the billing units are *kilowatt-hours*. A kilowatt is 1000 watts, and one kilowatt-hour is the energy consumed by running a 1000-watt appliance for one hour. If you run a 1000-watt hair dryer for three hours a month, you have consumed 3000 watt-hours or 3 kilowatt-hours of energy. The formula for energy consumption is generally written as (watts/1000)*hours. Remember to divide watts by 1000 when converting to kilowatts.

To estimate the monthly energy cost of an appliance, multiply the kilowatt-hours it consumes by the cost per kilowatt-hour. With typical residential electric rates, electricity costs between $0.03 and $0.15 per kilowatt-hour. Check an electric bill or call your utility company to find out the rate for your area.

You have already entered an electric rate of 8 cents ($0.08) per kilowatt-hour in cell A3. The monthly cost of the hair dryer mentioned above is 24 cents. As you can see in Figure 4.1, large appliances used for heating (or cooling) are the major consumers of electricity in the home.

To build the formula for operating hours per month:

1 Select cell J7, which will contain the operating hours per month for the heat pump.

2 Type `+@SUM(`

3 Using Point mode, select the range to be summed, C7..I7, Monday's operating hours through Sunday's.

4 Type `)*4` and then press (ENTER)
The meaning of this formula is: total the seven cells to the left and multiply the total by 4. The formula's relative addressing will work when you copy it to the other cells in the column. The result of this formula is 128.

Pasting to a Range

The formula you have just created needs to be copied to calculate operating hours per month for the other appliances. You could use the Copy Down command to copy the formula down the entire range; however, this would copy the formula into certain cells that should be blank (J10, for example). You will instead use the Copy command to first make a copy of the cell and then use the Paste command to copy the formula into each cell in the correct ranges.

To paste a cell to a range:

1 Select cell J7, which contains the formula to be copied.

2 Choose Copy from the Edit menu.

3 Select the range J8..J9.

4 Choose Paste from the Edit menu.
The range will be filled with copies of the formula.

5 Select the range J11..J14 and then choose Paste from the Edit menu. Continue by selecting the remaining ranges one at a time (J11..J14, J16..J17, J19..J21, and J23..J24) and then choosing Paste. You can also issue the Paste command by pressing (CTRL)+V.
Your screen should resemble Figure 4.11.

Appliance	Wattage	| Hours Cycled-On							Operating Hours per Month	Kilowatt-hours per Month	Estimated Cost per Month
		Mon	Tue	Wed	Thu	Fri	Sat	Sun			
Residential Electricity Usage											
Cost per kilowatt-hour:											
0.08											
Heating/Cooling											
Heat pump (3 ton)	4800	4	4	4	4	4	6	6	128		
Portable heater	1500	1	1	1	1	1	2	2	36		
Water heater	4100	2	2	2	2	2	4	4	72		
Kitchen											
Frost-free refrigerator	460	15	15	15	15	15	15	15	420		
Convection oven	3000	0	0	0	0	0	3	3	24		
Microwave oven	1500	0.25	0.25	0.25	0.25	0.25	0.5	1	11		
Dishwasher	1200	1	0	1	0	1	1	1	20		
Laundry											
Washing machine	510	0	0	0	0	0	3	3	24		
Clothes dryer	4850	0	0	0	0	0	3	3	24		
Lighting											
Incandescent	150	5	5	5	5	5	5	5	140		
Fluorescent (twin)	96	5	5	5	5	5	5	5	140		
Fluorescent (compact)	18	5	5	5	5	5	5	5	140		
Electronics											
Color television	145	2	2	2	2	4	6	7	100		
Personal computer	160	1	1	1	1	1	2	3	40		
Total											

Figure 4.11

Calculating Kilowatt-Hours per Month

The kilowatt-hours of energy used by an appliance in a month is the number of kilowatts it consumes multiplied by the number of hours it is cycled-on.

 ### *To build the formula for kilowatt-hours per month:*

1 Select cell K7, which will contain kilowatt-hours per month for the heat pump.

2 Type **+(**

3 Point to the wattage for this appliance, in cell B7.

4 Type **/1000)***

5 Point to the operating hours per month for this appliance, in cell J7.

6 Press (ENTER)

This formula's relative addressing will work when the formula is copied to other cells. The completed formula, +(B7/1000)*J7, can be interpreted as: Take what is nine cells to the left, divide it by 1000, and multiply that result by what is one cell to the left.

7 Copy the completed formula to the cells in column K that should contain it.

The parentheses inserted in this formula are not required by the rules of operator priority, nor do they affect the result of the formula. They are used to help convey the logic of the computation to people who might later examine the formula.

Computing Estimated Cost per Month

The final column of your spreadsheet will compute the monthly cost of operating each appliance. This is calculated by multiplying the cost per kilowatt-hour (currently 0.08, in cell A3) by the kilowatt-hours per month calculated for each appliance in column K.

Follow the next steps carefully. To illustrate a common error, you will build a formula that is mathematically correct but does not work when copied to other cells. Later, you will correct the formula and copy it again.

To build the formula for estimated cost per month (first attempt):

1 Select cell L7, which will contain the cost per month of the heat pump.

Reminder The cost per month is the cost per kilowatt-hour multiplied by the number of kilowatt-hours used in a month.

2 Type +

3 Point to the cost per kilowatt-hour, in cell A3.

4 Type *

5 Point to the number of kilowatt-hours used, in cell K7.

6 Press (ENTER)

The completed formula reads +A3*K7

7 Using the skills you learned earlier for copying cells, copy this formula to the other cells that require it in column L.

Your worksheet should now resemble Figure 4.12.

	A	B	C	D	E	F	G	H	I	J	K	L
1	Residential Electricity Usage											
2	Cost per kilowatt-hour:											
3		0.08										
4				Hours Cycled-On								
5	Appliance	Wattage	Mon	Tue	Wed	Thu	Fri	Sat	Sun	Operating Hours per Month	Kilowatt-hours per Month	Estimated Cost per Month
6	Heating/Cooling											
7	Heat pump (3 ton)	4800	4	4	4	4	4	6	6	128	614.4	49.152
8	Portable heater	1500	1	1	1	1	1	2	2	36	54	0
9	Water heater	4100	2	2	2	2	2	4	4	72	295.2	0
10	Kitchen											
11	Frost-free refrigerator	460	15	15	15	15	15	15	15	420	193.2	0
12	Convection oven	3000	0	0	0	0	0	3	3	24	72	0
13	Microwave oven	1500	0.25	0.25	0.25	0.25	0.25	0.5	1	11	16.5	0
14	Dishwasher	1200	1	0	1	0	1	1	1	20	24	0
15	Laundry											
16	Washing machine	510	0	0	0	0	0	3	3	24	12.24	0
17	Clothes dryer	4850	0	0	0	0	0	3	3	24	116.4	0
18	Lighting											
19	Incandescent	150	5	5	5	5	5	5	5	140	21	0
20	Fluorescent (twin)	96	5	5	5	5	5	5	5	140	13.44	0
21	Fluorescent (compact)	18	5	5	5	5	5	5	5	140	2.52	0
22	Electronics											
23	Color television	145	2	2	2	2	4	6	7	100	14.5	0
24	Personal computer	160	1	1	1	1	1	2	3	40	6.4	0
25	Total											
26												

Figure 4.12

Using Absolute Cell References

There is obviously something wrong with the copied formulas. While the result of the original formula in cell L7 is correct, all the other formulas in column L result in 0 (zero).

Consider the original formula in cell L7. As with the other formulas you have created, +A3*K7 uses relative cell references. The formula means: take what is 4 cells up and 11 cells to the left, and multiply that by what is 1 cell to the left.

Now consider the copy of the formula in cell L8. It attempts to take the contents of cell A4, which is 4 cells up and 11 cells to the left, and multiply it by cell K8, which is 1 cell to the left.

The K8 part is correct; the A4 reference is wrong. Cell A4 is blank, and because blank cells have a value of zero, the result of the formula is 0. The results of the other formulas are 0, because the other formulas attempt to multiply by cells that contain text, which are also considered to have a value of zero.

The formula in cell L8 (and in all the other cells) should instead mean: take what is in cell A3, and multiply it by what is one cell to the left of the cell in which this formula is located. Using 1-2-3 terminology, the reference to cell A3 should not be a relative reference, but an *absolute reference.*

An absolute cell reference in a formula is frozen so that it will not change even if the formula that contains it is copied. A fully absolute reference is indicated with dollar signs preceding both the column letter and row number. For example, in $A$3, the dollar sign in front of the A means: don't change the A. The dollar sign in front of the 3 means: don't change the 3.

You can type the dollar signs within a cell, but the most convenient way to make a reference absolute is to use the absolute function key, (F4), which will work either when you are editing a formula or when you are in point mode. In the steps that follow you will rebuild the formula, this time making the reference to cell A3 absolute.

> *Tip* Any time you are pointing to a cell while building a formula and that cell alone provides the required information for the formula and for future copies of the formula, the reference to the cell should be absolute. In short: if you're building a formula to be copied, any references to specific cells should be made absolute.

To build the formula for estimated cost per month (second attempt):

1 Select cell L7, which will contain the cost per month of the heat pump.

2 Type +

3 Point to the cost per kilowatt-hour, in cell A3, and press (F4)
Notice that the dollar signs for absolute addressing appear in the contents box.

> *Tip* Don't hold down (F4), because it will cycle through absolute, mixed, and relative address forms. If this happens, tap (F4) several times to cycle back to where both the row and column part of the address are frozen.

4 Type *

5 Point to the number of kilowatt-hours used, in cell K7.

6 Press (ENTER)
The completed formula reads +$A$3*K7

7 Copy this formula to the other cells in column L that require it.
Your worksheet should now resemble Figure 4.13.

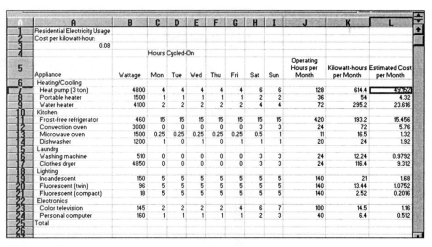

Figure 4.13

Once again, the formula you just created and copied means: take what is in cell A3 and multiply it by what is one cell to the left of the cell containing this formula.

Building the Total Formula

The only formula remaining for you to enter on the spreadsheet is the total of estimated monthly electricity costs.

To build the total formula:

1 Select cell L25, which will contain the total monthly cost of all appliances.

2 Type **+@SUM(**

3 Select the range encompassing all the cost formulas, L24..L7.

> *Tip* Select the range by moving backward. It's okay for the range to include blank cells—they won't affect the total.

4 Type **)** and press (ENTER)
The completed formula reads @SUM(L24..L7). Your worksheet should now resemble Figure 4.14.

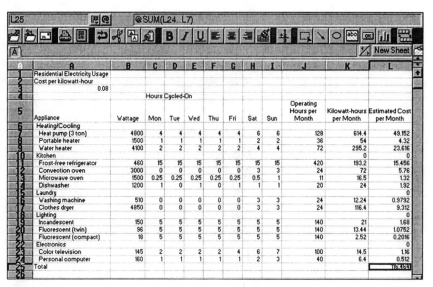

Figure 4.14

5 Save the worksheet.

EXIT If necessary, you can quit 1-2-3 now and continue this project later.

FORMATTING THE WORKSHEET

As you can see in Figure 4.1, the finished worksheet has several formatting features. In the remainder of this project, you will assign formats to the worksheet and arrive at a completed document that appears very similar to Figure 4.1.

Changing Number Formats

Three kinds of number formats are appropriate for this worksheet:

- A comma-punctuated format, called Comma, with zero decimal places, used for wattage, operating hours per month, and kilowatt-hours per month.
- A format showing two digits to the right of the decimal used for the hours cycled-on and for most of the values in the estimated cost per month column. Although the values in these areas are currently small numbers, in later uses of the worksheet they could become larger and so a comma-punctuated format could be helpful.
- A U.S. Dollar number format, showing two decimal places, used for the cells showing the first entry and the total in the estimated cost per month column.

In the following steps, you will apply a Comma number format to a collection composed of the columns for wattage, operating hours per month, and kilowatt-hours per month.

To apply the Comma number format to a collection:

1 Select a collection of cells that includes all the values in the wattage, operating hours per month, and kilowatt-hours per month columns (cells B7..B24, and J7..K24).

2 Choose Number Format from the Style menu.
The Number Format dialog box appears.

3 Select Comma format, and then select 0 decimal places as shown in Figure 4.15.

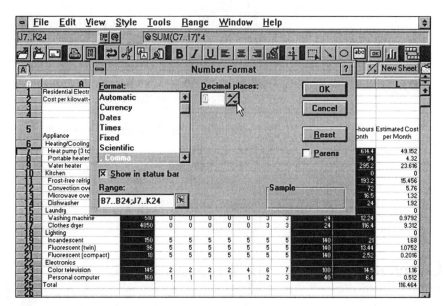

Figure 4.15

4 Select OK.
The affected values will now always appear with no digits to the right of the decimal and with commas inserted in values of 1000 and higher.

To apply a number format from the status bar:

1 Select C7..I24, the range for hours cycled-on for Monday through Sunday.

2 Choose Comma from the Number Format box on the status bar.
The numbers for hours cycled-on now appears with two digits to the right of the decimal point. When accessed through the status bar, the Comma number format defaults to two decimal places.

The final number formatting you will do is for the column for estimated cost per month and the cell for cost per kilowatt-hour. Because the values in these cells are dollar amounts, they should appear with two digits to the right of the decimal. Even though all the figures in the column represent dollar amounts, preceding each by a dollar sign would make the column more difficult to read. In traditional financial-spreadsheet style, a dollar sign is used only in the first entry and the total of this column.

> **Reminder** The regular Comma number format displays two digits to the right of the decimal; the regular Currency number format is similar to Comma, except that a dollar sign precedes the displayed value.

To apply the Comma number format to a range:

1 Select L8..L24, the values for estimated cost per month, *excluding* the first and last figures, cells L7 and L25.

2 Apply the Comma number format by using either the Number Format option from the Style menu or the Number Format box on the status bar.

To apply the Currency number format to a collection:

1 Select the estimated cost per month for the heat pump in L7, the total estimated cost in L25, and the cost per kilowatt-hour in cell A3.

2 Apply the Currency number format by using either the Number Format item from the Style menu or the Number Format box on the status bar. Select two decimal places.

Your worksheet should resemble Figure 4.16.

	A	B	C	D	E	F	G	H	I	J	K	L
1	Residential Electricity Usage											
2	Cost per kilowatt-hour:											
3		$0.08										
4					Hours Cycled-On							
5	Appliance	Wattage	Mon	Tue	Wed	Thu	Fri	Sat	Sun	Operating Hours per Month	Kilowatt-hours per Month	Estimated Cost per Month
6	Heating/Cooling											
7	Heat pump (3 ton)	4,800	4.00	4.00	4.00	4.00	4.00	6.00	6.00	128	614	$49.15
8	Portable heater	1,500	1.00	1.00	1.00	1.00	1.00	2.00	2.00	36	54	4.32
9	Water heater	4,100	2.00	2.00	2.00	2.00	2.00	4.00	4.00	72	295	23.62
10	Kitchen											
11	Frost-free refrigerator	460	15.00	15.00	15.00	15.00	15.00	15.00	15.00	420	193	15.46
12	Convection oven	3,000	0.00	0.00	0.00	0.00	0.00	3.00	3.00	24	72	5.76
13	Microwave oven	1,500	0.25	0.25	0.25	0.25	0.25	0.50	1.00	11	17	1.32
14	Dishwasher	1,200	1.00	0.00	1.00	0.00	1.00	1.00	1.00	20	24	1.92
15	Laundry											
16	Washing machine	510	0.00	0.00	0.00	0.00	0.00	3.00	3.00	24	12	0.98
17	Clothes dryer	4,850	0.00	0.00	0.00	0.00	0.00	3.00	3.00	24	116	9.31
18	Lighting											
19	Incandescent	150	5.00	5.00	5.00	5.00	5.00	5.00	5.00	140	21	1.68
20	Fluorescent (twin)	96	5.00	5.00	5.00	5.00	5.00	5.00	5.00	140	13	1.08
21	Fluorescent (compact)	18	5.00	5.00	5.00	5.00	5.00	5.00	5.00	140	3	0.20
22	Electronics											
23	Color television	145	2.00	2.00	2.00	2.00	4.00	6.00	7.00	100	15	1.16
24	Personal computer	160	1.00	1.00	1.00	1.00	1.00	2.00	3.00	40	6	0.51
25	Total											$116.46
26												

Figure 4.16

3 Save the worksheet.

Changing Font Style and Size

As you learned earlier in this project, a font is a typeface design. Arial, Courier, and Times New Roman are names of different fonts.

In addition to choosing a font, you can decide whether it should appear having a particular **attribute**. The basic font attributes are **Bold,** *Italic,* and <u>Underlined</u>. The size of a font is measured in units called **points**. One point is 1/72 of an inch; the default font size in 1-2-3 is 12 points.

The standard SmartIcon set contains a group of three convenient buttons that can be used for the following functions: turning the bold attribute on or off; turning the italic attribute on or off; and adding or removing underlining. Extensive control over fonts is available in the Font and Attributes dialog box, which you can access from the Style menu.

The only font used in the completed version of this worksheet is Arial, although a variety of point sizes and font styles are employed. In the next series of steps, you will change the main title to appear in 18-point, bold, italic text.

To change the font attribute and size for the main title:

1 Select cell A1, which contains the title *Residential Electricity Usage.*

2 Choose Font & Attributes from the Style menu.
The Font & Attributes dialog box appears.

3 Select Bold and Italics from the Attributes list box.

4 Select 18 points for the type size.
Your screen should resemble Figure 4.17.

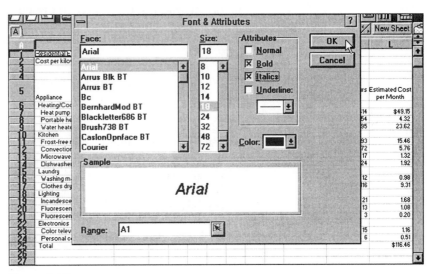

Figure 4.17

5 Select OK.
The title text should now appear in bold and italic, as well as in a larger point size.

Changing Font Attributes and Size for Other Cell Entries

Here's a list of the remaining cell entries having font attributes and font sizes that need to be changed:

- The title *Hours Cycled-On* should be bold.
- All the column titles should be italic.
- The titles *Appliance* and *Total* should be 18-point bold.
- The titles *Heating/Cooling, Kitchen, Laundry, Lighting,* and *Electronics* should be bold font style.
- The value for the total in the Estimated Cost per Month column should be bold.

To change font attributes in the worksheet:

1 Select cell C4, which contains the text *Hours Cycled-On.*

2 Click the Bold SmartIcon.
This changes the font style to bold.

3 Select the range B5..L5, which contains the column titles.

4 Click the Italic SmartIcon.
This changes the font style to italic.

5 Select cell A5, which contains the text *Appliance*.

6 Choose the Bold SmartIcon, and then choose 18 points from the Font Size box on the status bar.

Copying Only the Format of a Cell

The title *Total* in cell A25 is supposed to have the same font style and size as the title *Appliance* in cell A5. Lotus 1-2-3 has the ability to copy just the format (and not the contents) of one cell to another cell.

To copy the format of cell A5 to cell A25:

1 Select cell A5, which contains *Appliance*.

2 Choose Copy from the Edit menu.

3 Select cell A25, which contains *Total*.

4 Choose Paste Special from the Edit menu.
The Paste Special dialog box appears.

5 Select Styles Only, as shown in Figure 4.18.

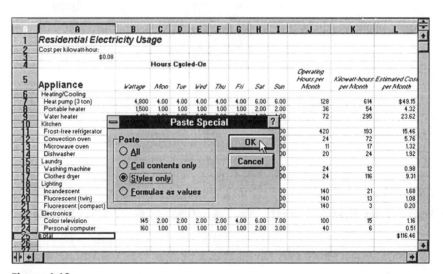

Figure 4.18

6 Select OK.
The format is copied.

To complete the font settings for the worksheet:

1 Select a collection of cells to include *Heating/Cooling* (A6), *Kitchen* (A10), *Laundry* (A15), *Lighting* (A18), and *Electronics* (A22).

2 Format these cells as bold.

Centering Selected Titles

The title in A1 should be centered across the whole worksheet; the title *Hours Cycled-On* should be centered across the weekday columns.

 ### *To center titles across selected columns:*

1 Select the range A1..L1.

2 Choose Alignment from the Style menu.
The Alignment dialog box appears.

3 Select the Center and Across Columns options, and then select OK, as shown in Figure 4.19.

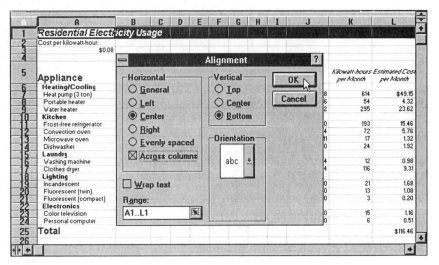

Figure 4.19

4 Select the range C4..I4.
This is the selection in which *Hours Cycled-On* should be centered.

5 Center *Hours Cycled-On* across the selection.

Adding Borders to a Worksheet

A *border* is a line that lends visual organization to the information in a worksheet. The completed worksheet will have several kinds of borders. You will turn cell gridlines off after setting the border, because the gridlines make it harder to see the borders.

> *Tip* It is usually a good idea to work from within the worksheet toward the outside perimeter: that is, you should create the innermost borders first and then proceed to the next layer, and so forth.

The innermost borders in this worksheet are those for the values in the hours cycled-on columns. Next you will add the horizontal section borders, separating appliance categories. Finally, you will set the outer border.

To add borders to the cells in the hours cycled-on columns:

1 Select the range C5..I24, the cells containing the hours cycled-on column headings and values.

2 Choose Lines & Color from the Style menu.
The Lines & Color dialog box appears.

3 Select Outline under the Border section.

4 Select Left under Border.
Your screen should resemble Figure 4.20.

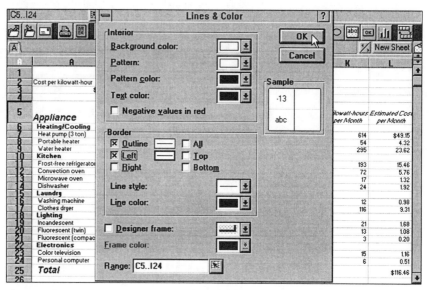

Figure 4.20

A thin line appears next to Line style indicating that this line will be used to form an outline around the selected area.

5 Select OK.

6 Select Set View Preferences from the View menu.

7 Clear the check box marked Grid Lines to turn off cell gridlines and then select OK.
The effect of the Border command is now more apparent, as shown in Figure 4.21.

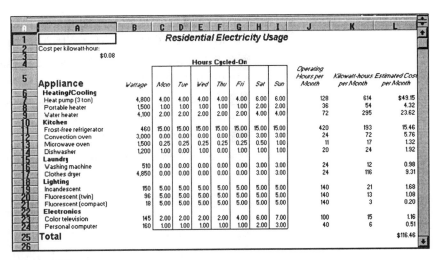

Figure 4.21

8 Turn gridlines back on to make it easier to position the active cell.

To set the horizontal section borders:

1 Select a collection to include the rows for the appliance categories and the total. The ranges are cells A6..L6, A10..L10, A15..L15, A18..L18, A22..L22, and A25..L25.

2 Choose Lines & Color from the Style menu and specify a thin top border, as shown in Figure 4.22.

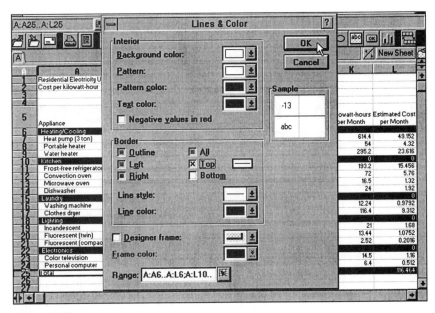

Figure 4.22

3 Select OK.

To set an outline around the entire worksheet:

1 Select the entire functional area of the worksheet, the cell range A1..L25.

2 Choose Lines & Color from the Style menu, and set an outline border for the worksheet.

3 Turn cell gridlines off.
Your worksheet should resemble Figure 4.23.

	A	B	C	D	E	F	G	H	I	J	K	L
1					*Residential Electricity Usage*							
2	Cost per kilowatt-hour:											
3		$0.08										
4						Hours Cycled-On						
5	**Appliance**	*Wattage*	*Mon*	*Tue*	*Wed*	*Thu*	*Fri*	*Sat*	*Sun*	*Operating Hours per Month*	*Kilowatt-hours per Month*	*Estimated Cost per Month*
6	**Heating/Cooling**											
7	Heat pump (3 ton)	4,800	4.00	4.00	4.00	4.00	4.00	6.00	6.00	128	614	$49.15
8	Portable heater	1,500	1.00	1.00	1.00	1.00	1.00	2.00	2.00	36	54	4.32
9	Water heater	4,100	2.00	2.00	2.00	2.00	2.00	4.00	4.00	72	295	23.62
10	**Kitchen**											
11	Frost-free refrigerator	460	15.00	15.00	15.00	15.00	15.00	15.00	15.00	420	193	15.46
12	Convection oven	3,000	0.00	0.00	0.00	0.00	0.00	3.00	3.00	24	72	5.76
13	Microwave oven	1,500	0.25	0.25	0.25	0.25	0.25	0.50	1.00	11	17	1.32
14	Dishwasher	1,200	1.00	0.00	1.00	0.00	1.00	1.00	1.00	20	24	1.92
15	**Laundry**											
16	Washing machine	510	0.00	0.00	0.00	0.00	0.00	3.00	3.00	24	12	0.98
17	Clothes dryer	4,850	0.00	0.00	0.00	0.00	0.00	3.00	3.00	24	116	9.31
18	**Lighting**											
19	Incandescent	150	5.00	5.00	5.00	5.00	5.00	5.00	5.00	140	21	1.68
20	Fluorescent (twin)	96	5.00	5.00	5.00	5.00	5.00	5.00	5.00	140	13	1.08
21	Fluorescent (compact)	18	5.00	5.00	5.00	5.00	5.00	5.00	5.00	140	3	0.20
22	**Electronics**											
23	Color television	145	2.00	2.00	2.00	2.00	4.00	6.00	7.00	100	15	1.16
24	Personal computer	160	1.00	1.00	1.00	1.00	1.00	2.00	3.00	40	6	0.51
25	**Total**											$116.46
26												

Figure 4.23

4 Turn cell gridlines back on.

5 Save the worksheet.

PRINTING AND FINAL MODIFICATIONS

In the steps that follow, you will print the worksheet. After examining the printout, you will notice areas that require adjustments. You will adjust them and then print the worksheet again.

To print the worksheet:

1 Make sure your printer is powered-on and is online.

2 Choose Print from the File menu.

3 Choose Current Worksheet, and then select OK.
Your worksheet prints on two pages.

Changing the Orientation of a Printout

Because the worksheet is printed on two pages, you would need to trim one of the sheets and tape the two pages together to have a single printed image of the worksheet. If you want this worksheet to fit on a single page, you can either change the *scaling* (reducing it to fit) or flip the *orientation* of the printout from *portrait* (the default) to **landscape**. Both the scaling and the orientation controls are in the Page Setup dialog box.

The text of a landscape printout reads along the long dimension of the paper. The terms *portrait* and *landscape* derive from the world of art, where portrait paintings are usually oriented with their long side on the vertical, and landscape paintings are oriented with their long side on the horizontal.

You will also notice that the cost per kilowatt-hour value in cell A3 might look better if it was aligned to the center, rather than aligned to the right. In the following steps, you will modify the alignment of cell A3 and instruct 1-2-3 to produce a landscape printout.

To adjust and reprint the worksheet:

1 Select cell A3, choose Alignment from the Style menu, and change the horizontal alignment to Center.

> *Reminder* Changing the alignment to center means to center the entry within its cell. Doing this does not center an entry across columns.

2 Save the worksheet.

3 Choose Print from the File menu.

4 Choose Current Worksheet, and then choose Page Setup.

5 Select the Landscape option under Orientation, and then select OK.

6 Select OK in the Page Setup dialog box, and then select OK from the Print dialog box.

Your completed landscape printout should resemble Figure 4.1.

Defining Range Names

To make your worksheet easier to maintain, you can define **range names** for single cells or larger ranges on the worksheet. You can then use the names as you enter new formulas. To use a range name within a formula, you type the name as part of the formula. When computing the formula's result, 1-2-3 automatically refers to the list of range names within the worksheet and substitutes the name with its definition.

Consider the formula for estimated cost per month in cell L7. It currently reads +$A$3*K7. The same reference, $A$3, is used in every one of the estimated-cost formulas. The formulas would be a little more understandable if they looked like this: +$COST_PER_KWH*K7. In the following steps, you will define the name COST_PER_KWH to refer to cell A3. Then 1-2-3 will refer automatically to the range name in all formulas within the worksheet. Because cell A3 is an absolute cell reference, 1-2-3 will display a dollar sign ($) in front of the range name in the formulas.

To define a range name:

1 Select cell A3, which contains the cost per kilowatt-hour.

2 Choose Name from the Range menu.
The Name dialog box appears.

3 Type **COST_PER_KWH** in the Name text box, and then choose Add. Choosing Add causes the name you typed to be added as a range name. Notice that the Range text box already contains the address A3, which is the cell being defined as a range name (see Figure 4.24).

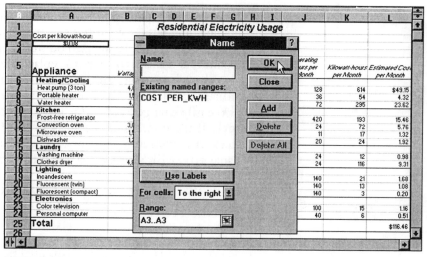

Figure 4.24

4 Select OK.

5 Select cell L7, the estimated cost per month for the heat pump.
Notice that the formula reads +$COST_PER_KWH*K7
If you examine any formula for estimated cost, you will discover that the
range name $COST_PER_KWH is used instead of $A$3.

6 Save the worksheet.
The list of defined range names is part of the worksheet. Because it has
changed, you should save it.

Tip   When you define a range name, follow these guidelines:

- Make the range name meaningful. Don't use names like "X" or "N."
  If a name refers to the tax rate, then make it TAX_RATE, not X.
- Make the name readable by using an underscore between words.
- Use only letters, underscores, and numbers in a range name, never
  use spaces, and do not make a name look like a cell address or formula.
  Range names such as F16, B1, and Quarter-1 are ambiguous.

Documenting Formulas

The total time an appliance is operated in a month is calculated by multiplying a week's operating time by four, because there are approximately
four weeks in a month. For example, to compute the total monthly operating
hours for the heat pump, the formula @SUM(C7..I7)*4 is used in cell J7.
The @SUM @function computes a week's hours, and the result is then
multiplied by 4.

It may seem that anyone examining the formula would understand that
the 4 represents the four weeks in a month, but the 4 is a rather benign
example of a *magic number*. Magic numbers are undocumented constants
that show up in formulas. The problem with magic numbers is twofold.
First, magic numbers carry little intrinsic meaning, and so when people
(even the worksheet's author) examine the worksheet long after it was first
created, they may not understand the purpose of the number. Second,
magic numbers buried inside formulas make it harder to change the work-

sheet. For example, suppose you created and copied the previously described formula and later wanted to use a more precise definition of a typical month as being 4.345 weeks. You would have to first edit or rebuild the formula, and then recopy it, to replace the old formula.

Although we won't do this in the current worksheet, one alternative to using magic numbers is to present such constants explicitly, in their own easily changed cells. This is the approach that you took when you entered the information about the cost of $0.08 per kilowatt-hour of electricity. Instead of remembering the cell address, you could use a range name of WEEKS_PER_MONTH in formulas within the worksheet.

THE NEXT STEP

Many of the commands that you used in this project will help in the construction and management of larger worksheets. When the functional part of a worksheet grows to encompass thousands of cells, the increased complexity can be tamed somewhat by initially spending time on design, using range names, and using the Zoom Out command to view the entire worksheet.

You have also worked with several sophisticated formatting features. Remember that the important thing about any worksheet is its results—usually numbers resulting from formulas. Fonts, font attributes, borders, and so on enhance the legibility of the worksheet and should not in themselves become a distraction to the person who reads it.

Perhaps one of the best ways to make worksheet results more legible is to present them graphically, using 1-2-3's superb charting capability. That is the subject of the next project.

SUMMARY AND EXERCISES

Summary

- You can use the Zoom In and Zoom Out commands to magnify or reduce your view of the worksheet. You can also set a customized magnification, which is saved with the worksheet. Zooming out is especially helpful for comprehending the arrangement of a large worksheet.
- You can use the Fill by Example command to fill a range based upon an example within one of the cells, or you can use the Fill command to fill a range with values based upon a starting number and an increment number.
- You can change the horizontal and vertical alignment of cell entries. Titles above columns of numbers are usually easiest to read if they are aligned to the right or to the center. You can also make the text in cells wrap onto several lines.
- You can assign names to single cells and ranges of cells. Range names make formulas more intelligible by eliminating constant numbers typed into formulas.
- You can copy a single cell and paste its contents into a range.

- Absolute cell references are usually necessary when you are copying a formula that contains a reference to a single cell on the worksheet.
- The font size (measured in points) and attributes (regular, italic, bold, or bold italic) can be changed in selected cells or in a range or collection of cells.
- Borders can be applied to cells and to larger selections of a worksheet.

Key Terms and Operations

Key Terms
absolute reference
attribute
border
range names
font
landscape orientation
point
portrait orientation
size
wrapping

Custom
Fill
Fill by Example
Font & Attributes
Lines & Color
Name
Number
Page Setup
Paste
Paste Special
Zoom In
Zoom Out

Operations
Alignment
Border

Study Questions

Multiple Choice

1. The Zoom In command will
   a. magnify the view of the worksheet by 10 percent.
   b. reduce the view of the worksheet by 10 percent.
   c. magnify the view of the worksheet around the selected cell.
   d. reduce the view of the worksheet around the selected cell.
   e. none of the above.

2. What command is used to conveniently enter a single value into a selected range?
   a. Paste
   b. Fill by Example
   c. Range Name
   d. Fill
   e. Paste by Example

3. In the formula +@SUM(G3..G12)*0.12115, the 0.12115 is called a(n)
   a. range name
   b. constant
   c. absolute address
   d. formula modifier
   e. relative address

4. In the formula +@SUM(G3..G12)*EXPENSE FACTOR, EXPENSE FACTOR is a(n)
   a. text constant
   b. manifest constant
   c. hidden number
   d. absolute address
   e. range name

5. In the formula +$A$3*K7, $A$3 is called a(n)
   a. defined constant
   b. range name
   c. absolute cell address
   d. relative cell address
   e. manifest constant

6. If the formula +A1+$A$2 is entered in cell A3 and then copied to cell B3, the copy in cell B3 will read
   a. +B1+$A$2
   b. +A1+$A$2
   c. +A1+$B$2
   d. +B1+$B$2
   e. +B1+B2

7. Bold and Italic are examples of:
   a. font attributes
   b. patterns
   c. alignments
   d. font names
   e. cell styles

8. When adding several levels of borders to a worksheet, it is best to
   a. start from the innermost level and work outward.
   b. start with the overall outline and work in.
   c. proceed column by column.
   d. zoom to a high magnification.
   e. print with cell gridlines on.

9. Printing that is oriented along the long dimension of the paper is referred to as
   a. portrait orientation.
   b. panoramic orientation.
   c. wide-angle printing.
   d. anisotopic mapping.
   e. landscape orientation.

10. Writing an incorrect formula that attempts to multiply a number by a text entry causes 1-2-3 to display what in the formula's cell?
   a. ERR
   b. 0
   c. *******
   d. 127
   e. !!!!!

Short Answer

1. What commands are used to reduce or magnify the worksheet on the screen?

2. What term is used to describe the breaking of a long text entry into several lines within its cell?

3. What type of number format should be used when a numeric entry, such as 45, needs to appear as a dollar amount?

4. What is the easiest way to enter the month names *Jan, Feb, Mar,* and so on in a range of cells?

5. Arial and Times New Roman are examples of what?

6. What unit of measurement is used when referring to the size of characters in a font?

7. If a formula refers to a specific, single cell, and the formula will be copied to other cells, how should the reference to the single cell appear in the formula?

8. If you want a border line to appear around all four sides of a selection, what steps should you follow?

9. How is a text entry normally aligned when it is entered into a cell?

10. How will numbers appear if they are formatted using the Comma number format?

For Discussion

1. Describe the difference between the Fill command and the Fill by Example command.

2. What is the difference between relative and absolute cell addressing? Under what circumstances should a formula contain an absolute cell reference?

3. Explain the difference between portrait and landscape orientation. When is landscape printing appropriate?

4. Under what circumstances would it be appropriate to use a range name?

Review Exercises

Coffee House Income Projection

Follow the steps below to construct a worksheet similar to that in Figure 4.25. The question marks in the figure indicate cells that will contain formulas.

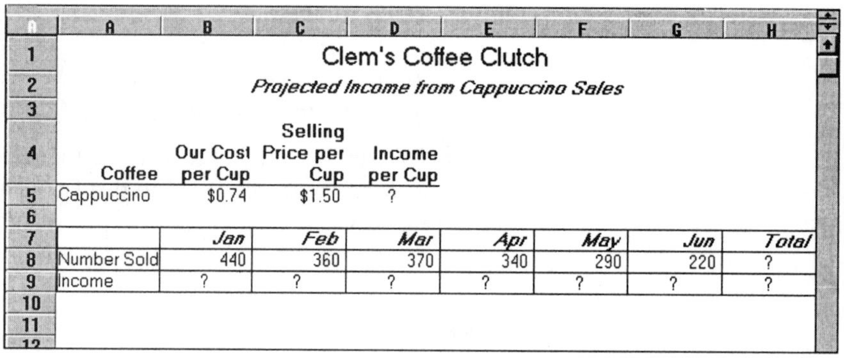

Figure 4.25

1. Enter all the text constants first. Use the Fill by Example command to enter the month names.

2. Enter the numbers for our cost per cup and selling price per cup.

3. Enter all the values for number sold.

4. Enter the formula for income per cup as selling price per cup minus our cost per cup.

5. Calculate the income for January by multiplying the number sold by the income per cup. Remember, the reference to income per cup should be absolute. Copy the formula to the cells for the other months.

6. Create formulas (using the @SUM @function) for total number sold and total income.

7. Center the title and subtitle across columns, and make them bold. Make the font size of the title larger than the font size of the subtitle, and make the subtitle italic.

8. Format the column headings *Coffee*, *Our Cost per Cup*, *Selling Price per Cup*, and *Income per Cup* as bold, aligned to the right, and set to wrap text.

9. Format the month names and Total as bold, italic, and aligned to the right.

10. Apply the U.S. Dollar number format to the cost, price, and income per cup cells. Apply the U.S. Dollar number format with zero decimal places to the monthly income formulas. Apply the Comma number format with zero decimal places to the values for number sold each month.

11. Adjust column widths and row heights as necessary, and, using the Lines & Color command from the Style menu, apply borders so that the worksheet resembles Figure 4.25.

12. Save the worksheet as COFFEE41.

13. Print the worksheet.

Coffee Brand Income as a Percent of Total Income

Figure 4.26 shows an enhanced version of the COFFEEX worksheet from Assignment 2 in Project 3.

	A	B	C	D	E	F	G	H
1	Coffee	Cost	Selling Price	No. Sold	Income	Percent of Total Income		
2	House Blend	$0.39	$0.95	60	$33.60	?		
3	Espresso	0.61	1.25	12	7.68	?		
4	Cappuccino	0.74	1.50	22	16.72	?		
5	Cafe Mocha	0.55	1.45	35	31.50	?		
6	Cafe Royale	0.68	1.85	55	64.35	?		
7	*Total*			184	$153.85	?		
8								
9								

Figure 4.26

A column has been added to show the income of each flavor of coffee expressed as a percent of the total income. This value is calculated by dividing a flavor's income amount by the total income. If this formula is to be successfully copied to all the cells in the Percent of Total Income column, the reference to the total income (Total) must be absolute.

The worksheet is also formatted with various alignments, borders, number formats, and font styles.

Refer to Figure 4.26 and build a similar worksheet. First, add the new column, Percent of Total Income, and then proceed with styling and borders. Apply the U.S. Dollar and Comma number formats as indicated in the figure. Use the Percent number format for the new column of formulas.

Define a range name of TOTAL_INCOME to refer to the cell containing the total income.

Save the worksheet under the name COFFEE42.

Assignments

Developing Your Own Electricity Worksheet

Construct a worksheet to calculate your own monthly consumption of electricity. If necessary, look up energy consumption figures for the appliances in your home, apartment, or dorm room. Can you affect the usage of any appliance to the extent that substantial amounts of electricity are saved? Save the worksheet under the name MYENERGY.

Municipal Waste Trends

Figure 4.27 shows an enhanced version of the EPA2 worksheet from the first review exercise in Project 3. The formula that computes the percent of the total for a particular category takes the 1990 value and divides it by the 1990 grand total (this is similar to the second review exercise in this project). Note that the borders have been customized, titles have been added, and number formatting has been adjusted.

Category	1960	1970	1980	1990	Percent of Grand Total (for 1990)
Municipal Waste Trends					
In pounds per day per person					
Nonfood Wastes					
Paper	0.91	1.19	1.32	1.60	?
Glass	0.20	0.34	0.36	0.28	?
Plastics	0.01	0.08	0.19	0.32	?
Metals	0.32	0.38	0.35	0.34	?
Total Nonfood	1.44	1.99	2.22	2.54	?
Other					?
Food	0.37	0.34	0.32	0.29	?
Yard	0.61	0.62	0.66	0.70	?
Total Other	0.98	0.96	0.98	0.99	?
Grand Total	2.42	2.95	3.20	3.53	?

Figure 4.27

Build the new formulas and adjust the formatting as necessary to create a completed worksheet similar to Figure 4.27. Use the Percent number format for the new formulas. Save the modified worksheet under the name EPA3.

Adapting to Off-Hours Discounts

Some electric utilities offer *energy-savings time*, a two-tier residential-electricity rate system, where customers who use electricity during off-peak hours receive a special reduced rate (for example, $0.05 per kilowatt-hour) and pay a premium rate (for example, $0.15 per kilowatt-hour) for electricity used during peak-demand hours. In the summer and fall, off-peak hours are usually 9:00 p.m. to noon on weekdays and all day on weekends; in the winter and spring, off-peak hours are 9:00 a.m. to 5:00 p.m. on weekdays and all day on weekends.

Adapt the ENERGY1 worksheet to accommodate a two-tier electricity-cost schedule. Save the worksheet under the name ENERGYDL.

PROJECT 5: VISUALIZING INFORMATION WITH CHARTS

Objectives

After completing this project, you should be able to:

▶ Translate a verbal description and a sketch of a chart into a Lotus 1-2-3 chart

▶ Identify the major components of a chart

▶ Create bar charts, pie charts, and 3-D perspective bar charts

▶ Resize, position, and customize charts

▶ Associate chart text with the worksheet

▶ Print charts

CASE STUDY: PRIME TIME TV SHOWS

Television has reigned as the predominant communications medium in the United States since shortly after the end of World War II. Figure 5.1 is a worksheet that shows the popularity of various kinds of prime time TV shows in the U.S. from 1950 through 1990. This information is a snapshot of mid- to late-twentieth-century American popular culture.

The Most Popular Prime Time TV Shows
Genre by Decade (1950–1990)

Genre	1950s	1960s	1970s	1980s
Crime	8	4	13	16
Drama	10	7	8	14
Variety	20	14	2	0
Western	21	16	2	0
SitCom	23	48	61	54
Other	18	11	14	16
Total	100	100	100	100

Figure 5.1

For purposes of the worksheet, a television program is considered popular if it was among the ten most-watched *prime time* (evening) programs each year. Each decade had 100 top programs. The worksheet condenses this data by considering decades and by classifying television shows by genre (category) of show.

It's possible to see patterns in this table of numbers, but for most people, the best way to identify trends and interrelationships in data is to present the data visually as a ***chart,*** using lines, bars, geometric symbols, and colors.

In this project, you will construct several types of charts to present the information shown in Figure 5.1. Each type of chart emphasizes a certain aspect of the data or lends itself to a particular way of viewing or interpreting the information. Lotus 1-2-3 offers many more chart types than you need for this project. Table 5.1 lists a few of the chart types you are likely to use for most of your charting needs.

Table 5.1

Chart Type	Use	Application
bar	Compares individual values at a specific time. Emphasizes comparison rather than time flow. Can also be used to emphasize data variation over a period of time.	product launch, budget, quarterly sales forecast
pie	Shows relationships between portions of a whole.	sales levels in various cities
line	Shows trends or changes over time. Emphasizes time flow and the rate of change rather than the amount of change.	price index

Designing the Solution

To build a chart, you will first decide what it is that you want to present in the chart and the type of chart that is most appropriate for the data you will plot. You can then figure out how the various aspects of the planned chart translate into 1-2-3 commands and charting options.

Suppose you want to show how the popularity of crime and drama shows changed between 1950 and 1990, and you want your chart to resemble Figure 5.2. Crime-show popularity and drama-show popularity are the variables that make up the data series that you want to plot as a chart. A *data series* is a set of related values that appear in either a worksheet column or row. Using a bar chart such as the one in Figure 5.2 is one way to show this kind of information.

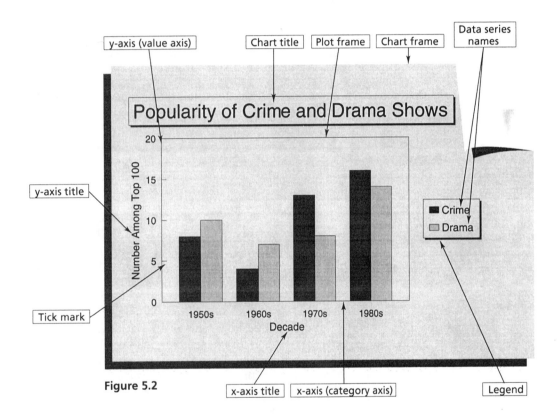

Figure 5.2

The labels along the bottom edge (the x-axis) of the chart often correspond to your worksheet column headings. They tell you what the chart categories are. Viewing the data in the category 1960s, you can see that the Drama data series has the value 7.

The elements of the plot area are graphically distinguished by the same pattern, color, or symbol. Each category, scale, or data series is marked on the axis with a tick mark. Generally, two axes create the major frame for plotting. The horizontal or category axis—also referred to as the *X-axis*—is the ruler for plotting categories of the data series. The vertical or value axis—also called the *Y-axis*—is the ruler for plotting data values. In addition to the graphical elements of the chart, text, such as titles, a legend, and labels, helps to convey the interpretation of the data you are plotting.

Chart categories correspond to worksheet rows or columns. Row or column titles become the chart ***data labels*** along the chart axes. As shown in Figure 5.3, the data labels for the example chart are 1950s, 1960s, 1970s, and 1980s.

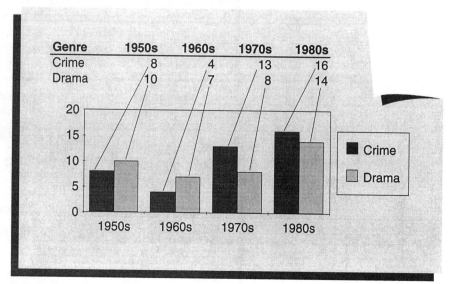

Figure 5.3

Figure 5.3 shows the relationship between a worksheet and a chart created from the worksheet. Each bar in the chart is a data marker. There are two data series: one for crime shows (represented by the dark bars on the chart and the values 8, 4, 13, and 16 on the worksheet), and the other for drama shows (the light bars on the chart, and the values 10, 7, 8, and 14 on the worksheet). On a worksheet, you can often identify the data series as a group of values, in a column or a row, that change over time.

If a data series is taken from a worksheet row, as is the data for the number of each genre of show each decade, the chart categories of that data series—the decades—will be represented in columns. Alternatively, if a data series is presented in a worksheet column, its chart categories are shown in rows. Figure 5.4 shows what the graph would look like if you switched the chart categories used in Figure 5.2 to the data series and the data series to the chart categories. Whether you make the chart categories rows or columns depends entirely on the focus of your chart.

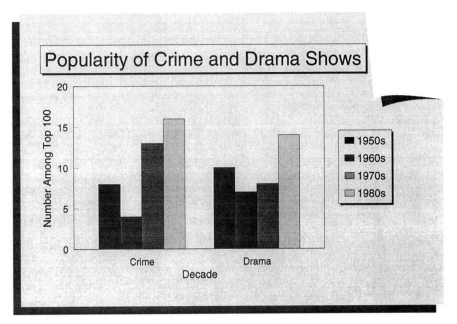

Figure 5.4

CREATING THE UNDERLYING WORKSHEET

In this section, you will make a worksheet similar to the one shown in Figure 5.1 and use it to create charts in the remainder of this project. You can refer to Figure 5.5 (which has been zoomed in) while typing the worksheet. The worksheet contains only four formulas, which compute totals for each column. The primary purpose of these formulas is to help you check that you correctly typed the number constants.

	A	B	C	D	E	F	G	
1	The Most Popular Prime Time TV Shows							
2	Genre by Decade (1950-1990)							
3	Genre	1950s	1960s	1970s	1980s			
4	Crime	8	4	13	16			
5	Drama	10	7	8	14			
6	Variety	20	14	2	0			
7	Western	21	16	2	0			
8	SitCom	23	48	61	54			
9	Other	18	11	14	16			
10	Total	100	100	100	100			
11								

Figure 5.5

To build the worksheet:

1 Enter the title **The Most Popular Prime Time TV Shows** in cell A1.

2 Make the title in cell A1 14-point bold.

3 Enter the subtitle **Genre by Decade (1950-1990)** in cell A2, and make it bold.

4 Refer to Figure 5.5 and enter the column titles (*Genre* in cell A3 through *1980s* in E3), and make them bold with a thin bottom border.

5 Align to the right the column headings from the 1950s column to the 1980s column.

6 Change the height of row 3 to 24 points.

7 Refer to Figure 5.5 and enter the row titles (Crime in cell A4 through Other in cell A9) and the number constants (in the range B4..E9).

8 Enter `Total` in cell A10, and make it bold.

9 Create an @SUM formula in cell B10 to total the column.

10 Copy the @SUM formula to the other cells that require it.

11 Assign a thin top border and a double-line bottom border to the range A10..E10.

12 Select A1..E2 and set the alignment to center text across columns.

13 Save the worksheet as TV1.

BUILDING A BAR CHART

In this section, you will build a bar chart based on Figure 5.2. Charts are saved with the worksheet.

To specify the range to be charted:

1 Select a custom zoom of 65-percent magnification.

2 Select the range A3..E5, as shown in Figure 5.6.
This range encompasses the data to be charted and the associated category and data series names. The corner cell containing the text *Genre* is neither a data series nor a chart category, so 1-2-3 will use it as the chart title.

	A	B	C	D	E	F	G	H	I	J	K	
1	The Most Popular Prime Time TV Shows											
2		Genre by Decade (1950-1990)										
3	Genre	1950s	1960s	1970s	1980s							
4	Crime	6	4	13	16							
5	Drama	10	7	6	14							
6	Variety	20	14	2	0							
7	Western	21	16	2	0							
8	SitCom	23	48	61	54							
9	Other	16	11	14	16							
10	Total	100	100	100	100							
11												
12												
13												

Figure 5.6

3 Select Chart from the Tools menu, or select the Chart SmartIcon. The mouse pointer changes to resemble a small chart, and the message *Click and drag where you want to display the chart* is displayed in the title bar. You can drag the mouse to select an area in which the chart will be created, or you can click the mouse button once to display the chart in its default size.

4 Position the mouse pointer crosshairs in the middle of cell F3, and then hold down the left mouse button and drag to the middle of cell J15, as shown in Figure 5.7.

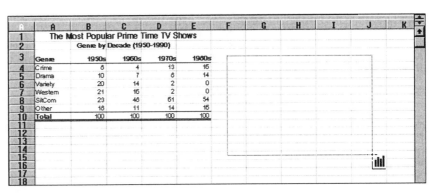

	A	B	C	D	E	F	G	H	I	J	K
1	The Most Popular Prime Time TV Shows										
2	Genre by Decade (1950-1990)										
3	Genre	1950s	1960s	1970s	1980s						
4	Crime	8	4	13	16						
5	Drama	10	7	8	14						
6	Variety	20	14	2	0						
7	Western	21	16	2	0						
8	SitCom	23	48	61	54						
9	Other	18	11	14	16						
10	Total	100	100	100	100						

Figure 5.7

5 Release the mouse button.
The chart appears within the rectangle you selected.

WORKING WITH CHARTS

Lotus 1-2-3 makes several decisions about how to display a chart. It decides the chart type, legend names, axes names, and titles. In the steps that follow, you will change several aspects of your chart's appearance.

Modifying a Chart

The chart is part of the worksheet, but it does not fill any cells and it doesn't have a cell address. Instead, think of a chart as existing in its own layer that floats on top of the worksheet cells. This means that it can easily be moved and resized. When you select a chart, small black squares, called **handles,** appear on its corners and sides. At the same time, the menu bar displays the Chart menu in place of the Range menu, and a set of SmartIcons used for manipulating charts appears.

You can select a chart by clicking in the chart background—that is, within the chart rectangle, but not in the chart itself. If you select the chart and then drag the mouse, you can reposition the chart on the worksheet. If you click and drag one of the handles, you can resize the chart window.

To reposition the chart:

1 Select cell A1.
Notice that the handles on the chart rectangle disappear—the chart is no longer selected.

2 Click inside the chart rectangle, but not any of the chart legends, frames, or titles (see Figure 5.8).

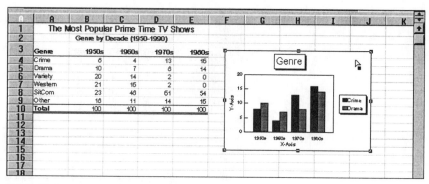

Figure 5.8

The handles reappear, signaling that the chart is selected.

3 Click and hold the mouse button with the pointer positioned inside the chart rectangle.

4 Drag the chart's outline so that it is below the worksheet data (in rows 12 to 24), as shown in Figure 5.9.

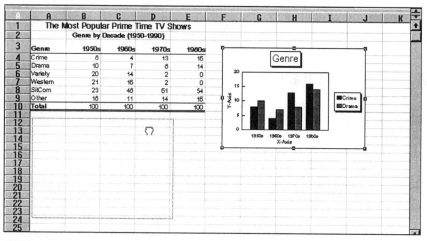

Figure 5.9

5 Release the mouse button.
The chart should now appear below the worksheet data.
The chart will be easier to read if you make it larger. To do this you can: change the width of the chart by dragging the middle handle of the left or right edges of the rectangle; change the height of the chart by dragging the middle handle at the top or bottom edges; and change both the width and the height of the chart simultaneously by dragging one of the corner handles.

To resize the chart:

1 Hold down the mouse button on the lower-right handle of the chart rectangle.

2 Drag the outline down and to the right so that the chart becomes wider and longer, as shown in Figure 5.10.

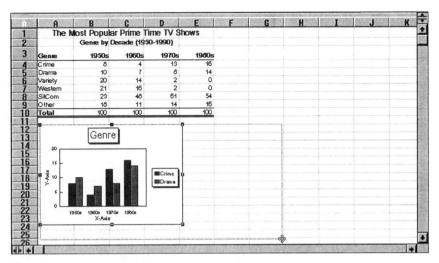

Figure 5.10

3 Release the mouse button.
The chart should now appear similar to Figure 5.11.

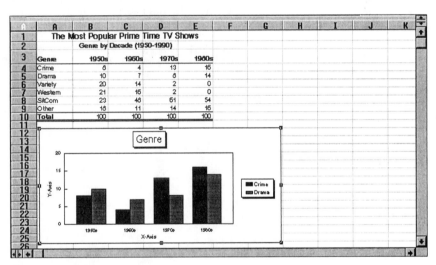

Figure 5.11

Setting the Chart Format

You can change whether the data series will be in rows or columns and whether cells in the initially selected range should be used for the data series and chart category names. Lotus 1-2-3 works on the assumption that you want fewer data series than chart categories, which means that for this worksheet, the data series are initially presented in rows.

To specify data series by column:

1 Choose Ranges from the Chart menu.
The Ranges dialog box appears.

2 Select By Column in the Assign Ranges drop-down list box, and then select OK as shown in Figure 5.12.

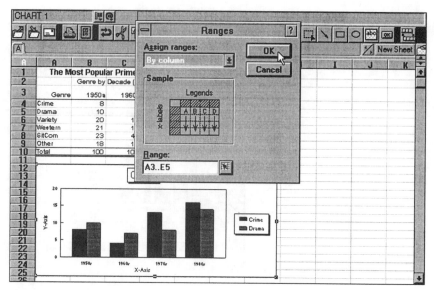

Figure 5.12

Your screen should resemble Figure 5.13. You can see what the chart looks like when the data series is presented in columns rather than in rows.

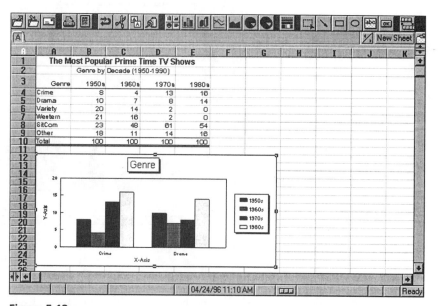

Figure 5.13

4 Again choose Ranges from the Chart menu.

5 Select By Row in the Assign Ranges drop-down list box, and then select OK.

Your screen should once again resemble Figure 5.11; the data series are again charted as rows.

Assigning Titles

By default, 1-2-3 assigns a *legend* and a *title* to your chart. A legend is a key that lists what each color or symbol stands for. The title of the chart is based on the label in the upper-left corner of the selected range. The chart title can be changed to refer to another cell in the worksheet, or you can type in the title manually. In the steps that follow, you will first change the chart title to refer to cell A1, which contains the worksheet title. You will then manually enter a different title to describe the chart ranges more accurately.

To change the default titles:

1 Choose Headings from the Chart menu.

The Headings dialog box appears. Note the cell reference in the Line 1 text box, A:A3, which indicates that the chart title is taken from the label in cell A3. The Cell check box immediately to the right of the Line 1 text box indicates that 1-2-3 is to display the contents of that cell.

2 Click the range selector (the box at the right end of the Line 1 text box) as shown in Figure 5.14.

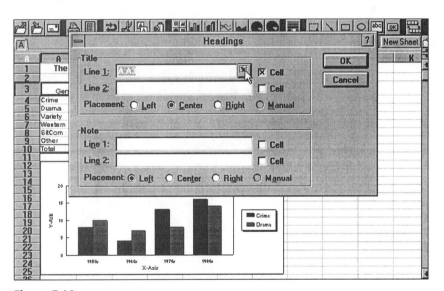

Figure 5.14

The Headings dialog box vanishes from the screen, and the mouse pointer changes to the shape used for selecting a range.

3 Click cell A1, where the worksheet title is stored, as shown in Figure 5.15.

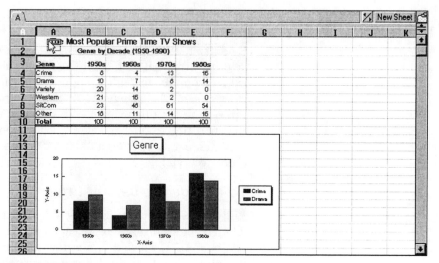

Figure 5.15

After you select cell A1, the Headings dialog box reappears with cell reference A1 in the Line 1 text box.

4 Select OK.

The chart appears, using the contents of cell A1 as the chart title. However, a more specific chart title would be better.

5 Choose Headings from the Chart menu.

6 Click to uncheck the Cell check box to the right of the Line 1 text box.

7 Type **Popularity of Crime and Drama Shows** in the Line 1 text box, and then select OK as shown in Figure 5.16.

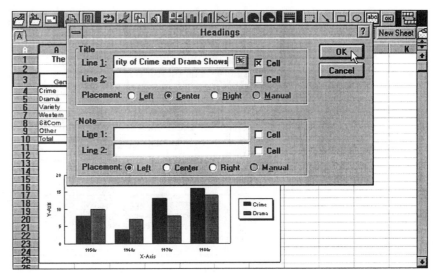

Figure 5.16

 To change the Axes labels:

1 Choose Axis from the Chart menu, and then choose X-Axis. The X-Axis dialog box appears.

2 Type **Decade** in the Axis Title text box (see Figure 5.17).

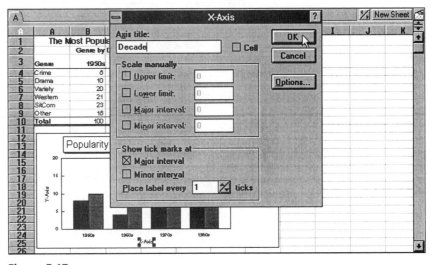

Figure 5.17

Although it might seem obvious that the categories along the X-axis are decades, an axis title makes this even clearer.

3 Select OK.
The X-axis is now labeled *Decade*.

An easier way to open the appropriate Axis dialog box is to double-click the axis label that you want to change.

4 Double-click the word *Y-Axis* within the chart.
The Y-Axis dialog box appears.

5 Type **Number Among Top 100** in the Axis Title text box, and then select OK.
Titles for the Y-axis are important, because they indicate what the qualifying units are—for example, what the height of a bar represents. Your chart should appear similar to that in Figure 5.18.

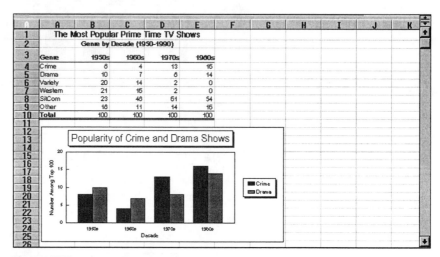

Figure 5.18

Linking

The chart you just created is part of your worksheet; if the data which the chart depends on changes, the chart will automatically update to reflect the change. In the following steps, you will change the value for Crime Shows in the 1960s to see the effect of this linkage. You will then use the Undo command to undo the entry and revert to the original value.

To observe the effect of linkage:

1 Select cell C4, which contains 4, the number of crime shows popular during the 1960s.
Note the bar on the chart that corresponds to this value.

2 Type **20** and press (ENTER)
The chart changes immediately to show the change in the worksheet.

3 Choose Undo from the Edit menu.

> *Reminder* Undo reverses the effect of the most recently performed command.

 EXIT If necessary, you can save the worksheet, quit 1-2-3 now and continue this project later.

Printing Charts

A chart is part of your worksheet, but it can be printed with or without the surrounding worksheet data. The printing commands you have learned to use with worksheets also work with charts. In the following steps, you will use the Print Preview command to see a simulated printout on-screen; then you will print the worksheet. Print Preview is useful, because it allows you to detect problems with your printout without wasting paper, ink, or time.

To print the chart with its worksheet:

1 Save the worksheet.

2 Choose Print Preview from the File menu.
The Print Preview dialog box appears.

3 Select Current Worksheet, and then select OK.
A simulated printout page appears on-screen, with a new set of SmartIcons displayed, as shown in Figure 5.19.

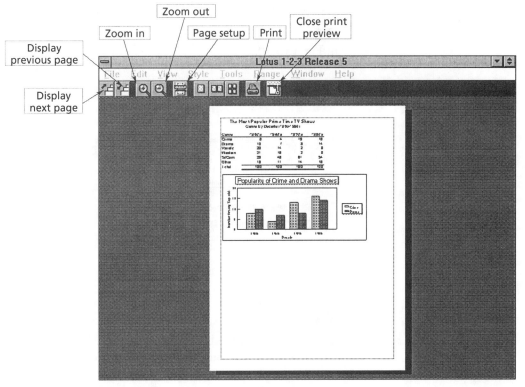

Figure 5.19

You can magnify or reduce your view of the page by selecting either the Zoom In or the Zoom Out SmartIcon. Using the SmartIcon with the plus sign magnifies the page, while the one with the minus sign reduces the page. You can also access other printing commands from the Print Preview window.

4 Position the pointer over the Zoom In SmartIcon and click.
This zooms in on the center of the page.

7 Select OK from the Print dialog box.

Deleting Charts

You can have many different charts on a worksheet. You can delete a chart by selecting it and pressing ⌈DEL⌋ or by choosing Clear from the Edit menu.

To delete the chart:

1 Select the chart background area.

2 Press ⌈DEL⌋

Building a Bar Chart from a Collection

The chart you created plotted Crime and Drama TV shows, but what if you wanted a chart that plotted Variety and SitCom TV shows? In the steps that follow, you will build a chart that uses a collection as the data series for the chart. You will then assign X-axis data labels to the chart.

To create a chart using a collection:

1 Select a collection of ranges consisting of A6..E6 and A8..E8, as shown in Figure 5.20.

> *Reminder* Be sure to drag to select multicell ranges.

	A	B	C	D	E	F	G	H	I	J	K
1	The Most Popular Prime Time TV Shows										
2		Genre by Decade (1950-1990)									
3	Genre	1950s	1960s	1970s	1980s						
4	Crime	6	4	13	16						
5	Drama	10	7	6	14						
6	Variety	20	14	2	0						
7	Western	21	16	2	0						
8	SitCom	23	48	61	54						
9	Other	16	11	14	16						
10	Total	100	100	100	100						
11											
12											

Figure 5.20

2 Choose Chart from the Tools menu, or select the Chart SmartIcon.

3 Click the mouse button once in cell F3.
Clicking the mouse button once creates a chart using 1-2-3's default chart size. Notice there are no dates along the bottom of the chart (the X-axis).

4 Choose Ranges from the Chart menu.
The Ranges dialog box appears. The first item in the Series list box is X-Axis Labels; you use this to select the range of labels to appear along the X-axis.

5 Click the Range Selector box.
The Ranges dialog box disappears from the screen, letting you select the range of cells for the X-axis.

6 Select the range B3..E3.
The Ranges dialog box reappears.

7 Select OK.

The chart now displays the date labels along the X-axis, as shown in Figure 5.21.

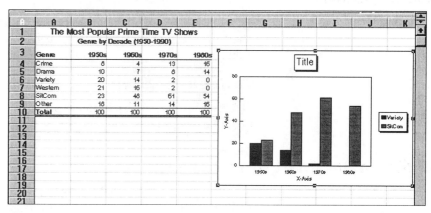

Figure 5.21

8 Delete the chart.

BUILDING PIE CHARTS

A pie chart is different from most other chart types, because it shows only one data series. Pie charts are ideal for showing the relationship between a part and the whole—the relative share that each category represents.

In the following steps, you will create a pie chart that shows the breakdown of different kinds of TV shows for the 1960s. This time, the data series will be in a column—the column for the 1960s—and the chart categories will be the different kinds of shows.

To build a pie chart:

1 Select a collection of ranges consisting of A4..A9 and C4..C9, as shown in Figure 5.22.

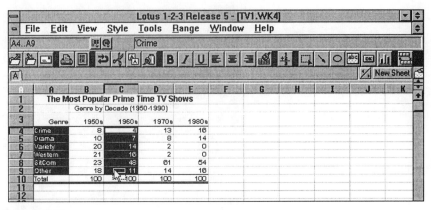

Figure 5.22

2 Choose Chart from the Tools menu, or click the Chart SmartIcon.

3 Drag to select a chart area from about F3 to K22.
As before, a bar chart is created.

4 Choose Type from the Chart menu.

5 Select Pie, and then select OK, as shown in Figure 5.23.

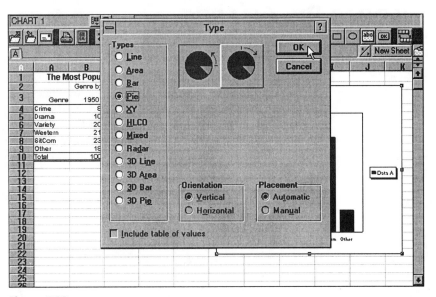

Figure 5.23

Your screen should now resemble Figure 5.24.

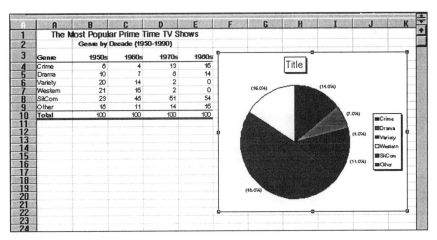

Figure 5.24

Changing Chart Type Styles

As with type appearing within cells, the type style of text within a chart can be enhanced to improve the overall appearance of the chart.

To change chart type styles:

1 Double-click the chart title (currently *Title*).
The Headings dialog box appears.

2 Type **The Most Popular TV Shows of the 1960s** in the Line 1 text box.

3 Select OK.
The title of the chart contains more characters than can fit within the chart's title box. To display all the characters, you can either make the box bigger (by dragging the title box handles) or reduce the size of the text within the box. In this example, you will reduce the size of the text.

4 Select the chart title (if necessary) by clicking anywhere within the title box.

5 Select a font size of 14 points from the status bar.
Your screen should resemble Figure 5.25.

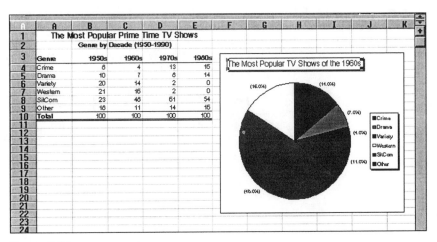

Figure 5.25

Labeling the Pie Slices

The chart would be easier to read if each pie slice were labeled with its corresponding label in the genre range. Lotus 1-2-3 can title each pie slice with values from a data series, with percentages of values from a data series, or with labels from a row or column of the worksheet.

To label each pie slice with values from the worksheet:

1 Select the chart.

2 Choose Data Labels from the Chart menu.
The Data Labels dialog box appears.

3 Select the Contents of X Data Range check box, clear the Percentages check box, and then select OK as shown in Figure 5.26.

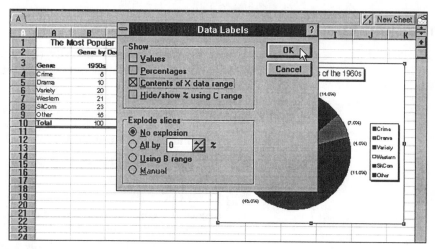

Figure 5.26

Notice that the legend box is no longer displayed on the chart. With each pie slice labeled individually, it is no longer necessary to refer to a legend to see what each pie slice represents.

Exploding a Pie Slice

Suppose you want to emphasize or draw attention to the slice for the Western category. One way to do this is to *explode*—or pull out—that slice from the pie.

To explode a pie chart slice:

1 Position the pointer on the middle of the slice for Western, click and hold down the mouse button, and drag slightly up and to the left, as shown in Figure 5.27.

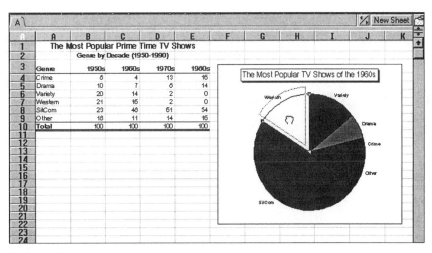

Figure 5.27

The slice for Western should now be pulled out from the pie. Once the mouse button is released, handles appear on the slice, which means that it is still selected within the chart.

2 Clear the slice handles by clicking anywhere else in the chart.

Changing the Chart Type

Perhaps a fancier pie chart—a 3-D pie chart—would look better. You can change the chart type in the Chart menu.

To change the type of chart:

1 Choose Type from the Chart menu.

2 Select 3D Pie, and then select OK.
The chart now appears as a 3-D pie chart, as shown in Figure 5.28.

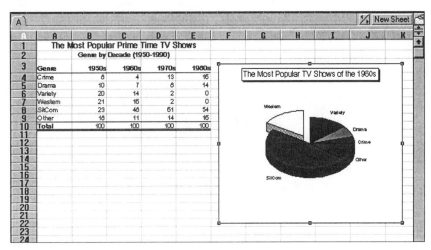

Figure 5.28

3 Save the file as 1960PIE1.

The worksheet containing the pie chart can be opened later and modified.

4 Delete the chart from the worksheet.

Building a 3-D Bar Chart

What type of chart would help you to visualize the changing popularity of all the genres of television programs for the entire time span of the worksheet? A regular bar chart would be cramped, as shown in Figure 5.29. A three-dimensional bar chart, which you can think of as a group of bar charts seen in 3-D perspective, might be better.

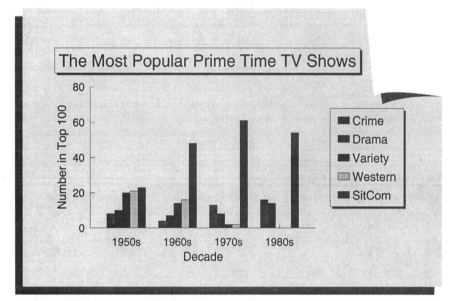

Figure 5.29

 To build a 3-D perspective bar chart:

1 Select the range A1..E8, as shown in Figure 5.30. *Do not include the Other category.*

A	B	C	D	E	F	G	H	I	J	K
1	The Most Popular Prime Time TV Shows									
2	Genre by Decade (1950-1990)									
3	Genre	1950s	1960s	1970s	1980s					
4	Crime	8	4	13	16					
5	Drama	10	7	8	14					
6	Variety	20	14	2	0					
7	Western	21	16	2	0					
8	SitCom	23	48	61	54					
9	Other	18	11	14	16					
10	Total	100	100	100	100					
11										

Figure 5.30

2 Choose Chart from the Tools menu, or click the Chart SmartIcon.

3 Drag from F3 to K22 to select a chart area.

As before, a bar chart is displayed. Notice this time that 1-2-3 has used the contents of cells A1 and A2 as titles for the chart.

4 Choose Type from the Chart menu.

5 Select the 3D Bar chart type, and then select the chart style shown in Figure 5.31.

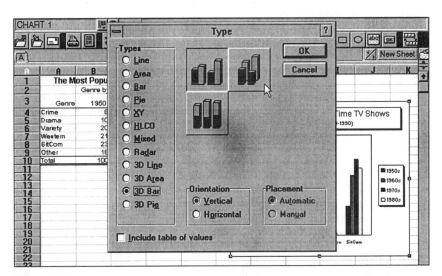

Figure 5.31

6 Select OK.

The chart appears as a 3-D bar. It will be easier to see the various columns of the chart if the data series is presented in rows, rather than in columns.

7 Choose Ranges from the Chart menu.

8 Select By Row from the Assign Ranges drop-down list box, and then select OK.

Your screen should resemble Figure 5.32.

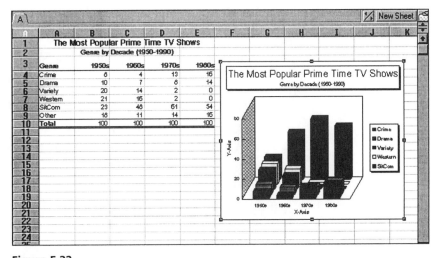

Figure 5.32

9 Change the Y-axis title to **Number in Top 100**

10 Change the X-axis title to **Decade**

11 Change the font size of the first line of the chart title from 18 to 14 points.

Adding Grid Lines to the Chart

Grid lines can be placed on the X and Y axes to help someone viewing the chart to better gauge data series values.

To add grid lines:

1 Choose Grids from the Chart menu.
The Grids dialog box appears.

2 Select Both from the X-axis drop-down list box.

3 Select Both from the Y-axis drop-down list box, and then select OK as shown in Figure 5.33.

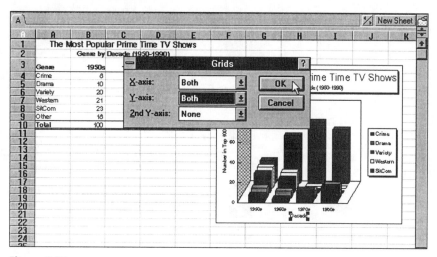

Figure 5.33

Printing the Chart

Often, you will want a printout that shows only the chart and none of the background worksheet.

To print only the chart:

1 Select the chart (if necessary).

2 Choose Print Preview from the File menu.

3 Choose the Selected Chart button.

4 Select OK.
A sample of the printout is displayed, showing the chart only.

5 Select the page layout SmartIcon.
The Page Layout dialog box appears.

6 Select Landscape under Orientation.

7 Select Fill Page but Keep Proportions from the Size drop-down list box, as shown in Figure 5.34.

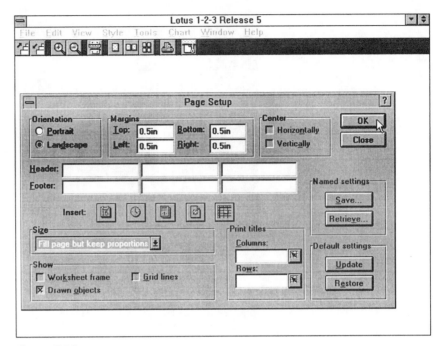

Figure 5.34

8 Select OK.

The chart should fill the page, as shown in Figure 5.35.

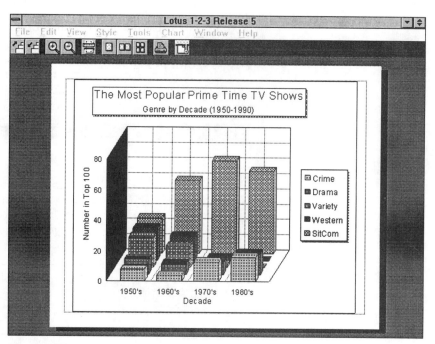

Figure 5.35

9 Print the worksheet by selecting the Print SmartIcon. Your printout should resemble Figure 5.36.

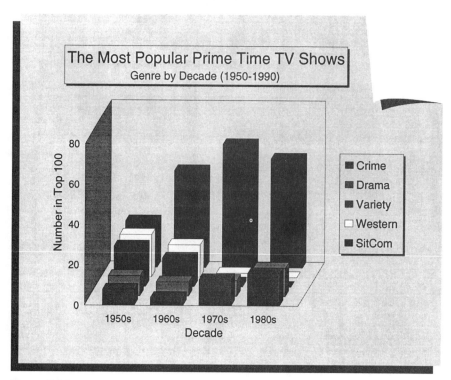

Figure 5.36

10 Save the worksheet as TV3D.

The 3-D bar chart conveys information more effectively than does the original table of numbers. If you follow a group of bars of a single color from left to right across the chart, you are tracing through time, following the changing popularity of a particular genre of TV show. If you read from the back to the front of the chart, you can examine the relative popularity of different kinds of shows for a particular decade.

THE NEXT STEP

Charts can help you analyze information, and they can also help you convey worksheet information more effectively to other people. If you are building a worksheet, the purpose of which is to make a point—to convince or educate other people about some conclusion or decision—charting can be a powerful tool.

However, you will encounter some worksheets—such as the one in the next project—for which a chart would not be of primary value. Use charting as you would use fonts and formatting: to support the understanding of information in worksheets, and not to distract or confuse.

SUMMARY AND EXERCISES

Summary

- Charting makes it easier to visualize and identify patterns in a table of numbers.
- Lotus 1-2-3 has 12 major types of charts, and many variations can be made from each type.
- The data you want to plot (display) in a chart is called a data series; each member of the data series corresponds to a chart category.
- If data series are in columns on the worksheet, their chart categories are in rows, and vice versa.
- Chart-category names appear along the horizontal (X) axis of a chart. The vertical axis is called the Y-axis.
- Using the Chart menu is the quickest way to build a basic chart. You select the range you want to chart, including any names that you want to appear on the chart.
- One or more charts can exist within a worksheet. Charts are saved along with the worksheet in a single file.
- Charts are linked to the worksheets on which they are based; if the data changes, the chart changes.
- Charts can be printed along with the worksheet, or by themselves.
- Charts can be repositioned and resized on the worksheet.

Key Terms and Operations

Key Terms
chart
data series
data labels
explode
handles

legend
title
X-axis
Y-axis

Operations
Print Preview

Study Questions

Multiple Choice

1. The labels that appear along the bottom edge of a chart are known as
   a. series
   b. variables
   c. data labels
   d. data markers
   e. data points

2. What must be done to a chart when the value of a worksheet cell is modified?
   a. The chart must be recreated.
   b. The data range must be reselected.
   c. The data label must be reselected.
   d. Nothing must be done; the chart will automatically adjust.
   e. You cannot change the value of a cell a chart depends on.

3. How many major chart types are there in 1-2-3?
   a. 1
   b. 2
   c. 3
   d. 4
   e. 12

4. On a chart, what is used to indicate what each color or symbol stands for?
   a. the X-axis
   b. a legend
   c. a data series
   d. a category
   e. a title

5. Line charts are most appropriate for
   a. showing trends or changes over time
   b. comparing individual values at specific times
   c. showing relationships between portions of a whole
   d. all of the above
   e. none of the above

6. Bar charts are most appropriate for
   a. comparing individual values at a specific time
   b. emphasizing variation over a period of time
   c. emphasizing comparison rather than time flow
   d. all of the above
   e. none of the above

7. Pie charts are most appropriate for
    a. showing trends or changes over time
    b. comparing individual values at specific times
    c. showing relationships between portions of a whole
    d. all of the above
    e. none of the above

8. The size of text in a chart title can be changed by
    a. selecting the title and then choosing Chart from the Edit menu
    b. selecting the title and then choosing Name from the Chart menu
    c. selecting the title and then choosing Fonts and Attributes from the Style menu
    d. selecting the chart and then choosing Fonts and Attributes from the Style menu
    e. none of the above

9. If you want to modify a chart, you must
    a. select Type from the Chart menu
    b. select the chart by clicking it
    c. choose Edit from the Chart menu
    d. choose Chart from the Edit menu
    e. select the worksheet window

10. To print a chart with its corresponding worksheet
    a. select the chart and then choose Current Worksheet in the Print dialog box
    b. select the worksheet and then choose Current Worksheet in the Print dialog box
    c. choose Selected Chart in the Print dialog box
    d. choose Current Worksheet in the Print dialog box
    e. none of the above

Short Answer

1. What chart type would you use to show trends and interrelationships in data?

2. If the data series is horizontal (in rows) on a worksheet, how are the chart categories arranged?

3. Which axis is the X-axis? The Y-axis?

4. What are chart handles used for?

5. How is a pie chart different from most other chart types?

6. What term is used to describe a pie slice that has been pulled out of the pie for emphasis?

7. What type of chart would be most appropriate for showing month-by-month profits for a 48-month series?

8. What type of chart would be most appropriate for showing the relative market share of various brands of automobile?

9. How do you delete a chart?

10. Can charts change if the worksheets on which they were originally built change?

For Discussion

1. In what ways might a bar chart provide a deceptive view of data? What about a 3-D bar chart? What do certain charts imply that may not really be present in the data?

2. When is a pie chart an appropriate chart type? A bar chart?

3. What is a chart legend, and why is it usually important?

Review Exercises

Bar Chart of Municipal Waste Trends for 1960–1990

Open the EPA3 worksheet that you completed in Project 4. Construct a bar chart that shows how waste of paper, glass, plastics, and metals changed over the time period of 1960 through 1990. The data series for this chart are in rows. The chart should resemble Figure 5.37. Print the chart by itself (without the worksheet), and save the file as EPACHART.

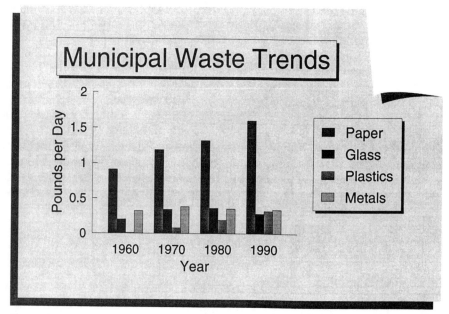

Figure 5.37

3-D Column Chart of Audio Sales for 1975–1990

Open the AUDIO2 worksheet from Project 3. Construct a 3-D bar chart showing sales of LP Albums, Singles, 8-Track Tapes, Cassette Tapes, and Regular CDs over the 1975 to 1990 time period. Print the worksheet with the chart.

Assignments

Pie Chart of Energy Usage of Home Appliances

Open the ENERGY1 worksheet from Project 4. Construct a pie chart, with a legend but without labels for each slice, showing the share of the total monthly energy bill for each appliance in the worksheet. Make another pie chart that graphs only the major users of electricity.

3-D Bar Chart of Daily Appliance Usage

Using the ENERGY1 worksheet from Project 4, construct a 3-D bar chart that shows, for each day of the week, the number of hours the following appliances are used: conventional oven, microwave oven, dishwasher, and clothes dryer. Format the chart as needed.

PROJECT 6: BUILDING DYNAMIC WORKSHEETS

Objectives

After completing this project, you should be able to:

▶ Work with calendar dates and date formats

▶ Build formulas that keep a running balance

▶ Use the @IF and @ISSTRING functions

▶ Use mixed cell references

▶ Hide columns

▶ Assign colors to cell contents

▶ Reconcile a checking account

▶ Work with multiple worksheets in a single file

CASE STUDY: BALANCING A CHECKBOOK

In this project, you will build a worksheet that will enable you to balance a checkbook easily. Suppose you have a checking account. The record of checks and other transactions in your checkbook is called a *check register*. Figure 6.1 illustrates a small check register. The withdrawal category includes checks, Automated Teller Machine (ATM) debits, Electronic Fund Transfer (EFT) payments, charges, fees, and so on. The deposit category includes ordinary deposits, automatic payroll transfers, credits, and refunds. Note that rounded-off numbers will be used in this project to make it easier to follow the examples.

		Register	Match	Withdrawal	Deposit	Balance Forward
Number	Date	Description				300.00
101	11/06/95	Kang Xi Grocery Store		50.00		250.00
DEP	11/11/95	Paycheck			1,200.00	1,450.00
102	11/14/95	Metro Electric Power		100.00		1,350.00
103	11/14/95	Imperial Apartments		400.00		950.00
DEP	11/18/95	Lottery Winnings			50.00	1,000.00

Figure 6.1

The list of transactions—deposits, checks paid, charges, and so on—that the bank sends to you each month is called a bank *statement*. Figure 6.2 shows a typical bank statement.

First Interdimensional Bank
Checking Account Statement

Deposits/Credits

Date	Description	Amount
11/11/95	Deposit	1,200.00

Checks/Withdrawals/Fees

Date	Description	Amount
11/9/95	Check 101	50.00
11/16/95	Check 103	400.00
11/17/95	Monthly Fee	10.00

Account Summary as of 11/17/95

Beginning Balance	300.00
Plus 1 Deposit/Credit	1,200.00
Less 3 Checks/Withdrawals/Fees	460.00
Ending Balance	1,040.00

Figure 6.2

The bank statement informs you that you have a certain amount of money in your account—this is the statement's ending *balance*. Your check register also has its own balance—how much money *you* think you have in the account— and it's likely that the two balances are different.

Why are they different? First, there were probably checks you wrote that had not yet been presented to the bank for payment by the time the statement was printed and mailed. In the example, the check to Metro Electric Power is one of these. Your check register also probably lists checks that you wrote or deposits that you made *after* the bank printed the statement, such as the deposit of lottery winnings in the example.

Second, the bank statement probably shows transactions such as charges, fees, and automatic payments that you might not have known about and did not record in the register. And of course, it's quite possible that you wrote a check or withdrew money from an ATM and forgot to record it in the register.

Reconciling the two balances—balancing the checkbook—means adjusting the register balance so that it is updated to reflect transactions appearing only on the bank statement and adjusting the statement balance so that it is updated to reflect transactions appearing only on the register. You can use one of several approaches to reconciling. The method you'll find described on the back of any bank statement is more suitable for pencil and paper than it is for electronic worksheets. The method you will implement in this project is one that uses an electronic worksheet (rather than a register booklet) as the actual check register. This eliminates the need for a complete paper register.

Designing the Solution

Your electronic check register will contain a record of all checking-account transactions that you know of. When a new statement arrives, any transactions appearing on the statement but not on the register should be entered into the register. This is how you inform the register about transactions appearing only on the bank statement. For example, suppose you receive a bank statement and you see that you were charged a $10.00 monthly service fee. You would record that fee in the register, as shown in Figure 6.3. Once you record transactions such as this in your check register, the register balance will be updated or adjusted to reflect the information in the bank statement.

		Register				Balance Forward
Number	Date	Description	Match	Withdrawal	Deposit	300.00
101	11/06/95	Kang Xi Grocery Store		50.00		250.00
DEP	11/11/95	Paycheck			1,200.00	1,450.00
102	11/14/95	Metro Electric Power		100.00		1,350.00
103	11/14/95	Imperial Apartments		400.00		950.00
DEP	11/18/95	Lottery Winnings			50.00	1,000.00
FEE	11/17/95	Monthly Fee		10.00		990.00

Figure 6.3

What about transactions that you made and recorded in the register *after* the bank printed its statement? How do you update the bank statement to reflect these? You don't modify the statement directly. Instead, you mark off in the register all withdrawals and deposits that also appear in the statement, as shown in Figure 6.4. Any unmarked entry is *unmatched*—it appears only on the register and not on the statement.

		Register				Balance Forward
Number	Date	Description	Match	Withdrawal	Deposit	300.00
101	11/06/95	Kang Xi Grocery Store	X	50.00		250.00
DEP	11/11/95	Paycheck	X		1,200.00	1,450.00
102	11/14/95	Metro Electric Power		100.00		1,350.00
103	11/14/95	Imperial Apartments	X	400.00		950.00
DEP	11/18/95	Lottery Winnings			50.00	1,000.00
FEE	11/17/95	Monthly Fee	X	10.00		990.00

Figure 6.4

You then total all unmatched entries— all the withdrawals and deposits that appear in the register but not on the statement. To produce an adjusted statement balance, you subtract the total withdrawals and add the total deposits to the bank statement's ending balance, as shown in Figure 6.5. The adjusted statement balance should equal the adjusted register balance.

Adjusted Register Balance:	$990.00
Bank Statement Ending Balance:	1,040.00
LESS Withdrawals in register not shown on statement:	100.00
PLUS Deposits in register not shown on statement:	50.00
Adjusted Statement Balance:	$990.00
Discrepancy:	$0.00

Figure 6.5

If the two adjusted balances agree, your checkbook is balanced. If not, some transaction or a group of transactions has not been correctly accounted for or contains mistakes. The worksheet you will build in this project cannot automatically correct such recording errors, although it can help find them.

In automating the task of balancing a checkbook, you will begin by constructing a check register similar to the one shown in Figure 6.1. It will contain columns for check number, date, description, match, withdrawal, deposit, and balance forward. The only formula in these columns will be one to compute the balance forward. Once the check register is complete, you will construct formulas that reconcile the register with information derived from a bank statement.

BUILDING A CHECK REGISTER

You will now make the initial text entries for the check register, as shown in Figure 6.6. Notice that some space is being preserved at the top of the worksheet; later, you will place the balancing formulas here. It makes more sense to put those formulas near the top (or perhaps to the right), because the top section of the worksheet is easy to find. Also, as you make new entries in the register, the worksheet will grow downward, and it would be inconvenient to have something else in the way.

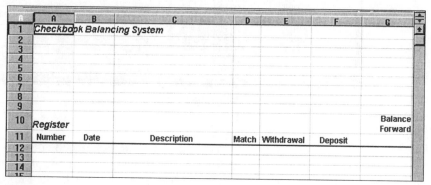

	A	B	C	D	E	F	G
1	Checkbook Balancing System						
2							
3							
4							
5							
6							
7							
8							
9							
10	Register						Balance Forward
11	Number	Date	Description	Match	Withdrawal	Deposit	
12							
13							
14							
15							

Figure 6.6

The sample data that you enter in the check register will be based on Figure 6.1.

To prepare the worksheet and enter the main headings:

1 Enter `Checkbook Balancing System` in cell A1.

2 Enter `Register` in cell A10.

3 Enter `Number` in cell A11.

4 Enter `Date` in cell B11.

5 Enter `Description` in cell C11.

6 Enter `Match` in cell D11.

7 Enter `Withdrawal` in cell E11.

8 Enter `Deposit` in cell F11.

9 Move to cell G10 and enter `Balance Forward`

10 Save the worksheet as CHKBAL1.

To format the column headings:

1 Set the format of the text *Checkbook Balancing System* in cell A1 and *Register* in cell A10 to 14 points, bold italic.

2 Set the format of *Balance Forward* in cell G10 to bold, right horizontal alignment, and wrap text.

3 Increase the height of row 11 to 18 points.

4 Select the other column titles in the range A11..F11, and set the format to bold.

5 Extend the range selection to include G11, and in the Border section of the Lines & Color dialog box, set a thick bottom border, as shown in Figure 6.7.

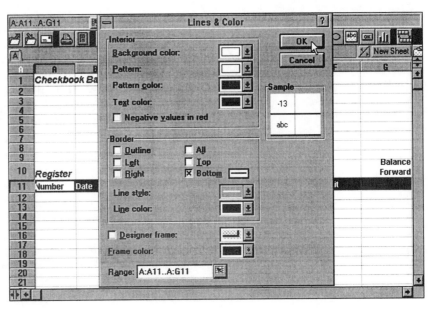

Figure 6.7

6 Set the horizontal alignment to center for the column titles in the range A11..F11.

7 Widen the Withdrawal, Deposit, and Balance Forward columns (E..G) to 10 points.

8 Widen the Description column (C) to 25 points.

9 Narrow the Match column (D) to 6 points.

10 Choose Zoom Out from the View menu.
Your worksheet should now resemble Figure 6.8.

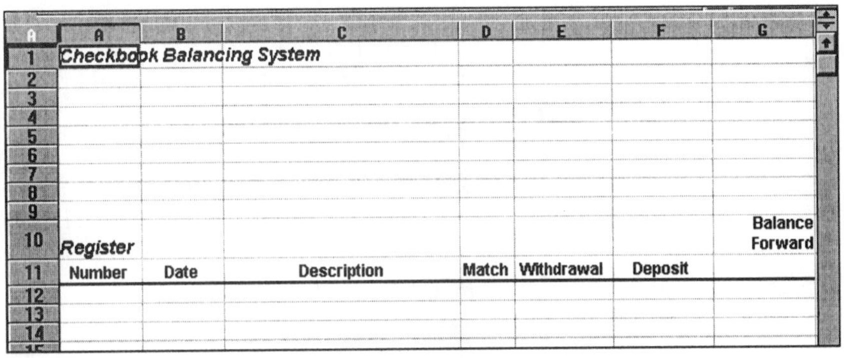

Figure 6.8

11 Save the worksheet.

Using Calendar Dates in 1-2-3

Lotus 1-2-3 lets you enter dates (and times) in a worksheet cell. A date is a special kind of number. Lotus 1-2-3 dates are useful in several respects.

You can perform *date arithmetic* with 1-2-3; that is, you can add days to a date, subtract days from a date, or subtract an earlier date from a later date (to determine the number of days between the two dates). For example, suppose the date May 7, 1995 is stored in cell A1, and the date December 16, 1994 is stored in cell A2. The formula +A1-A2 will result in 142, the number of days between the two dates.

Lotus 1-2-3 stores dates within the worksheet as *date numbers.* A date number can be any number from 1 through 73050, representing dates from January 1, 1900 through December 31, 2099. For example, the date May 7, 1995 is stored in the worksheet as 34826. You assign a date-number format to show the date in a more readable form, such as 05-May-95.

To enter a specific, constant date—such as 5/7/95—into a cell, type the date directly: for example, you could type 5/7/95 or 7-May-95. Lotus 1-2-3 will attempt to convert your entry to a date number, and it will automatically assign a date format consistent with the way you entered the date.

If you want today's date—which changes daily—to appear in a cell, type the formula +@NOW. The @NOW function shows a date number that can be formatted with one of the date formats to make the date readable. The result of this @NOW function depends on whatever date the computer system is set to. Lotus 1-2-3 offers a number of functions to help with date calculations. Table 6.1 lists a few of them; the examples presume that cell X15 contains a valid date, such as 05/07/95.

Table 6.1

Task	Function
To display the current date	@NOW
To extract the month (1 to 12) from a date in another cell	@MONTH(X15)
To extract the day of the month from a date in another cell	@DAY(X15)
To extract the year from a date in another cell	@YEAR(X15)
To extract the day of the week (0 to 6, where 0 is Monday) from a date in another cell	@WEEKDAY(X15)

In the following steps, you will enter a date for the first check and then assign a date number format to the Date column of the check register.

To enter and format a date:

1 Enter **11/6/95** in cell B12.
Notice that this entry appears as 11/06/95. Lotus 1-2-3 automatically interprets the entry as a date and assigns a default format of m/d/y.

2 Select all of column B.

3 Choose Number Format from the Style menu.
The Number Format dialog box appears.

4 Select Dates from the Format list box.
The Dates list box appears.

5 Select 12/31/93 in the Dates list box, and then select OK, as shown in Figure 6.9.

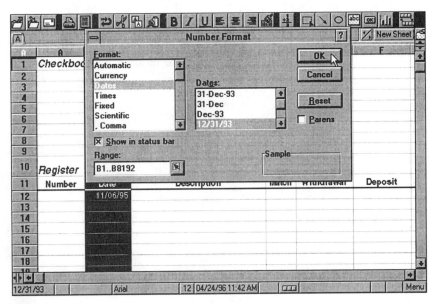

Figure 6.9

Formatting a Column as Labels

Column A of the worksheet will contain check numbers. Ordinarily, entering a number into a cell will cause 1-2-3 to interpret the number as a value. It would be better if the entire column were formatted so that any entry in the column would be interpreted as a label. In the following steps, you will format the column so that any entry in the column will be interpreted as a label.

To format a column for entering labels:

1 Select all of column A.

2 Choose Label from the status bar Number Format box.

3 Enter **101** in cell A12.
The number will be interpreted by 1-2-3 as a label and will be aligned to the left within the cell.

To enter the check description and withdrawal amount:

1 Enter **Kang Xi Grocery Store** in cell C12 as the description of this entry.
Note that the match column will be left blank for now.

2 Type **50** in cell E12.
A check is the most common kind of account withdrawal.

Using Comma Number Format

Values appearing in the Withdrawal, Deposit, and Balance Forward columns are dollar amounts and should appear consistently with two digits to the right of the decimal. In the following steps, you will assign the Comma number format to these three columns.

To assign the Comma number format:

1 Select columns E, F, and G.

2 Select the Comma number format from the status bar, as shown in Figure 6.10.

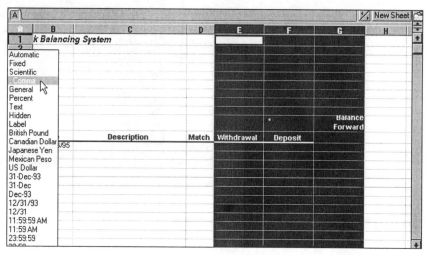

Figure 6.10

Keeping a Running Balance

The Balance Forward column in the check register is a typical example of a *running balance*—a value that appears on each line of an account or register to show the current balance. The starting balance for this register will be entered in cell G11. Calculation of the balance for each line of the register will involve taking the previous balance, subtracting any withdrawals, and adding any deposits.

Such a formula uses relative addressing and can be copied to provide a running balance for each line of the register. In the steps that follow, you will copy the formula downward so that ten rows of the worksheet will be ready to contain check-register entries.

Ten is an arbitrary number of rows: if new rows are needed later in the register, the formula can be copied easily to them. The advantage of copying the formula in advance to a large number of rows is that you won't have to remember to copy it each time the worksheet grows. The disadvantage is that the extra formulas (until they are needed) can use up memory and slow down the calculation of the worksheet.

 To build the formula for Balance Forward:

1 Enter **300** for the starting balance in cell G11.

2 Select cell G12.
This cell will contain a formula to compute the balance forward for the first line of the register.

3 Type +

4 Select the previous balance (300, in cell G11).

5 Type -

6 Select the withdrawal amount (50, in cell E12).

7 Type +

8 Select the deposit amount (cell F12, which is blank), and then press (ENTER)

9 Copy the formula down column G to cell G21. Your screen should look like Figure 6.11.

	A	B	C	D	E	F	G
1	Checkbook Balancing System						
2							
3							
4							
5							
6							
7							
8							
9							Balance Forward
10	Register						
11	Number	Date	Description	Match	Withdrawal	Deposit	300.00
12	101	11/06/95	Kang Xi Grocery Store		50.00		250.00
13							250.00
14							250.00
15							250.00
16							250.00
17							250.00
18							250.00
19							250.00
20							250.00
21							250.00

Figure 6.11

The result of the formula is 250.00. This relative formula means: take what is one cell above the formula, subtract what is two cells to the left, and add what is one cell to the left. Because no further deposits or withdrawals are currently entered in later lines of the register, the balance forward is 250 in each remaining cell.

The first line of the register contains only a withdrawal—so why bother having the balance forward formula add the blank deposit cell? You should design your formulas for flexibility; this single formula will work for either a deposit or a withdrawal entry in the register. This flexibility lets the formula be used in any line of the register, without regard to the type of register entry.

Completing the Remaining Register Entries

In the following steps, you can refer to Figure 6.12 to complete the other four check-register entries.

	A	B	C	D	E	F	G
1	Checkbook Balancing System						
2							
3							
4							
5							
6							
7							
8							
9							
10	Register						Balance Forward
11	Number	Date	Description	Match	Withdrawal	Deposit	300.00
12	101	11/06/95	Kang Xi Grocery Store		50.00		250.00
13	DEP	11/11/95	Paycheck			1,200.00	1,450.00
14	102	11/14/95	Metro Electric Power		100.00		1,350.00
15	103	11/14/95	Imperial Apartments		400.00		950.00
16	DEP	11/18/95	Lottery Winnings			50.00	1,000.00
17							1,000.00
18							1,000.00
19							1,000.00
20							1,000.00
21							1,000.00

Figure 6.12

To make the other check-register entries:

1 Enter **DEP** (an abbreviation for *deposit*) in cell A13.

2 Enter **11/11/95** for the date in cell B13.

3 Enter **Paycheck** for the description in cell C13.

4 Enter **1200** for the deposit amount in cell F13.

5 Enter the information for the other three lines of the check register, referring to Figure 6.12. Remember not to enter the Balance Forward amounts; these are formulas.

Your screen should now resemble Figure 6.12.

6 Save the worksheet.

 EXIT   If necessary, you can quit 1-2-3 now and continue this project later.

BUILDING THE RECONCILIATION SYSTEM

How can the check register you've just completed be made to work as part of a checking-account balancing system? Suppose a statement arrives from the bank, as illustrated in Figure 6.13. You will recall that the first step in reconciling the electronic check register is to add to the register any entries that appear only on the statement. This is simply a matter of entering some new lines of information in the register. Using the example statement, only one item, a $10.00 monthly fee, needs to be added to the register.

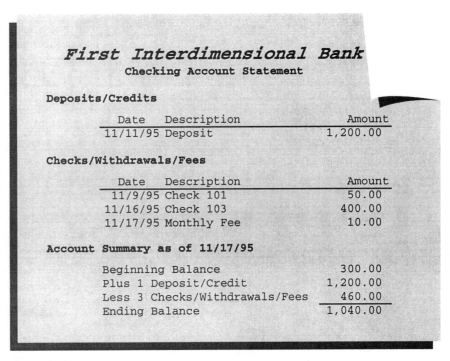

First Interdimensional Bank
Checking Account Statement

Deposits/Credits

Date	Description	Amount
11/11/95	Deposit	1,200.00

Checks/Withdrawals/Fees

Date	Description	Amount
11/9/95	Check 101	50.00
11/16/95	Check 103	400.00
11/17/95	Monthly Fee	10.00

Account Summary as of 11/17/95

Beginning Balance	300.00
Plus 1 Deposit/Credit	1,200.00
Less 3 Checks/Withdrawals/Fees	460.00
Ending Balance	1,040.00

Figure 6.13

To add entries to the register from the statement:

1 Enter **FEE** in cell A17.

2 Enter **11/17/95** in cell B17.

3 Enter **Monthly Fee** in cell C17.

4 Enter **10** in cell E17 (the withdrawal column).

Your screen should now resemble Figure 6.14.

	A	B	C	D	E	F	G
1	Checkbook Balancing System						
10	Register						Balance Forward
11	Number	Date	Description	Match	Withdrawal	Deposit	300.00
12	101	11/06/95	Kang Xi Grocery Store		50.00		250.00
13	DEP	11/11/95	Paycheck			1,200.00	1,450.00
14	102	11/14/95	Metro Electric Power		100.00		1,350.00
15	103	11/14/95	Imperial Apartments		400.00		950.00
16	DEP	11/18/95	Lottery Winnings			50.00	1,000.00
17	FEE	11/17/95	Monthly Fee		10.00		990.00
18							990.00
19							990.00
20							990.00
21							990.00

Figure 6.14

Setting Up the Match Column

You would repeat the procedure you just completed—adding items that appear only on the statement to the checkbook register—each time a new statement arrived. What about items that appear on the register but not on the statement? You will recall that entries that *do* appear on both the register and the statement should be checked off in the match column of the electronic register. Any unmatched entries identify those items that appear only in the register.

In this check register, a letter X will be used as the checkmark. In the steps below, you will format and then fill in the match column of the register.

To prepare the match column:

1 Select all of column D.

2 Set the horizontal alignment to center.

3 Refer to the sample bank statement in Figure 6.13 and mark off entries in the register that are matched on the statement. Use an uppercase X to mark matches.

Your worksheet should now resemble Figure 6.15.

	A	B	C	D	E	F	G
1	Checkbook Balancing System						
2							
3							
4							
5							
6							
7							
8							
9							
10	Register						Balance Forward
11	Number	Date	Description	Match	Withdrawal	Deposit	300.00
12	101	11/06/95	Kang Xi Grocery Store	X	50.00		250.00
13	DEP	11/11/95	Paycheck	X		1,200.00	1,450.00
14	102	11/14/95	Metro Electric Power		100.00		1,350.00
15	103	11/14/95	Imperial Apartments	X	400.00		950.00
16	DEP	11/18/95	Lottery Winnings			50.00	1,000.00
17	FEE	11/17/95	Monthly Fee	X	10.00		990.00
18							990.00
19							990.00
20							990.00
21							990.00

Figure 6.15

Setting Up the Columns for Unmatched Entries

To reconcile the account, you will need to know the total of withdrawals shown on the register but not on the statement and the total of deposits shown on the register but not on the statement. In other words, you need to identify and total the unmatched withdrawals and the unmatched deposits.

In the steps that follow, you will set up two special columns to the right of the register. One column will contain unmatched withdrawals, and the other will contain unmatched deposits. Note that the titles for these columns will be placed a couple of cells above the top border of the column.

To set up the reconciliation columns:

1 Select a Custom Zoom percent of 55.

2 Enter `Withdrawals in Register Unmatched on Statement` in cell H9.

3 Enter `Deposits in Register Unmatched on Statement` in cell I9.

4 Widen columns H and I to 12.

5 Set the format of H9 and I9 to align to the right horizontally and wrap text.
Your screen should resemble Figure 6.16.

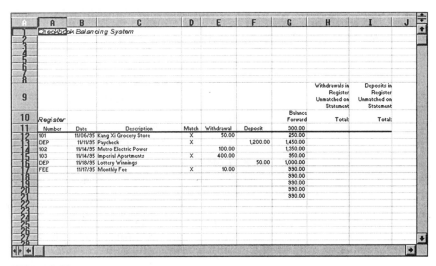

Figure 6.16

6 Enter **Total:** in cells H10 and I10, and set the horizontal alignment to right in cells H10 and I10.

7 Select all of columns H and I, and assign the Comma number format.

8 Set a thick bottom border in cells H11 and I11.
Your screen should resemble Figure 6.17.

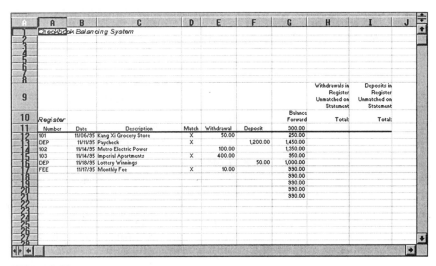

Figure 6.17

9 Save the worksheet.

Creating Formulas that Make Decisions

Consider how the new column for unmatched withdrawals should work. If a particular withdrawal in the register is not matched on the statement (that is, if there is no *X* in the match cell), that amount should appear in the Unmatched Withdrawals column. In the small sample register you have built, there is only one place in the unmatched withdrawals column where a nonzero number should appear: 100 should display in cell H14, because Metro Electric Power had not presented the check for payment before the bank printed the statement.

If the task of identifying unmatched entries is going to be automated, a special formula is required for each cell in the unmatched withdrawals column. The formula must be capable of performing a simple test: if the match cell in this row contains an *X*, then display zero; otherwise display the withdrawal amount.

Using the @IF Function

In 1-2-3, the @IF function can automate simple decisions. The syntax of the @IF function is described as:

@IF(logical___test, value___if___true, value___if___false)

This means that the @IF function takes three arguments: the first argument expresses a test or question; the second argument expresses what to do if the test result is true; and the third argument expresses what to do if the test result is false.

The @IF function can be applied several ways to solve the problem of identifying unmatched entries. In the following sections, you will try two approaches. The first version will produce a formula that can be understood this way: if there is an *X* in the match cell, then display zero; otherwise display the withdrawal amount.

To build the @IF formula for unmatched withdrawals (version 1):

1 Select cell H12, the first cell in the unmatched withdrawals column.

2 Type **+@IF(**

3 Select the match cell, D12.

4 Type **="X",0,**
Note that the *X* is uppercase.

5 Select the withdrawal cell, E12.

6 Type **)** and press (ENTER)

The completed formula in cell H12 is + @IF(D12 = "X",0,E12)

Ignoring relative cell reference terminology for the moment, this formula can be interpreted as meaning: if what's in cell D12 equals an *X*, then display a 0; otherwise display what's in cell E12. The *X* appears in quotes because it is a ***string***—a sequence of one or more characters to be taken literally—and not a range name or the name of a function.

Because the match cell contains an *X*, the result of the formula is 0.00. This formula is straightforward, but it is also brittle—it is sensitive to slight variations in the tested condition and could give unwanted results to an unsuspecting or careless user. In the steps that follow, you will test the formula to see how it responds to other kinds of entries in the match cell.

To test the first @IF formula:

1 Select the match cell, D12.

2 Type **x** and press ENTER

Make sure you enter a lowercase *X*. The result of the @IF formula is still 0.00, which is correct. You can conclude that the formula is not *case sensitive*—that is, it doesn't care whether a letter is entered in uppercase or lowercase. But suppose someone used an *m* to mark matching entries.

3 Select cell D12.

4 Type **m** and press ENTER

The result of the @IF formula is now 50.00, which is wrong. The problem is that the tested condition is too particular; this would be a more robust formula if it tested simply whether any label was in the cell. Lotus 1-2-3 provides a special function to do this: @ISSTRING(D12) will return (result in) 1 (True) if cell D12 is a string, and 0 (False) otherwise.

To build the @IF formula for unmatched withdrawals (version 2):

1 Select cell H12, the first cell in the unmatched withdrawals column.

2 Type **+@IF(@ISSTRING(**

3 Select the match cell, D12.

4 Type **),0,**

5 Select the withdrawal cell, E12.

6 Type **)** and press ENTER

The formula reads @IF(@ISSTRING(D12,),0,E12). Your screen should resemble Figure 6.18. The formula's result is correct, even though an *m* rather than an *X* was used in the match cell.

	A	B	C	D	E	F	G	H	I	J
1	Checkbook Balancing System									
9								Withdrawals in Register Unmatched on Statement	Deposits in Register Unmatched on Statement	
10	Register						Balance Forward			
11	Number	Date	Description	Match	Withdrawal	Deposit	300.00	Total:	Total:	
12	101	11/06/95	Kang Xi Grocery Store	m	50.00		250.00	0.00		
13	DEP	11/11/95	Paycheck	X		1,200.00	1,450.00			
14	102	11/14/95	Metro Electric Power		100.00		1,350.00			
15	103	11/14/95	Imperial Apartments	X	400.00		950.00			
16	DEP	11/18/95	Lottery Winnings			50.00	1,000.00			
17	FEE	11/17/95	Monthly Fee	X	10.00		990.00			
18							990.00			
19							990.00			
20							990.00			
21							990.00			
22										
23										

Figure 6.18

7 Enter **X** in cell D12.

Using Mixed Cell References

The @IF formula uses relative cell references and should work without a problem for the other cells in the unmatched withdrawals column. It might seem as if it would work for the unmatched deposits column as well, because the same basic @IF test is needed. The best way to understand why the formula won't correctly duplicate in its present form is to copy it and examine the results.

In the steps that follow, you will copy the formula in cell H12 to the range H12..I21 and study the resulting formulas.

To copy a range of cells:

1 Select cell H12.

2 Choose Copy from the Edit menu.

3 Select the range H12..I21.

4 Choose Paste from the Edit menu.
Your screen should resemble Figure 6.19.

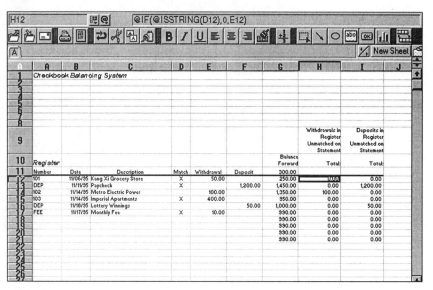

Figure 6.19

5 Select cell I12.

The formula in cell I12 reads @IF(@ISSTRING(E12),0,F12), which can be read as: if the cell four columns to the left is blank, then display zero; otherwise display the value in the cell three columns to the left.

The cell that *should* be tested by @ISSTRING is D12, not E12. It is correct, however, that the formula displays the value of F12 if the match cell is blank. The relative cell reference to F12 in this formula is correct, but a relative reference does not work for the cell being tested by @ISSTRING.

If you look at the results in the unmatched deposits column, you will see that they are incorrect. Will a fully absolute reference to D12 solve the problem? In the following steps, you will modify and recopy the @IF formula to find out if it will.

To modify the @IF formula (using fully absolute cell references):

1 Select cell H12.

You will now edit the function in this cell.

2 Click the text *D12* in the contents box.

3 Press (F4) to make the reference fully absolute. The formula now reads @IF(@ISSTRING($A:$D$12),0,E12)

The $A: in the above formula refers to worksheet A. If there was more than one worksheet in the file, the reference to cell D12 would refer to cell D12 in worksheet A.

4 Press (ENTER)

Notice that the reference to $A: disappeared; 1-2-3 recognizes that there is only one worksheet active.

5 Copy the formula, and then paste it across and down to replace the old @IF formulas in the range H12..I21. Your screen should look like Figure 6.20.

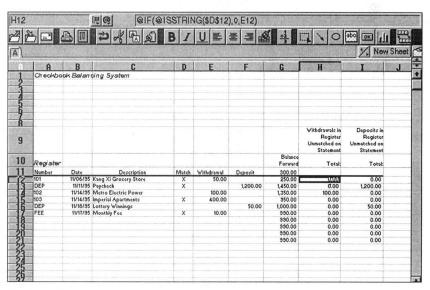

Figure 6.20

6 Select cell I17.

Now the formula has trouble in both the unmatched withdrawals and the unmatched deposits columns. Consider the formula in cell I17, which reads @IF(@ISSTRING($D$12),0,F17). The @ISSTRING part of this formula, like all the other new @IF formulas, tests cell D12. It should be testing D17, the match cell in its own row.

Now consider the original formula in cell H12:
@IF(@ISSTRING($D$12),0,E12)

You will recall that any time you are referring to a cell while building a formula and that cell *alone* provides the required information for the formula and for future copies of the formula, the reference to the cell should be absolute. In this case, it is not only cell D12 that all the copied formulas will need to refer to.

What can be said about the copied formulas? Each one will have to refer to the cell in the Match column (D) of its own current row. In other words, the cell tested by @ISSTRING will always be D*something*. Only the *column* part of the cell reference should be absolute. The row should be allowed to adjust as the formula is copied. This is an example of a ***mixed cell reference***—a cell reference where only the column or only the row is static. Only one dollar sign appears in a mixed reference; for example, $D12 or F$3. In the steps that follow, you will rebuild and recopy the formula once again, this time using a mixed reference where appropriate.

To modify the @IF formula:

1 Select cell H12.

2 Select the text $D$12 in the contents box.

3 Press F4 until the mixed reference A:$D12 appears.
The formula now reads @IF(@ISSTRING(A:$D12),0,E12). The $D12 in the new formula can be interpreted as: column D, current row. Once again, the A: refers to worksheet A. If multiple worksheets existed in the file, you would want to refer to cell D12 in the current worksheet.

4 Press ENTER

5 Copy the formula, and then paste it across and down to replace all the old @IF formulas in the range H12..I21.

6 Save the worksheet.

Tip The general rule is to use an ordinary, fully relative cell reference. If, when you copy a formula, you get incorrect results from the duplicated formulas, follow these guidelines to rebuild and recopy the original formula:

- Any time you are pointing to a cell while building a formula, and that cell alone provides the required information for the formula (and for future copies of the formula), the reference to the cell should be fully absolute.
- If all the required information is in one column, then make the column reference absolute.
- If all the required information is in one row, then make the row reference absolute.

Calculating the Total Unmatched Withdrawals and Deposits

The totals of unmatched withdrawals and deposits are required to balance the checkbook. In the following steps, you will build an @SUM formula, first using a keyboard shortcut to speed the selection of the range to be summed. Using the keyboard shortcut, 1-2-3 moves along adjacent non-empty cells until it finds an empty cell; it will stop immediately before the empty cell.

To build the formula:

1 Select cell H11, which will contain the total unmatched withdrawals.

2 Type +@SUM(

3 Press ↓ . END ↓

Lotus 1-2-3 automatically finds the bottom of the block of nonempty cells and extends the range selection to that point.

4 Type **)** and press (ENTER)
The formula is @SUM(H12..H21). Although this formula could be copied to calculate the total unmatched deposits, you will instead experiment with another shortcut selection technique.

5 Select cell I11, which will contain the total unmatched deposits.

6 Type **+@SUM(**

7 Click cell I12, position (do not drag) the pointer in cell I21, hold down (SHFT) and click the mouse button, and then type **)** and press (ENTER)
The formula reads @SUM(I12..I21)

Building the Reconciliation Formulas

The formulas that perform the calculations to balance the account will be placed in the top section of the worksheet. The method used will be the same as the one discussed at the beginning of this project. You have already adjusted the register balance (you added items appearing at first only on the statement to the register). Now you will create formulas to adjust the statement balance to reflect unmatched withdrawals and deposits. Use the Zoom In command if you are having trouble seeing individual worksheet cells.

To enter the row titles:

1 Enter **Adjusted Register Balance** in cell D2.

2 Enter **Bank Statement Ending Balance** in cell D3.

3 Enter **LESS Withdrawals** in cell D4.

4 Enter **PLUS Deposits** in D5.

5 Enter **Adjusted Statement Balance** in cell D6.

6 Enter **Discrepancy** in D7.

7 Align to the right the text you just entered in D2..D7.

8 Increase the height of row 1 to 30 points.

9 Center the main worksheet title, *Checkbook Balancing System*, across the selection A1..G1.

10 Change the *vertical* alignment of cell A1 to Top.

11 Increase the height of row 3 to 25 points.
Your screen should resemble Figure 6.21.

	A	B	C	D	E	F	G	H	I	J
1			Checkbook Balancing System							
2			Adjusted Register Balance							
3			Bank Statement Ending Balance							
4			LESS Withdrawals							
5			PLUS Deposits							
6			Adjusted Statement Balance							
7			Discrepancy							
8										
9								Withdrawals in Register Unmatched on Statement	Deposits in Register Unmatched on Statement	
10	Register						Balance Forward			
11	Number	Date	Description	Match	Withdrawal	Deposit	300.00	Total: 100.00	Total: 50.00	
12	101	11/06/95	Kang Xi Grocery Store	X	50.00		250.00	100.00	0.00	
13	DEP	11/11/95	Paycheck	X		1,200.00	1,450.00	0.00	0.00	
14	102	11/14/95	Metro Electric Power		100.00		1,350.00	100.00	0.00	
15	103	11/14/95	Imperial Apartments	X	400.00		950.00	0.00	0.00	
16	DEP	11/18/95	Lottery Winnings			50.00	1,000.00	0.00	50.00	
17	FEE	11/17/95	Monthly Fee	X	10.00		990.00	0.00	0.00	
18							990.00	0.00	0.00	
19							990.00	0.00	0.00	
20							990.00	0.00	0.00	
21							990.00	0.00	0.00	
22										

Figure 6.21

12 Save the worksheet.

The adjusted register balance is the current balance shown in the register. The very short formula to calculate this, +G21, simply takes the value of the bottom cell (G21) of the balance forward section of the register. If new rows are inserted within the register, they will push the bottom cell downward, and 1-2-3 will adjust the formula so that it still refers to the bottom cell.

To calculate the adjusted register balance:

1 Select cell E2.

2 Type +

3 Select the last entry in the Balance Forward column, G21.

4 Press (ENTER)
The formula reads +G21, and its result is 990.00.

The bank statement's ending balance is not a formula; it is a value specified on the bank statement. Refer to Figure 6.13 or 6.2 to obtain this number.

To enter the bank statement ending balance:

1 Select cell E3.

2 Enter **1040**

The totals of unmatched withdrawals and deposits are already calculated by the @SUM formulas in cells H11 and I11. The formulas in the reconciliation section will refer to these cells.

To show unmatched withdrawals and deposits:

1 Select cell E4 (which will contain the total of withdrawals recorded in the register but not shown on the statement) and type +

2 Select the total unmatched withdrawals (cell H11), and press (ENTER)
The completed formula is +H11, and its result is 100.00.

3 Select cell E5 (which will contain the total of deposits recorded in the register but not shown on the statement), and type +

4 Select the total unmatched deposits (cell I11), and press (ENTER)
The completed formula is +I11, and its result is 50.00.

The adjusted statement balance is computed by taking the bank statement ending balance, subtracting unmatched withdrawals, and adding unmatched deposits.

To compute the adjusted statement balance:

1 Select cell E6, which will contain a formula to compute the adjusted statement balance.

2 Type +

3 Select the bank statement ending balance (in cell E3), and then type –

4 Select the LESS Withdrawals amount (in cell E4), and then type +

5 Select the PLUS Deposits amount (in cell E5), and then press (ENTER)
The completed formula is +E3-E4+E5, and its result is 990.00.
The discrepancy is the difference between the Adjusted Register Balance and the Adjusted Statement Balance. If the discrepancy is zero, the account is balanced.

To calculate the discrepancy:

1 Select cell E7 and type +

2 Point to the Adjusted Register Balance (in cell E2) and type –

3 Point to the Adjusted Statement Balance (in cell E6) and press (ENTER)
The formula is +E2-E6, and its result is 0.00; the account balances.

4 Assign the U.S. Dollar number format to the adjusted register and statement balances in cells E2 and E7.

5 Set a thin top border and a thick bottom border for the Adjusted Statement Balance in cell E6.
Your screen should resemble Figure 6.22.

	A	B	C	D	E	F	G	H	I	J
1			Checkbook Balancing System							
2			Adjusted Register Balance		$990.00					
3			Bank Statement Ending Balance		1,040.00					
4			LESS Withdrawals		100.00					
5			PLUS Deposits		50.00					
6			Adjusted Statement Balance		990.00					
7			Discrepancy		$0.00					
8										
9								Withdrawals in Register Unmatched on Statement	Deposits in Register Unmatched on Statement	
10	Register							Balance Forward	Total:	Total:
11	Number	Date	Description	Match	Withdrawal	Deposit		300.00	100.00	50.00
	101	11/06/95	Kang Xi Grocery Store	X	50.00			250.00	0.00	0.00
	DEP	11/11/95	Paycheck	X		1,200.00		1,450.00	0.00	0.00
	102	11/14/95	Metro Electric Power		100.00			1,350.00	100.00	0.00
	103	11/14/95	Imperial Apartments	X	400.00			950.00	0.00	0.00
	DEP	11/18/95	Lottery Winnings			50.00		1,000.00	0.00	50.00
	FEE	11/17/95	Monthly Fee	X	10.00			990.00	0.00	0.00
								990.00	0.00	0.00
								990.00	0.00	0.00
								990.00	0.00	0.00

Figure 6.22

Now that you have learned about the @IF function, you can create a formula that displays a message about whether the account balances.

To build an @IF formula for the balancing message:

1 Select cell C9 and type `+@IF(`

2 Point to the Discrepancy cell (E7), type `=0, "The account balances!", "The account does NOT balance!")` and press (ENTER)

3 Set the attributes of cell C9 to bold, with center horizontal alignment, and center vertical alignment.
Your screen should resemble Figure 6.23.

Figure 6.23

4 Save the worksheet.

EXIT If necessary, you can quit 1-2-3 now and continue this project later.

STREAMLINING A WORKSHEET

Your worksheet is now fully functional, but several improvements are possible. You should give some consideration to making a worksheet easy to use and error-resistant. This is especially true if the worksheet might be used by people other than yourself.

Hiding Columns

Certain parts of this worksheet—for example, the columns for calculating the unmatched totals—hold little interest for someone who just wants to know whether an account balances. In the following steps, you will learn how to hide columns on the worksheet so that they are not distractions.

To hide selected columns:

1 Select cells H1 and I1.

2 Choose Hide from the Style menu.
The Hide dialog box appears.

3 Select Column, as shown in Figure 6.24.

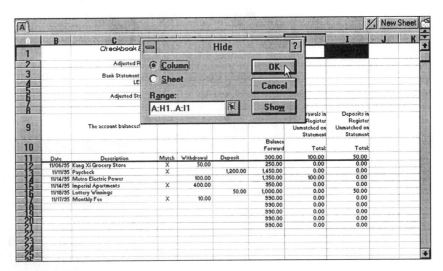

Figure 6.24

4 Select OK.

Columns H and I are no longer visible, but they still exist and cells within them can be referred to by formulas in the worksheet.

You can magnify the worksheet so that it is easier to read.

5 Select a Custom Zoom percent of 70.

> *Tip* You can disclose hidden columns by selecting a column range spanning the hidden columns (adjacent cells in columns G and J), choosing Hide from the Style menu, and selecting Show.

Protecting Cells

With so many formulas on the worksheet, a user could easily wipe out a formula by accidentally entering something else in its cell. Therefore, users should be allowed to change only certain cells. In the following steps, you will learn how to *seal,* or ***protect,*** the entire worksheet and *unprotect* only the cells for which changes are allowed. By default, all cells are initially protected, but protected and unprotected settings have no effect until the file is sealed. The general approach to using cell protection is to designate the cells that the user is allowed to change as being unprotected, and then to seal the file. The file is sealed using a password so only those users who have the password can unseal the file.

Several cells in the worksheet should remain unprotected once the file is sealed. The user must be allowed to make entries in cell E3, the bank statement ending balance; in cell G11, the balance forward; and in all the cells in the range A12..F21 where the user enters deposit and withdrawal information.

To unprotect a collection:

1 Select a collection of cells to include cell E3, cell G11, and the range A12..F21.

2 Choose Protection from the Style menu.
The Protection dialog box appears.

3 Select Keep Data Unprotected After File Is Sealed as shown in Figure 6.25.

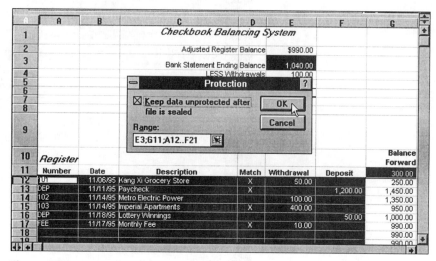

Figure 6.25

4 Select OK.
The collection of cells is now unlocked, but this setting will have no effect until the file is sealed with a password. Notice that the contents of unprotected cells in the worksheet are colored blue.

To seal a file:

1 Choose Protect from the File menu.
The Protect dialog box appears.

2 Select the Seal File check box (see Figure 6.26).

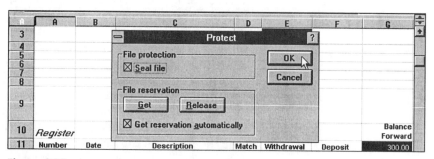

Figure 6.26

3 Select OK.
The Password dialog box appears.

4 Think of a password, type it in the Password text box, press (TAB) and then retype the same password in the Verify text box.

The password is entered twice to make sure it is typed correctly. Passwords are case-sensitive, so be sure you remember whether you typed your password in uppercase or lowercase characters.

5 Select OK.

6 Select cell E6, the adjusted statement balance, and type **3**
A message box appears indicating that this is a protected cell.

7 Select OK to clear the message box.

8 Select cell E3, type **1030** and press (ENTER)
Observe that changes *can* be made to the unlocked cell, and the formulas in the worksheet display different results. Even if formulas are protected, they still recalculate and can display new results.

9 Choose Undo from the Edit menu.
You can undo certain actions immediately after performing them if you change your mind. In this case, choosing Undo will revert to the original entry of 1040.

The file should be unsealed so that you can make further modifications to the worksheet.

To unseal the file:

1 Choose Protect from the File menu.

2 Clear the Seal File check box, and then select OK.

3 Enter the password you used to seal the file in the Password dialog box, and then select OK.

Assigning Cell Background Colors

The worksheet would be easier to use if unlocked cells that required or allowed entry appeared marked with something more visible than blue text. In the steps that follow, you will assign an outline and a background color to all the unprotected cells.

To assign a cell border and a cell background color:

1 Select a collection of cells to include cell E3, cell G11, and the range A12..F21.

2 Choose Lines & Color from the Style menu.

3 Set a thin outline border, and then select a light color (such as light yellow) or a light shade (if you have a monochrome monitor) from the Background Color list box, as shown in Figure 6.27

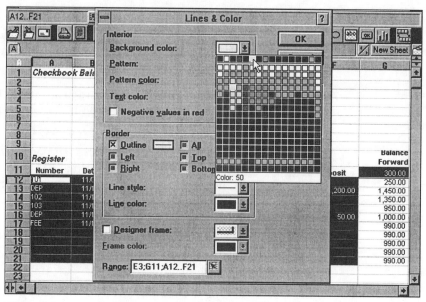

Figure 6.27

4 Select OK.

The collection now appears with a different color or shade.

5 Save the file.

CREATING A 3-D WORKSHEET

The worksheet you have created can now be used to keep track of your checking account, but what about a savings account? One way to create a savings account worksheet is to modify the titles of the original worksheet and save it as a separate file. An easier method would be to use 1-2-3's 3-D worksheet feature, which lets you place up to 255 worksheets within a single file.

In the steps that follow, you will copy the entire working area of the checking-account worksheet to another worksheet within the same file. You will then modify the second worksheet to accommodate a savings-account register. Finally, you will create another worksheet that will contain a summary for the other two worksheets.

Creating a Second Worksheet

Because the savings-account worksheet will be almost identical to the checking-account worksheet, you will make a duplicate of the checking-account worksheet.

To create a separate worksheet:

1 Double-click the worksheet A tab in the upper-left corner of the worksheet.

An insertion point will appear in the worksheet tab, letting you type in a name for the worksheet.

2 Type **Checking** and press (ENTER)

The worksheet is now labeled *Checking*.

3 Select the New Sheet box in the upper-right corner of the worksheet. A new, blank worksheet, named B appears.

4 Double-click the B worksheet tab, and name it **Savings**

5 Click the Checking worksheet tab.
The checking account worksheet now appears.

6 Select the entire working area of the Checking worksheet, cells A1..J21. Remember, the two hidden columns, H and I, must be included in the selection.

7 Choose Copy from the Edit menu.

8 Select the Savings worksheet tab.
The empty Savings worksheet appears.

9 Choose Paste from the Edit menu.
The Checking account worksheet is now duplicated in a new worksheet.

Setting Group Mode

The worksheet contents have been copied, but not all the attributes from the original worksheet were carried over. Notice that the column widths are not like the originals, and columns H and I are no longer hidden. Lotus 1-2-3 allows you to work with separate worksheets in *Group mode*, which will apply the formatting of the current worksheet to all the worksheets in the file.

To set Group mode:

1 Save the file.
Group mode is a global command; saving the worksheet first ensures that you can return to the original if the command has an undesired effect.

2 Select the Checking worksheet tab.

3 Choose Worksheet Defaults from the Style menu.
The Worksheet Defaults dialog box appears.

4 Select Group mode, and then select OK (see Figure 6.28).

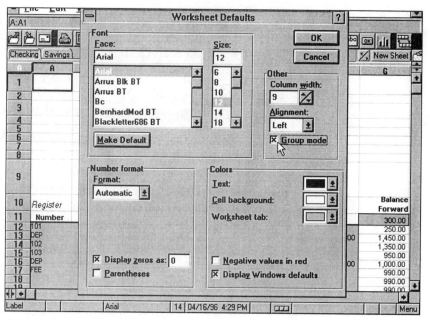

Figure 6.28

5 Select the Savings worksheet tab.
Notice that the column widths are now the same as those of the Checking worksheet, and that columns H and I are now hidden.

With Group mode on, any changes to styles, column widths, or attributes will affect all worksheets in the file. Because you will be creating another worksheet with different styling, you will now turn off Group mode.

> **Tip** Activating Group Mode changes all worksheets within a file to the style settings of the current worksheet. Be certain the active worksheet contains the style settings you want before you activate Group mode.

To turn off Group Mode:

1 Choose Worksheet Defaults from the Style menu.

2 Clear the Group mode check box, and then select OK.
The worksheet attributes will remain set in the Savings account worksheet.

Modifying the Savings Worksheet

The transactions that appear in the Savings worksheet should be deleted because they were copied from the Checking worksheet. You will now modify the Savings worksheet title, enter a new balance forward and bank statement ending balance, and then enter some sample transactions.

To modify the Savings worksheet:

1 Select the Savings worksheet tab.

2 Double-click cell A1, where the worksheet title is stored, and position the insertion point after the word Checkbook.

3 Delete the word Checkbook, type **Savings Account** and press ENTER

4 Select the range A12..F17, and then press (DEL)
Notice that the cell reference in the selection indicator displays
B:A12..B:F17, which means that the selected range is A12..F17 in
worksheet B.

5 Enter a new bank statement ending balance of **3609** in cell E3.

6 Enter a new balance forward of **3000** in cell G11.

To enter the remaining savings transactions:

1 Enter **DEP** (deposit) in cell A12.

2 Enter **11/20/95** for the date in cell B12.

3 Enter **Insurance Reimbursement** for the description in cell C12.

4 Enter **X** in cell D12.

5 Enter **87** for the deposit amount in cell F12.

6 Enter **DEP** in cell A13.

7 Enter **11/21/95** in cell B13.

8 Enter **Commission** in cell C13.

9 Enter **X** in cell D13.

10 Enter **522** in cell F13.

Your worksheet should resemble Figure 6.29.

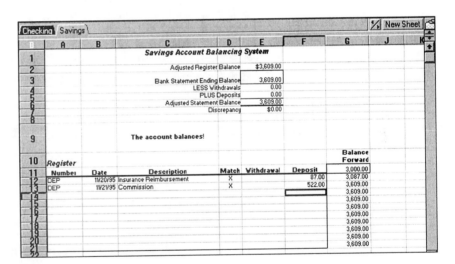

Figure 6.29

Creating a Summary Worksheet

You will now create a third worksheet that contains a summary of the
Checking and Savings worksheets. You can refer to Figure 6.30 as you
type.

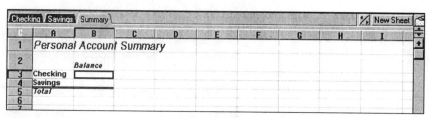

Figure 6.30

To create the Summary worksheet:

1 Select the Savings worksheet tab.

2 Select the New Sheet box to create a third worksheet.

3 Double-click the new worksheet tab, and name it `Summary`

4 In cell A1, enter `Personal Account Summary`

5 In cell B2, enter `Balance`

6 In cell A3, enter `Checking`

7 In cell A4, enter `Savings`

8 In cell A5, enter `Total`

To format the Summary worksheet:

1 Make cell A1 18-point bold italic.

2 Make cells A3 and A4 bold.

3 Make cells A5 and B2 bold italic.

4 Increase the height of row 2 to 30 points.

5 Create a double-line top border in cells A5..B5.

Your worksheet should resemble Figure 6.30.

Adding Cell References to the Summary Worksheet

The Summary worksheet should reflect the account balances from the Checking and Savings worksheets. You will use the Point mode to specify the account-balance cells in the other worksheets. You will then create an @SUM formula that will total the two amounts, and you will apply appropriate number formats to the cells.

To use point mode to specify cells in a different worksheet:

1 Select cell B3

This cell will contain the checking-account balance.

2 Type +

3 Select the worksheet tab for Checking.

4 Select cell E6.

5 Press (ENTER)

Cell B3 now refers to cell E6 in the Checking worksheet. The formula reads: +Checking:E6.

6 Select cell B4, which will contain the savings account balance.

7 Type +

8 Select the worksheet tab for Savings.

9 Select cell E6, and then press (ENTER)

Cell B4 now refers to cell E6 in the Savings worksheet. The formula reads: +Savings:E6.

To create the Total entry and apply number formats:

1 Select cell B5 in the Summary worksheet, and create an @SUM formula that will total the checking and savings amounts.

2 Apply the U.S. Dollar number format to cells B3 and B5.

3 Apply the Comma number format to cell B4.

Your worksheet should now resemble Figure 6.31.

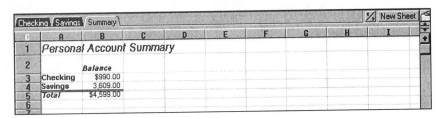

Figure 6.31

4 Save the worksheet.

THE NEXT STEP

You can extend and refine this worksheet in several ways. For example, you could use range names in many of the formulas to make them easier to understand. The worksheet could also be adapted to slightly different applications, such as record keeping of credit-card accounts.

In the next project, you will automate this worksheet using 1-2-3's database and macro capabilities. Using these features, you will find it much easier to handle the check register as the number of entries increases.

SUMMARY AND EXERCISES

Summary

- Lotus 1-2-3 can manipulate calendar dates, performing math on them and formatting them to appear in a variety of ways.
- Formulas that keep a running balance typically refer to the previous balance one row above and then adjust by adding or subtracting values that appear in the current row.
- The @IF function performs a test and will give different results depending on whether the test result is true or false.
- Mixed cell references in a formula keep only the row or only the column constant when the formula is copied.

- You can hide columns from view, but they still exist, and cells within them can still be referred to by formulas.
- You can protect cells from change, or assign cells customized colors and patterns.
- You can create multiple worksheets within a single file.
- You can build a formula that refers to cells in a worksheet other than the current worksheet.

Key Terms and Operations

Key Terms	Operations
case sensitive	cell protection
date arithmetic	Group Mode
date number	Hide
mixed cell reference	Protect document
protect	
string	

Study Questions

Multiple Choice

1. How would you enter the date 11/15/95 into a cell?
   a. enter the date number
   b. spell out the date
   c. 11/15/95
   d. enter the date as a label
   e. November 15, 1995

2. What @function is used to display the current date number?
   a. @DATE
   b. @SUM
   c. @CURRENT
   d. @NOW
   e. @RIGHTNOW

3. If cell G12 contains the formula +G11-E12+F12, and this formula is copied down one cell to G13, the newly copied formula in G13 would be
   a. +G12-E13+F13
   b. +G11-E12+F12
   c. +G11-E13+F13
   d. +G12-E12+F12
   e. +G12-E12+F13

4. If cell A5 is empty, what would be the result of the formula +@IF(@ISSTRING(A5),50,100) ?
   a. 50
   b. 100
   c. 0
   d. 150
   e. A5

5. In the formula +A1+A$2, the A$2 is referred to as a(n)
   a. absolute cell reference
   b. relative cell reference
   c. mixed cell reference
   d. currency cell
   e. static cell address

6. Suppose cell A3 contains the formula $+A1+A\$2$. If the formula were copied to B3, the copy in B3 would read
   a. $+B1+B\$2$
   b. $+B1+A\$2$
   c. $+B1+A\$3$
   d. $+A1+B\$2$
   e. $+B1+B2$

7. To hide a column, you first select the column and then
   a. choose Column Width from the Style menu
   b. choose Hide from the Style menu
   c. choose Column Width from the Edit menu
   d. choose Hide/Unhide from the Window menu
   e. choose Style from the Column Width menu

8. How does 1-2-3 indicate that a cell is protected?
   a. There is no indication.
   b. A border appears around the cell.
   c. A small dot appears in the upper-right corner of the cell.
   d. The cell text is colored blue.
   e. The cell appears with a light yellow background.

9. To have a cell appear with a different background color, choose
   a. Color from the Style menu
   b. Patterns from the Style menu
   c. Number format from the Style menu
   d. Font & Attributes from the Style menu
   e. Lines & Color from the Style menu

10. When building a formula in worksheet A of a file with multiple worksheets, to refer to cell A1 in worksheet B you would
    a. select cell A1, and then the B worksheet tab
    b. select the B worksheet tab, and then select cell A1
    c. select cell A1, and then select GoTo A1
    d. point to cell A1, and then choose Worksheet from the View menu
    e. none of the above

Short Answer

1. Under what circumstances will 1-2-3 recognize a cell entry as a date?

2. Why should you enter a date as a date number and not as a label?

3. Describe the steps required to display a date number as a readable date.

4. Before sealing a worksheet, what should you do to the cells to which changes will be allowed?

5. What is the difference between sealing a file and protecting cells?

6. What happens if you try to enter characters into a protected cell?

7. Describe the steps required to hide a column.

8. Which function is used to test whether a cell contains text?

9. How many arguments does the @IF function have? What do these arguments do?

10. How many worksheets can be in a file?

For Discussion

1. Can 1-2-3 perform math on dates? If so, give an example. Describe three ways to format a date.

2. What are the general steps involved in protecting a worksheet? Why would you want to protect certain cells in a worksheet?

3. Under what circumstances would you use relative cell references?

Review Exercises

Personal Budget

Refer to Figure 6.32 and construct a personal budget for the first six months of a year. Use the Fill by Example command to save typing when entering the month names. Add whatever income and expense items that are appropriate for your situation.

Design a single net cash formula for January and copy it to the other cells in the Net Cash row. This formula should account for any savings (or deficit) from the previous month. The Start column is used to show the amount of cash on hand at the beginning of January. This is similar to the starting-balance amount in the checkbook register. The net cash formula for a particular month will take the previous month's net cash, add the current month's income, and subtract the current month's expenses. Negative amounts for net cash can be interpreted as being sums borrowed from another source, such as savings or credit-card overdraft accounts. Format the worksheet and save it under the name PBUDGET.

	A	B	C	D	E	F	G	H
1				**Personal Budget**				
2		Start	Jan	Feb	Mar	Apr	May	Jun
3	Income							
4	Salary		$1,200	$1,200	$1,200	$1,200	$1,200	$1,200
5	Expenses							
6	Rent		450	450	450	450	450	450
7	Food		250	250	250	250	250	250
8	Utilities		75	75	75	75	75	75
9	Telephone		30	30	30	30	30	30
10	Transportation		50	50	50	50	50	50
11	Entertainment		50	50	50	50	50	50
12	Other		100	100	100	100	100	100
13	Net Cash	$100	?	?	?	?	?	?
14								
15								

Figure 6.32

Report of Accounts Past Due

Construct a spreadsheet, similar to Figure 6.33, that computes the total of accounts that are greater than 30 days overdue. Use the @NOW function to show today's date, and apply the 31-Dec-93 number format. You can make up your own due dates.

The formulas in the Past 30 column perform a test: if today's date (which is computed in cell B2) minus the due date is greater than 30, then the amount is overdue and should be displayed; otherwise, 0 should be displayed. Note that an absolute address will be required if a single formula is to be built and copied successfully. The totals are each @SUM formulas.

Format the worksheet and save it under the name PASTDUE.

	A	B	C	D	E	F	G
1	*Report of Accounts Past Due*						
2	Today's Date	?					
3							
4	Account	Due	Amount	Past 30			
5	993-21-9147	14-Nov-95	$2,750	?			
6	994-58-6273	02-Dec-95	880	?			
7	992-45-6363	23-Oct-94	975	?			
8	998-46-4489	09-Dec-94	1,320	?			
9	Total		?	?			
10							
11							
12							

Figure 6.33

Assignments

Birthdays and Ages

Construct a worksheet similar to Figure 6.34. Use the @NOW function for today's date; apply the 31-Dec-93 number format.

The Age column contains formulas that calculate each person's current age in years. A person's age in days is calculated by subtracting his or her birth date from today's date. The age in years is calculated by dividing the age in days by the number of days in a year (365.25, to adjust for leap years). Note that the result of these calculations yields the fractional part of the age as a decimal fraction: for example, age 22.5 is 22 years 6 months and not 22 years 5 months. Format this column with the Comma number format.

The formula in the Birthday this Month? column performs a test using @IF and the @MONTH function: if the month of today's date is equal to the month of the birth date, then return "Yes"; otherwise, return a space, " ".

Format the worksheet and save it as BDAY.

	A	B	C	D	E	F	G	H
1	Today's Date	?						
2	Name	Birth Date	Age	Birthday this Month?				
3	Carmen	14-Mar-68	?	?				
4	Clem	29-Oct-59	?	?				
5	Govinda	08-Nov-72	?	?				
6	Gwendolyn	01-Jul-73	?	?				
7	Jane	03-Jun-73	?	?				
8	Mei Ling	27-May-71	?	?				
9	Rahula	15-Jan-74	?	?				
10	Rolf	17-Sep-74	?	?				
11	Sarvipali	14-Dec-70	?	?				
12	Xu	02-Apr-72	?	?				
13	Zhi	23-Feb-75	?	?				
14								

Figure 6.34

Commercial Lease Payments

The worksheet shown in Figure 6.35 shows the monthly payments due for commercial tenants in a small shopping mall. Each tenant pays the discount rate per square foot during the first year of the lease; the regular rate per square foot applies after the first year.

Construct a worksheet similar to the figure. Assign an appropriate number format for the cells in the Leased Space column.

The formulas in the Payment column check to see whether more than one year (365 days) has elapsed between the start date and today's date. The appropriate rate is multiplied by the tenant's amount of leased space.

Format the worksheet and save it under the name RENT.

	A	B	C	D	E
1	Today's Date	?			
2					
3	Regular Rate	$16.00			
4	1st Year Discount Rate	$5.00			
5					
6	Tenant	Leased Space (Square feet)	Start Date	Payment	
7	Clem's Fish Emporium	1,200	01-Dec-93	?	
8	Kang Xi Grocery Store	5,330	01-Jan-94	?	
9	Govinda's Gift Shop	1,450	01-Oct-93	?	
10	First Interdimensional Bank	3,180	01-Mar-94	?	
11	Total	11,160		?	
12					

Figure 6.35

Balancing Your Own Checkbook

If you have a checking account, use the CHKBAL1 worksheet to reconcile it. As you use the spreadsheet, note any improvements that would make it a more effective tool. Consider how it could be adapted to reconcile other accounts, such as credit-card accounts.

Objectives

After completing this project, you should be able to:

▶ Describe a 1-2-3 database and its components

▶ Create a database range

▶ Use database commands to add, delete, and find records

▶ Use the Sort command to rearrange records

▶ Create macros using the macro recorder

▶ Create and modify customized push buttons and assign macros to them

▶ Run macros using the menu, shortcut key assignments, and custom buttons

CASE STUDY: AUTOMATING A CHECKBOOK REGISTER

In this project, you will use two advanced features of 1-2-3—database management and macros—to enhance the checkbook-balancing worksheet that you built in Project 6. You will begin by considering how the checkbook register could be implemented as a 1-2-3 database. After the register is converted to function as a database, you will construct macros to automate the sorting of the register.

Recognizing Databases

A 1-2-3 *database* is a collection of information, organized in a list. Everyday examples of databases abound: telephone directories, inventory lists, parts lists, customer lists, library catalogs, and so forth. Table 7.1 illustrates a typical customer-list database.

Table 7.1

LastName	FirstName	Street	City	State	ZIP
Rogers	Bruce	1916 Centaur St.	New York	NY	01011
Twombly	Carol	89 Lithos Pwky.	Charlemagne	CA	92373
Gill	Eric	16 Joanna Rd. #30	Pilgrim	MA	21707
Kis	Miklos	1650 Janson Ave	Minneapolis	MN	66192
Almeida	Jose	1926 Convention Ctr.	Mendoza	TX	73105

Each row of a database is called a *record*. A database record describes something—for example, a customer, a part in an inventory, or a book. The columns of a database, called *fields*, break the record down into various aspects or categories. The fields in Table 7.1 are last name, first name, street, city, state, and zip. Each field has a *field name*, which is the formal designation of the field and in 1-2-3 appears as a column title. For example, the field name for the last-name field is LastName.

When you design a database, it's usually best to have lots of simple, discrete fields rather than only a few complex fields. For example, a database that has a single-address field containing the entire address (street address, city, state, and zip) would be harder to search and sort than a database that has separate fields for each of the components of an address.

What do people do with databases? Typically they *search* or *sort* the records in a database. *Searching* means finding all records that match a certain criterion, such as finding all records in the customer database that have Phoenix as the city. *Sorting* means shuffling the records into a different order: for example, ordering all the records alphabetically, based on the customer's last name.

Designing the Solution

If you consider the check register built in Project 6, you will realize that it is a kind of database. Its fields are check Number, Date, Description, Match, Withdrawal, and Deposit. The balance forward and unmatched withdrawal and unmatched deposit columns could also be considered fields, but in this project you will confine the database to the register's first six columns.

Both searching and sorting would be useful operations to perform on a check register. For example, you might want to find all deposits made after November 14, 1995, or you might want to sort all the register entries in alphabetical order by description. In the sections that follow, you will make some initial modifications to the check register to make it compatible with 1-2-3's database commands.

TRANSFORMING THE CHECK REGISTER INTO A DATABASE

A 1-2-3 database is a list of records entered into an ordinary worksheet. The first row of the database must contain field names. Ordinary text titles for columns will work for field names. Other information—such as the account-reconciliation system in CHKBAL1—can be on the worksheet along with the database itself.

The data records start just below the field names row. The *database range* consists of the field names row and the data records below it.

If you plan to add new records to the database, you should have some blank rows below the database to accommodate the new records. Lotus 1-2-3 databases grow downward; this growth is obstructed if something else, such as information related to another part of the worksheet, is in the way.

In the following steps, you will prepare the Checking worksheet for use as a 1-2-3 database. Because you will be working only with the Checking worksheet, you will delete the Savings and Summary worksheets. Some of the other changes you will make are cosmetic and are intended to make the worksheet easier to read while you work with the new commands.

To prepare the worksheet:

1 Open the worksheet CHKBAL1.

2 Select the Summary worksheet tab.

3 Choose Delete from the Edit menu.
The Delete dialog box appears.

4 Select Sheet, and then select OK (see Figure 7.1).

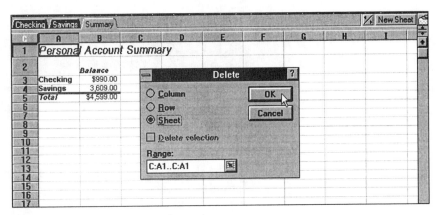

Figure 7.1

5 Select the Savings worksheet (if necessary), and then delete it.
The Checking worksheet should be the only remaining worksheet.

6 Set a Custom Zoom percent of 60.

7 Select cells G1 and J1, choose Hide from the Style menu, and then select Show.
Columns H and I are now visible.

8 Choose Save As from the File menu, and save the worksheet as CHKBAL2.WK4
Your screen should resemble Figure 7.2.

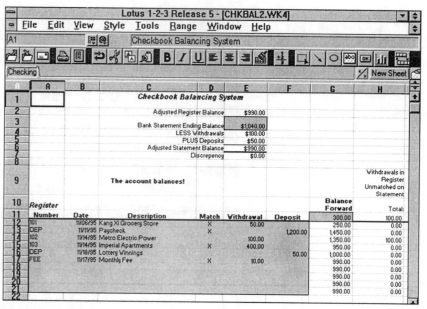

Figure 7.2

The database range will consist of the register itself, excluding the formulas for balance forward, unmatched withdrawals, and unmatched deposits. The database should not include blank rows. When this worksheet was built in the previous project, rows 18 through 21 were assigned a background color, but they do not contain information. In the following steps, you will clear these cells and then define the range A11..F17 as the database. Later, when records are added, you will see how to automatically expand the defined database range to include the new records.

Clearing Cell Contents and Styles

The Clear command lets you clear (erase) the contents of a cell, the styles applied to a cell, or both.

To clear the unused database records:

1 Select the range A18..F21.

2 Choose Clear from the Edit menu, select Both, and then select OK.

The formulas to the right of the register must be copied down so that they are present for however many records you anticipate the database will contain. You will arbitrarily set the maximum number of records to 100; this means that the formulas must be copied down through row 111. The @SUM formulas in the unmatched columns will need to be rewritten to accommodate the new register size, and the formula that shows the adjusted register balance in cell E2 will also have to be updated so that it refers to the new bottom cell of the Balance Forward column.

In the following steps, you will use several shortcuts to handle large areas on the worksheet.

To copy the formulas downward:

1 Scroll the worksheet so that columns G through I are visible.

2 Select the formulas in the range G21..I21, as shown in Figure 7.3.

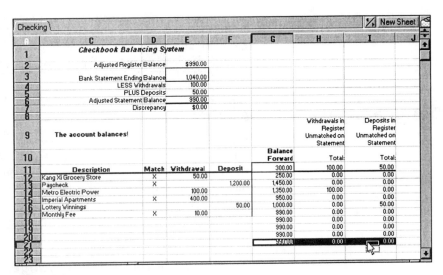

Figure 7.3

3 Choose Copy from the Edit menu.

4 Select the range G22..I111 by first selecting G22..I22, and then dragging the pointer down to row 111.
As you drag past the bottom of the worksheet window, the worksheet will scroll up.

5 Choose Paste from the Edit menu.

6 Press (HOME) to return to the upper-left area of the worksheet.

To rebuild the @SUM formulas for the unmatched columns:

1 Select cell H11, which contains the total unmatched withdrawals.

2 Type +@SUM(

3 Press ⊕ . (END) ⊕
Lotus 1-2-3 automatically finds the bottom of the block of nonempty cells and extends the selection to that point.

4 Type) and press (ENTER)
The formula is @SUM(H12..H111)

5 Copy this relative cell reference formula to cell I11 so the total unmatched deposits are computed correctly.

To rebuild the formula for the adjusted register balance:

1 Press (HOME)

2 Select cell E2, which contains a formula that refers to the bottom cell of the Balance Forward column of the register.

3 Type +
You will now use Point mode to complete the formula.

4 Select cell G10, which contains the text *Balance Forward*.

5 Press (END) ⊕ and then press (ENTER)
The new formula reads +G111.

6 Select columns H and I, choose Hide from the Style menu, select Column, and then select OK.

As in Project 6, the person who uses this worksheet to balance a checking account doesn't need to see these formulas.

Designating the Database Range

Most of your work so far has been to expand the size of the worksheet to accommodate more check-register entries. You can now tell 1-2-3 what the database range is; once this is done, you can access some of the database-management commands. The database range is the field names row and the data records below it, A11..F17. The database will be defined as a range name. The range name will then be used whenever commands or formulas refer to the database.

To designate the database range:

1 Select A11..F17.

2 Choose Name from the Range menu.

The Name dialog box appears. You will now enter the name REGISTER to refer to the selected range.

3 Type **register** in the Name text box, select Add, and then select OK as shown in Figure 7.4.

Because 1-2-3 converts range names to uppercase, the name can be entered in either uppercase or lowercase.

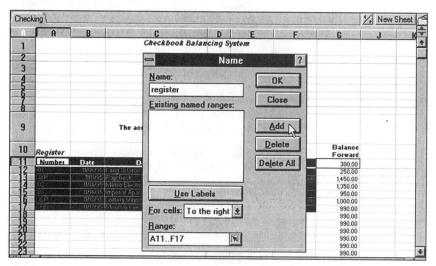

Figure 7.4

Now you can refer to the range A11 to F17 simply by using the name REGISTER.

FINDING RECORDS IN A DATABASE

You can use 1-2-3's database commands to find only records that meet a particular search criterion. For example, you might want to see only records that are dated prior to 11/15/94. Or you might want to see all the records that are matched in bank statements. In the steps that follow, you will construct a criterion that finds any records where the Number field contains the code DEP (deposit). You will also find any records with FEE in the number field. You will then use the Delete Record command to delete a record.

To set search criteria:

1 Press (HOME)

2 Choose Go To from the Edit menu.
The Go To dialog box appears.

3 Select REGISTER, and then select OK as shown in Figure 7.5.

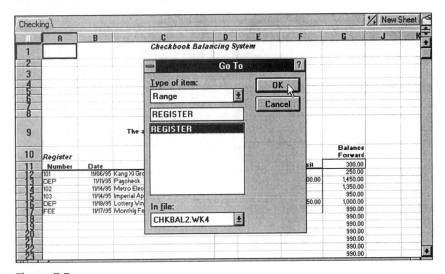

Figure 7.5

The Go To command selects REGISTER on the worksheet.

4 Choose Database from the Tools menu, and then choose Find Records. The Find Records dialog box appears. By default, 1-2-3 selects the first cell of the database range as the criterion for the search.
You will modify this criterion to find database records with DEP in the Number field.

5 Select DEP from the Value list box, and then select OK as shown in Figure 7.6.

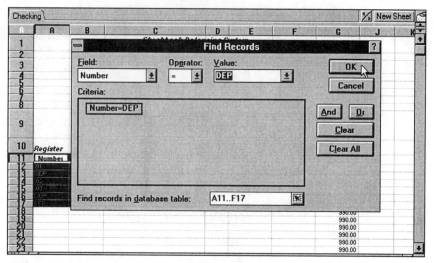

Figure 7.6

The two records containing DEP in the Number field are now selected.

To find all records unmatched with bank statements:

1 Choose Go To from the Edit menu.

2 Select REGISTER, and then select OK.

3 Choose Database from the Tools menu, and then choose Find Records.

4 Select MATCH from the Field list box, <> (not equal) from the Operator list box, and X from the Value list box.

5 Select OK.

All records without an X in the Match field are now selected.

Using Complex Criteria

In the following steps, you will construct criteria to search for all DEP transactions (ordinary deposits) made after 11/11/95.

To find all DEP transactions made after 11/11/95:

1 Choose Go To from the Edit menu.

2 Select REGISTER, and then select OK.

3 Choose Database from the Tools menu, and then choose Find Records.

4 Select DEP from the Value list box.

5 Select And.

You wish to find records that are deposits *and* that have dates later than 11/11/95.

6 Select Date from the Field list box.

7 Select > (greater than) as the Operator.

8 Select 11/11/95 from the Value list box, and then select OK as shown in Figure 7.7.

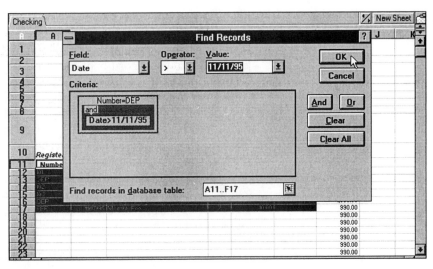

Figure 7.7

The single record containing DEP in the Number field and dated after 11/11/95 is now selected.

Deleting Database Records

Deleting records from a database uses a set of steps similar to those for finding records. Before deleting records, it is a good idea to perform a database Find command using the same search criteria. That way, if the criteria are specified incorrectly, you will see the selected records before you delete them. It is also a good idea to save the worksheet before performing any record deletion commands. In the following steps, you will use the Find command to select records with FEE in the Number field, and then use the Delete Records command to delete the record from the database.

To delete a database record:

1 Save the worksheet.

2 Choose Go To from the Edit menu.

3 Select REGISTER, and then select OK.

4 Choose Database from the Tools menu, and then choose Find Records.

5 Select FEE from the Value list box, and then select OK.
The single record containing FEE in the Number field is now selected.

6 Choose Go To from the Edit menu.

7 Select REGISTER, and then select OK.

8 Choose Database from the Tools menu, and then choose Delete Records.

9 Select FEE from the Value list box, and then select OK.
The record containing FEE in the Number field is now deleted from the database.

10 Choose Undo from the Edit menu.
Undo reverses the database Delete Records command and restores the record to the worksheet.

Adding Records to a Database

Adding a record to a database can be done in two ways. The first is to type the new database record beneath the last record of the current database and then redefine the REGISTER range name to include the new record. The other way is to use 1-2-3's Append Records command, which will automatically redefine the range name to include the new record. To use the Append Records command, you first create and name a range that contains the record (or records) to be added. You then tell 1-2-3 to append that range to the database.

You will begin by inserting rows to accommodate the database-entry range. The range should have column headings identical to those of the database. You will then assign to the range a name that can be used in the Append database command.

To create the range of records to be inserted:

1 Select all of rows 10, 11, and 12.

2 Choose Insert from the Edit menu.
Three new rows are inserted into the worksheet.

3 Select the three new rows (10, 11, and 12), and change the row height to 16 points.

4 Enter `Register Entry Area` in cell A10, and make it 14-point bold italic.

5 Center the title *Register Entry Area* across columns A through F.

6 Select the range A14..F15, which contains the column headings and the first database record, and then choose Copy from the Edit menu.

7 Select cell A11, and then select Paste from the Edit menu.

8 Select the range A12..F12, which will be used to contain new register entries, and clear it by pressing (DEL)

9 Remove the top border from the range A12..F12 using Lines & Color from the Style menu.
Your worksheet should resemble Figure 7.8.

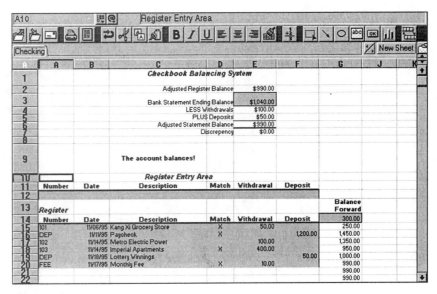

Figure 7.8

 ### To name the data-entry range:

1 Select the range A11..F12, which will be the register entry range.

2 Select Name from the Range menu, name the range **ENTRY** and then select OK.

 ### To insert data in the entry range:

1 Enter **104** in cell A12 for the Number of the check.

2 Enter **11/19/95** in cell B12 for the Date.

3 Enter **Clem's Auto Repair** in cell C12 for the Description.

4 Skip the Match field, and enter **425** in cell E12 for the Withdrawal amount.
The record is now ready to be appended to the database.

 ### To enter the record into the database:

1 Choose Database from the Tools menu, and then choose Append Records.

2 Type **ENTRY** in the Append Records From text box.

3 Type **REGISTER** in the To Database Table text box, and then select OK as shown in Figure 7.9.

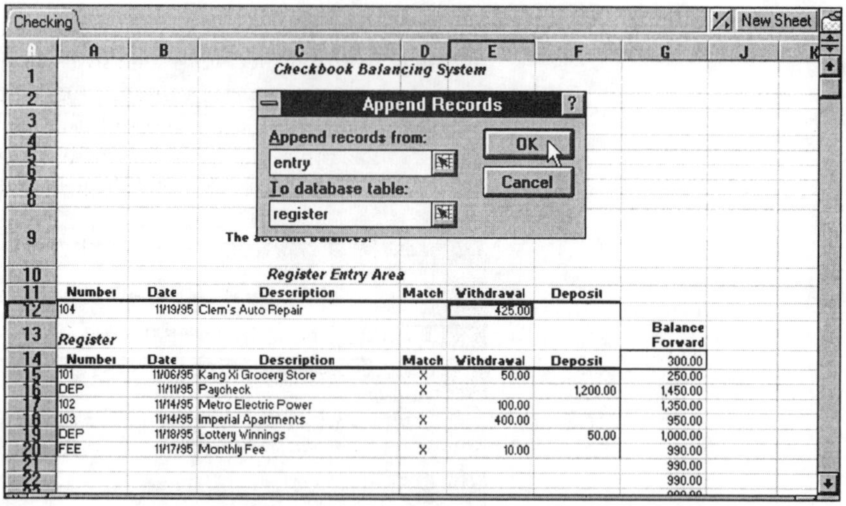

Figure 7.9

The record is now added to the database, and the REGISTER range name has been automatically extended to include the new record.

SORTING A DATABASE

Sorting rearranges the records in the database, putting them into a particular order according to what you specify as the sorting *key*. A key is the column or field that you want to be used as the basis for the sort. For example, the sorting key for a residential telephone directory is last name, because the records in the phone book are in ascending (alphabetical) order by last name.

Often, a single sorting key is not sufficient for a large database. For example, in a telephone directory, many people might have the same last name. What order should they be listed in? The first key used is called the *primary key;* if another key is needed as a tiebreaker, it can be specified as a *secondary key*. The primary key for a phone book is last name, the secondary key is first name (a group of people with the same last name will be listed alphabetically by first name). Lotus 1-2-3 allows up to 255 sort keys.

Lotus 1-2-3's sorting command can be used on any worksheet data, not just on databases, but database sorting is certainly the most common application of the command. The range to be sorted should include all the records to be sorted, *but not the field names*. If the field names are included, they will be sorted along with everything else.

> *Tip* Sorting can be a dangerous operation, because it shuffles so much data around in the worksheet. Before doing a sort, save the worksheet. When you select a range of records to be sorted, make sure you extend the selection far enough to the right to include every field in the database—otherwise, the sort will break apart each record.

In the following steps, you will first create a range name that specifies the area to be sorted. You will then use the Go To command to select the range and the Sort command to complete the sort. You will sort the records by the check Number field. The *second* key will be Date; that is, if a group of records have the same value in the Number field (for example, two records have the same DEP code), they will be put in order by date. The REGISTER range name that was previously created cannot be used because it includes field names that should not be a part of the sort range.

To create a named range for sorting:

1 Select the range A15..F21, which is the range that will be sorted.

2 Choose Name from the Range menu.

3 Type **SORTRANGE** for the Name, select Add, and then select OK. You are not required to use a named range with sorting, although it can make the process easier.

4 Press (HOME) to return the cell pointer to A1.

To sort the database by the Number and Date fields:

1 Save the worksheet.

2 Select Go To from the Edit menu, select SORTRANGE from the list, and then select OK.

3 Choose Sort from the Range menu.
The Sort Dialog box appears. Notice that the default first key is the first column of SORTRANGE, which is correct in this case, because the first key should be the Number field. The second key should be the Date field. Ascending means alphabetical order or increasing numbers.

4 Select Add Key.

5 Select the Sort By range selector box.
The Sort dialog box disappears, letting you select the cell that has the column that will be the second key.

6 Click cell B15.
The Sort dialog box reappears.

7 Select Add Key and then select OK, as shown in Figure 7.10.

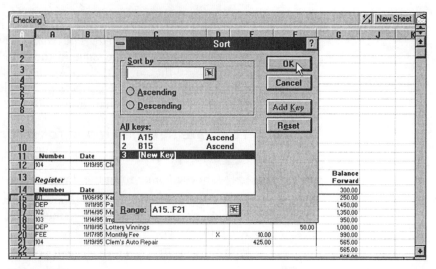

Figure 7.10

8 Press (HOME)

The database is now sorted, based on the Number field. The two DEP (deposit) transactions have the same value in the Number field; these are put in order based on the second key, Date.

EXIT If necessary, you can save the worksheet, quit 1-2-3 now and continue this project later.

USING MACROS

As someone works with this checkbook register, he or she might want to enter register entries one after another. You can simplify any repetitive task, such as appending records to the database, by the use of 1-2-3 macros. A *macro* is similar to a small computer program; it is a list of instructions that tells 1-2-3 to perform a sequence of commands and operations.

When you create a macro, you give it a name. You can also assign to the macro a keystroke combination that will run or *execute* the macro when the user presses that key. Mouse users can also create and assign customized buttons that can be used to run the macro. The convenience of a macro is in being able to have a series of operations performed by pressing a single key or button.

The easiest way to create simple macros is to *record* them rather than to write them from scratch. Before you record a macro, you should think carefully about exactly what steps you want to perform while the recorder is on.

In the following steps, you will type a new register entry and then record a macro that appends the entry to the database. With 1-2-3's macro recorder activated, you will perform the Database Append command; everything you do while the recorder is on will be written into a macro. Once you have completed the database append, you will turn the recorder off and examine the macro. You can then run the macro at a later time.

To insert data in the entry range:

1 Enter **ATM** in cell A12 for the check number.

2 Enter **11/17/95** in cell B12 for the date.

3 Enter **Cash Machine** in cell C12 for the description.

4 Skip the Match field, and enter **100** in cell E12 for the withdrawal amount.

To record a macro to append the record to the database:

1 Save the worksheet.

2 Choose Macro from the Tools menu, and then choose Record. Now every command you issue will be recorded. Carefully follow the next steps, which perform the database append commands. Notice that "Rec" appears in the status bar, indicating that a macro is being recorded.

3 Choose Database from the Tools menu, and then choose Append Records.

4 Type **ENTRY** in the Append Records From text box.

5 Type **REGISTER** in the To Database Table text box, and then select OK.

6 Choose Macro from the Tools menu, and then choose Stop Recording. The steps for appending a database record have now been recorded.

The steps you performed have been recorded into the Transcript window, a window similar to a worksheet window, designed to hold macros. You must make the Transcript window active to examine or modify the macro. In the steps that follow, you will switch to the Transcript window, examine the new macro, and copy the macro to another worksheet.

To switch to the Transcript window:

1 Choose Macro from the Tools menu, and then choose Show Transcript.
The Transcript window appears, as in Figure 7.11.

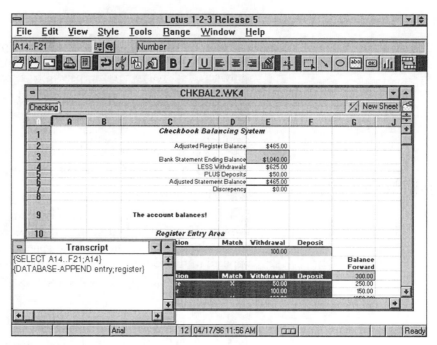

Figure 7.11

Interpreting a Recorded Macro

A macro describes a series of operations to be performed. Lotus 1-2-3 macros are composed mostly of special programming commands, called macro commands, that specify various 1-2-3 commands. In this project, you will record macros; writing macros using the macro commands directly is an advanced topic beyond the scope of this module.

The first line of the macro contains the text {SELECT A14..F21;A14}. This means that the first recorded command selected the range from A14..F21. The final cell reference, A14, refers to where the active cell in the selected range should appear. Notice that the range selected on the worksheet when the Append command was completed was A14..F21.

The second line in the Transcript window is {DATABASE-APPEND entry;register}, which is the command that appended the named range *entry* to the range *register*.

Running a Macro

You can run a macro by first selecting the text within the Transcript window, and then choosing Playback from the Transcript menu (the Transcript menu replaces the Range menu when the Transcript window is active).

> *Tip* It's wise to save a worksheet before running a macro in case the macro does some damage to the worksheet.

To run the macro using the Transcript window:

1 Select the Checking worksheet by clicking anywhere in it.

2 Save the worksheet.

3 Select the Transcript window.

4 Select all the text within the Transcript window by dragging the mouse pointer over the commands.
Only selected macro commands will be executed.

5 Choose Playback from the Transcript menu.
The macro executes, again appending the same register entry to the database.

6 Select Undo from the Edit menu.

Assigning a Macro to a Key

The Transcript window stores macros temporarily; closing the worksheet or exiting 1-2-3 will erase the recorded macro. You can select and then copy the macro to a worksheet so that it is saved when the worksheet is saved. It's a good idea to store macros in a separate worksheet within the current file so that the macro won't be overwritten accidentally. Once the macro is copied to a worksheet, you can assign a range name to the macro and run the macro whenever the file is open.

To run a macro, the macro commands must be assigned a range name. If the range name consists of a backslash followed by a single character, the macro can be executed by pressing (CTRL) and the assigned character. For example, naming a range \a causes 1-2-3 to execute the macro when (CTRL) + a is pressed.

In the steps that follow, you will first create a new worksheet and then copy the macro from the Transcript window to the new worksheet. You will then assign a range name to the macro so that it can be executed with a single key.

To create a macro worksheet:

1 Select the Checking worksheet (if necessary).

2 Select New Sheet.

3 Name the new worksheet **Macros**

To copy the macro to the macro worksheet:

1 Select the Transcript window.

2 Select all the macro commands within the Transcript window by dragging the mouse pointer over the text.

3 Choose Copy from the Edit menu.

4 Select the Macros worksheet.
Use the Zoom In command if the worksheet text is difficult to read.

5 Select cell B3.

6 Choose Paste from the Edit menu.
The macro is now part of the worksheet. Saving the worksheet will also save the macro.

7 Save the worksheet.

To assign a name to the macro:

1 Select the range B3..B4

2 Choose Name from the Range menu.

3 Type \a in the Name text box, select Add, and then select OK.

To run the macro using the assigned key:

1 Select the Checking worksheet.

2 Press (CTRL) + A

3 Scroll the worksheet down to verify that another copy of the register entry was appended to the bottom of the database range.
Because the macro is being tested, you will now undo the change made to the database by the macro.

4 Choose Undo from the Edit menu.
Choosing Undo switches back to the Macros worksheet.

Documenting a Macro

The macro was pasted to cell B3 in the Macros worksheet to leave room for describing, or documenting, the macro. Documenting macros can help users unfamiliar with the worksheet understand the purpose of the macro and what effect the macro will have on the worksheet. Complete documentation for a macro includes the range name assigned to the macro, the purpose of the macro, and a description of each macro command.

To document the macro:

1 Select the Macros worksheet (if necessary).

2 In cell A3, enter `'\a` as the macro range name.
Be sure to enter the apostrophe before the backslash.

> *Reminder* The apostrophe is a label prefix character. Without it, entering a backslash would cause the label to be repeated within the cell.

3 In cell B1, enter `Macro to append single record to database` the purpose of the macro.

4 In cell C3, enter `Select database range` to describe the first line of the macro.

5 In cell C4, enter `Append record to database` to describe the next line.

6 Widen column B to accommodate the widest entry in the column as shown in Figure 7.12.

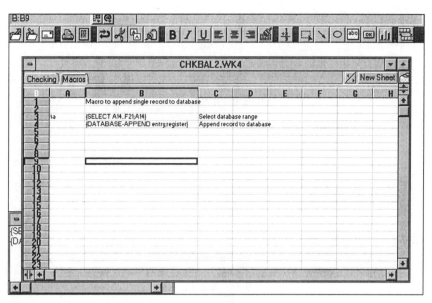

Figure 7.12

Creating Customized Buttons

An alternative to using a macro shortcut key is to place a button (resembling a dialog box command button) directly on the worksheet and assign a macro to the button. You can determine what the button text and format will be, as well as the button's size and location.

In this section, you will create a button and place it to the right of the register data entry range.

 ### To create and assign a button:

1 Maximize the worksheet window, and then select the Checking worksheet.

2 Return to the 60 percent custom zoom setting (if necessary).

3 Choose Draw from the Tools menu, and then choose Button. The pointer changes to crosshairs.

4 Referring to Figure 7.13, drag the crosshairs to form an outline for the button in cells G11 and G12.

10			*Register Entry Area*				
11	Number	Date	Description	Match	Withdrawal	Deposit	
12	ATM	11/17/95	Cash Machine		100.00		
13	Register						Balance Forward
14	Number	Date	Description	Match	Withdrawal	Deposit	300.00
15	101	11/06/95	Kang Xi Grocery Store	X	50.00		250.00

Figure 7.13

5 Release the mouse button. The Assign to Button dialog box appears.

6 Select the Button Text text box, and type **Add**

7 Select the Assign Macro From list box, and then select Range. All the ranges currently defined appear.

8 Select \A, the range name of the macro in the Macros worksheet, and then select OK as shown in Figure 7.14.

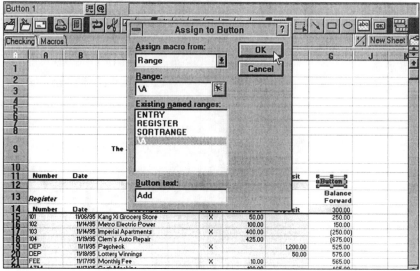

Figure 7.14

The button is currently selected. The handles let you reposition and resize the button.

9 Select cell A1.

Now the button is not selected. If you position the pointer on the button and click the mouse button, the macro assigned to the button will run.

10 Position the pointer over the button.

The pointer shape changes to a hand.

11 Click the mouse button.

The macro runs, and the register entry is appended to the database.

12 Choose Undo from the Edit menu.

13 Save the worksheet.

If you want to reselect the button to change its position or resize it, you can hold down (CTRL) and click the button.

Modifying a Macro

The macro now appends records to the database, but it would be more useful to the user if the entry range was erased each time the macro runs (so the same entry could not be entered more than once). In the steps that follow, you will record additional macro commands and paste them below the existing macro commands in the Macros worksheet. You will then redefine the macro range name to include the additional commands.

To append additional commands to a macro:

1 Select the Maximize/Restore button in the upper-right corner of the worksheet.

The worksheet window shrinks, and the Transcript window is visible behind the worksheet window.

2 Select the Transcript window.

3 With the mouse pointer positioned within the window, press the right mouse button, and choose Clear All.
The previously recorded macro is erased (the macro button and the macro in the Macros worksheet remain unaffected).

4 Select the worksheet window.

5 Choose Macro from the Tools menu, and then choose Record.

6 Select the range A12..F12 in the Checking worksheet.

7 Press (DEL) to clear the range.

8 Choose Macro from the Tools menu, and then choose Stop Recording.

9 Select the Transcript window.

10 Select the macro commands in the Transcript window by dragging, and then choose Copy from the Edit menu.

To modify the macro:

1 Select the Macros worksheet.

2 Select cell B5, which will contain the additional macro commands.

3 Choose Paste from the Edit menu.
The screen should resemble Figure 7.15.

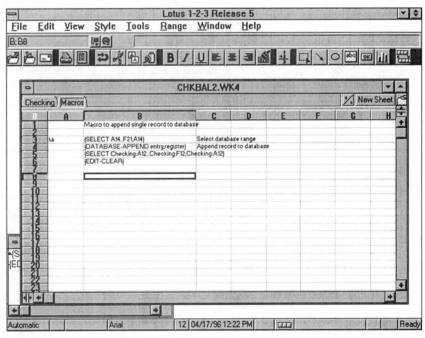

Figure 7.15

4 Select B3..B6, the range containing all the macro commands.

5 Choose Name from the Range menu.

6 Select the range named \A
Notice that the current range defined for \A is B3..B4.

7 Select the Range range selector, and then select B3..B6.

8 Select OK.

9 Select the Checking worksheet tab.

10 Try out the Add macro button by entering a register entry and then selecting the Add button. The register contents will be erased after being appended to the database.

THE NEXT STEP

You will occasionally create worksheets that can benefit from 1-2-3 database functions. However, 1-2-3's primary value is as a spreadsheet program, and if your 1-2-3 databases grow large, you should consider using an application dedicated to database management.

You can use macros to automate repetitive tasks in almost any worksheet. As you build worksheets, look for opportunities to optimize them with macros. Macros should not, however, take the place of fundamental worksheet components such as well-designed formulas.

SUMMARY AND EXERCISES

Summary

- A database is a tabular list of information. Rows are called records, and columns are called fields. Each field has a field name, which in 1-2-3 is the title used to head the column.
- It is better to have more simple fields than fewer complicated fields.
- Databases can be searched so that only those records that meet specific criteria are selected.
- A 1-2-3 database range consists of the field names row and the data records below it. The database will grow downward as more entries are added.
- The Clear command can erase a cell's contents, style, or both.
- Once a 1-2-3 database is defined, database commands can be used to add, delete, and search for records.
- Databases can be sorted, their records put in a different order. The field used as the basis for ordering the records is called a key. If two records have the same value for the first key field, a second key may be used as a tiebreaker.
- The range to be sorted should not include the field names row and should extend far enough to the right to encompass all the fields of the database. You should always save before sorting.
- Macros are similar to computer programs: they specify a sequence of operations for 1-2-3 to perform. You can record your actions and have them translated into macro form; this is easier than writing macros from scratch.
- You can run a macro from the Transcript window, by assigning a range name or by including the macro in a button. You should save the worksheet before running a macro.

- You can create customized buttons and assign macros to them.
- Macros can be edited and customized.

Key Terms and Operations

Key Terms	**Operations**
database	Append Records
database range	Clear
execute	Delete Records
field	Find Records
key	Record (macro)
macro	Sort
record (database)	
search	
sort	

Study Questions

Multiple Choice

1. In a 1-2-3 database, a row of information is referred to as
   - a. a field
   - b. a record
   - c. a form
   - d. criteria
   - e. a data list

2. The database range consists of
   - a. only the database records.
   - b. only the field names row.
   - c. the database records and the field names row.
   - d. the field names row and the first database record.
   - e. the first column of the database.

3. A database range to be sorted consists of
   - a. all database records but not the field names row.
   - b. all database records, including the field names row.
   - c. the key field column only.
   - d. the field names row and the first record.
   - e. the first column of the database.

4. Macros are recorded in the
   - a. Criterion range.
   - b. Edit window.
   - c. Information window.
   - d. Transcript window.
   - e. Macro window.

5. The field or column that serves as the basis for a sort is referred to as the
   - a. sort key.
   - b. sort criterion.
   - c. Sort Definition column.
   - d. Sort button.
   - e. Sort macro.

6. What is used as a tiebreaker to determine the ordering of records that have the same value for the primary sort key?
    a. the secondary key
    b. the tertiary key
    c. the primary criterion
    d. the secondary criterion
    e. the fallback criterion

7. What command can be used to remove only the styles from a cell (and not its contents)?
    a. Clear from the Edit menu
    b. Erase from the Edit menu
    c. Clear from the Format menu
    d. Format from the Clear menu
    e. None of the above

8. What is the result of a Find Records command?
    a. the first record of the database is selected
    b. the rows specified by the criterion are selected
    c. the field names are selected
    d. the columns specified by the criterion are selected
    e. the Find dialog box is displayed

9. What command is used to run a recorded macro from the Transcript window?
    a. Run from the Options menu
    b. Execute from the Macro menu
    c. Run from the Transcript menu
    d. Playback from the Transcript menu
    e. Macro Run from the Data menu

10. Macros are stored in
    a. a worksheet file
    b. a transcript file
    c. a macro file
    d. a macro dialog box
    e. any of the above

Short Answer

1. The column titles in a 1-2-3 database are used to identify what database component?

2. What field(s) would be most appropriate for keeping track of people's full names?

3. The telephone Yellow Pages uses what field as its primary key? Secondary key?

4. What does a 1-2-3 database range consist of? How does this differ from a sorting range?

5. Can sorting be used outside the context of databases?

6. Can a recorded macro be examined and edited? If so, where is it stored?

7. Is 1-2-3 case-sensitive in its use of range names?

8. If a new record is added by means of an Append Records command, will 1-2-3 adjust the definition of the database range?

9. What command is used to specify the range for a 1-2-3 database?

10. What steps are required to create customized buttons?

For Discussion

1. Why is sorting a dangerous operation? What steps can you take to minimize its hazards?

2. Explain the general steps involved in planning, recording, and executing a macro.

3. When you are designing a database, what principles should guide your specification of its fields?

Review Exercises

Creating a Macro to Sort by the Match Field

If the worksheet is not already loaded, open CHKBAL2.WK4, and create a range name called CHKREG for the database (be sure not to include the column headings in the range). Choose Macro from the Tools menu, and then select Record.

Record a macro that sorts the database by the Number field. Copy and then paste the macro to a separate worksheet. Assign a range name to the macro called SORTBYNUMBER. Create a button, similar to the Add button already on the worksheet, to run the macro. Save the worksheet before running the macro.

Birthday Database

Open the BDAY worksheet that you created in an assignment at the end of Project 6. Modify the worksheet to include a column *Last Name*, as shown in 7.16.

	A	B	C	D	E	F	G
1	Today's Date	25-Feb-94					
2	First Name	Last Name	Birth Date	Age	Birthday this Month?		
3	Carmen	Hunter	14-Mar-68	26	No		
4	Clem	Richardson	29-Oct-59	34	No		
5	Govinda	Smithers	08-Nov-72	21	No		
6	Gwendolyn	Jones	01-Jul-73	21	No		
7	Jane	Jones	03-Jun-73	21	No		
8	Mei Ling	Hsu	27-May-71	23	No		
9	Rahula	Jet	15-Jan-74	20	No		
10	Rolf	Johanson	17-Sep-74	19	No		
11	Sarvipali	Oman	14-Dec-70	23	No		
12	Xu	Chang	02-Apr-72	22	No		
13	Zhi	Hsu	23-Feb-75	19	Yes		
14							

Figure 7.16

Assign a range name, BIRTHDAYS, that consists of the column headings and rows for first and last name, birth date, and age. Use the Find Records command to display the names of people in the database who are 21 or older. Sort the names alphabetically by last name (remember not to include column headings in the sort).

Assignments

Macros for Commonly Typed Text

One common use for short macros is to type boilerplate text—that is, frequently used words or phrases. With a new worksheet, start the Macro Recorder. While the Recorder is running, type and enter your full name in a cell, and then format the cell to display text in the Times New Roman font, with an italic font style and a size of 14 points. Then type your social security number in the next cell down, and type information identifying your class section in the cell below that. The lower two cells should be formatted as Courier New, regular, and 12 points. Turn the recorder off.

Test the macro in various cells. Copy and then paste the the macro to a worksheet named BOILERPLATE.

Movie Database

Listing movies is a natural and common database application for small computers. Make a database listing your own top-ten movies or TV shows. Include fields for title, leading actor, genre, year produced, and any other aspect that you want to track. Create macros for adding movies to the database. Save the worksheet under the name MOVIE.WK4.

College Class Database

Design and construct a database that lists college classes you have taken or are currently enrolled in. Include such fields as course number, instructor, location, credit hours, and grade received. Write macros (with customized buttons) that sort the database in several different orders. Save the worksheet under the name CLASSES.WK4.

Operations Reference

FILE

Menu item	Mouse/SmartIcon	Keyboard	Description
New			Creates a new worksheet.
Open		CTRL + O	Opens an existing worksheet file on disk.
Close	Double-click worksheet's Control-menu box.	ALT + -	Closes the current worksheet.
Save		CTRL + S	Saves the current worksheet to disk.
Save As			Saves the current worksheet under a new name.
Protect			Seals (protects with a password) the current worksheet file.
Print Preview			Shows simulated printout of pages on-screen.
Page Setup			Specifies print size, orientation (portrait or landscape), and whether grid lines are to be printed.
Print		CTRL + P	Prints current worksheet, all worksheets, or currently selected range.
Exit		ALT + 4	Exits (ends) the Lotus 1-2-3 program.
	Double-click application's Control-menu box.		

EDIT

Menu item	Mouse/SmartIcon	Keyboard	Description
Undo		CTRL + Z	Undoes the previous command or action (not always possible).
Cut		CTRL + X	Removes information and places it in the clipboard.
Copy		CTRL + C	Copies information to the clipboard.
Paste		CTRL + V	Pastes information from the clipboard to a selection.
Clear		DEL	Clears cell contents, cell styles, or both.
Paste Special			Pastes cell contents, styles, or both from the clipboard to a range.
Copy Down	Select range, press right mouse button, and choose Copy Down.		Copies the topmost cell in a range to the other cells within the range.
Copy Right	Select range, press right mouse button, and choose Copy Right.		Copies the leftmost cell in a range to the other cells within the range.
Insert		CTRL + +	Inserts a row, column, or new worksheet.
Delete		CTRL + −	Deletes a row, column, or worksheet.
Go To		F5	Positions the active cell to a new position or to a named range.

VIEW

Menu item	Mouse/SmartIcon	Keyboard	Description
Zoom In			Magnifies the view of the worksheet by 10 percent.
Zoom Out			Reduces the view of the worksheet by 10 percent.
Custom			Sets a custom magnification of the worksheet.
Set View Preferences			Selects a new custom zoom percent and allows changing various window controls.

Style

Menu item	Mouse/SmartIcon	Keyboard	Description
Number Format	Click leftmost box on status bar.		Controls the appearance of values (formulas and numbers).
Font & Attributes	 Click within status bar.		Controls the typeface, size, and attributes of cell entries.
Lines & Color			Sets shading, colors, and borders of a selection.
Alignment			Sets the horizontal/vertical alignment and orientation of cell entries.
Gallery			Assigns combinations of cell styles automatically.
Column Width	Drag right edge of column heading to change column width; double-click edge for "best fit."		Sets the width of a column.
Row Height	Drag bottom edge of row number to change row height.		Sets the height of a row.
Protection			Controls whether cells in a range or collection are locked after the file is sealed.
Hide			Displays/hides columns or worksheets.
Worksheet Defaults			Sets default font and attribute settings for worksheets.

TOOLS

Menu item	Mouse/SmartIcon	Keyboard	Description
Chart			Creates a chart from the selected range.
Draw Button			Creates a button that can be assigned to a macro.
Database Find Records			Searches a database based upon selected criteria.
Delete Records			Deletes database records based upon selected criteria.
Append Records			Adds records to a database from a specified range.
Spell Check			Checks the spelling of the worksheet.
Audit	Click on *Circ* within status bar.		Finds cell dependents, formula precedents, and circular references in a worksheet.
Macro Run			Executes a macro.
Record			Records a macro.
Show			Displays recorded macro commands.
Transcript			

RANGE

Menu item	Mouse/SmartIcon	Keyboard	Description
Fill			Fills a range with values based on a starting value and increment.
Fill by Example			Fills a range with a sequence based on example data.
Sort			Sorts information in a range.
Name			Creates a range name.

WINDOW

Menu item	Mouse/SmartIcon	Keyboard	Description
Tile			Arranges worksheet windows so that all windows are displayed.
Cascade			Arranges worksheet windows in a cascaded fashion.

HELP

Menu item	Mouse/SmartIcon	Keyboard	Description
Contents			Displays table of contents for Help system.
Search			Displays searchable, alphabetical index of all Help topics.

Glossary

@function A built-in mathematical operation. Lotus 1-2-3 has more than 200 @functions with many uses. Perhaps the most common @function is @SUM, which totals the values in a range of cells. Example: @SUM(A3..A7) sums the range of cells from A3 to A7.

absolute cell reference A cell reference that does not change, even when the formula that contains the reference is copied. Either the row, column, or both the row and the column of an address may be absolute. Examples: A$1, $A1, $A$1. Also called an *absolute address*. Contrast with relative cell reference.

active cell *See* current cell.

application window The window that represents the Lotus 1-2-3 program.

argument (to a function) A piece of information provided to an @function. Some @functions, such as @NOW, require no arguments; others require one or several. Multiple arguments are separated by commas, as in @IF(A3>5,1,0).

border A decorative line attached to one or more sides of a cell. A variety of line styles are available.

case sensitive A computer program or function within a program that distinguishes between capital and lowercase letters is said to be case sensitive. Case sensitivity can affect the outcome of sorting operations and formulas that perform logical tests.

category name In charting, a category describes a certain circumstance for a variable, which means a variable has a particular value under a certain category. The categories appear along the bottom edge (X-axis) of a chart. Each category is labeled with a category name.

cell The basic building block of an electronic spreadsheet; the intersection of a column and a row. Cells are referred to by indicating their column and row. A cell is a holding place where you can store information.

cell dependent Cell (containing formulas) that depends on a particular cell for information.

cell reference A cell's address, usually expressed in terms of its column and row on the worksheet. For example, the cell at the intersection of column C and row 15 has the reference C15. A file with multiple worksheets may refer to a cell in any worksheet by specifying the worksheet name as part of the cell reference. For example, cell B:C15 refers to cell C15 in worksheet B.

chart A graph that displays quantitative information visually rather than using text and numbers.

circular reference A formula that directly or indirectly refers to itself. Circular references are almost always mistakes. Example: the formula +0.08*C15, if contained in cell C15, would be a circular reference.

collection A selection of cells consisting of several ranges.

column The vertical subdivision of a worksheet; columns are labeled with letters of the alphabet.

Contents box The area of the Lotus 1-2-3 window that displays the contents of the active cell.

current cell The active cell, as outlined by the thick border of the current-cell rectangle. The current cell is the place where the next action or command will occur. The current cell's address is displayed in the selection indicator.

data labels Labels appearing along chart axes, usually row or column headings corresponding to chart categories.

data series A set of related data values or observations used in constructing charts. The gross national product for each of the years 1970 through 1990 is an example of a data series.

database An organized table or list of information. The rows of a database are called records and the columns are called fields.

database range A range name consisting of database rows and row headings.

date arithmetic Use of calendar dates in mathematical calculations. For example, Lotus 1-2-3 dates can be subtracted from one another to determine the number of days between the two dates.

date number A number that represents the number of days since January 1, 1900. For example, May 7, 1995, is stored as a date number of 34826. Date numbers are most useful when assigned a number format appropriate for dates.

drag and drop The ability to "drag" the contents of a cell from one location to another and to "drop" the information into another cell. May be used to copy or move data.

edit line The area of the Lotus 1-2-3 window containing the Selection indicator, Contents box, and the Cancel and Confirm buttons.

execute To run a program or macro; to cause the program or macro to perform the instructions that comprise the program or macro.

explode   In pie charts, to emphasize a particular pie slice by pulling it out from the pie.

field   Within a database record, a field is a specific category (usually a column) of information. For example, a personnel record will contain fields for Social Security number, first name, last name, street address, and so forth.

file   A named collection of data stored on disk. In Lotus 1-2-3, a file may contain one or more worksheets.

font   A typeface; a kind of letterform. In Lotus 1-2-3, each font has a name (such as Arial), a size (such as 10 points), and an attribute (such as italic). Effects such as underlining and color can also be applied to a font.

formula   A type of cell entry that performs a calculation. All formulas begin with an @ (at) sign. Normally, the result of the formula (as opposed to the formula itself) appears within the worksheet. Formulas automatically change their result if there are changes in the cells upon which they depend. Formulas are the main reason that electronic spreadsheets are so useful.

formula precedent   Cell upon which formulas in other cells depend. A change in a formula precedent can cause the result of a dependent formula to change.

handles   Small black squares appearing around a chart or drawn object in a worksheet. Handles may be dragged with the mouse to resize the object.

I-beam   The shape of the pointer when the pointer is positioned within the Contents box, or when editing a cell.

key   In database sorting, a key is a field used to determine the ordering of records. The primary key determines the major sorting order; records having the same primary key can be ordered using a secondary key. In a telephone book, the primary key is the last name and the secondary key is the first name.

label   A text constant, usually representing comments, titles, or other nonmathematical information.

label prefix character   An indicator to Lotus 1-2-3 that the contents of a cell must be a label. Normally, 1-2-3 determines whether a cell entry is a label or a value based on the first character entered into a cell. If a label prefix character is entered as the first character of a cell, 1-2-3 will make that cell a label. Label prefix characters are also used to align cell contents.

landscape orientation   The orientation of a page with the long edge positioned horizontally.

legend   On a chart, a legend shows how different colors and data markers correspond to the data series used to make the chart.

linked text   On a chart, linked text is derived from a worksheet. If the original text changes in the worksheet, the linked text in the chart changes as well.

macro   A kind of computer program written specifically to run within Lotus 1-2-3. Simple macros consist of recorded 1-2-3 commands.

main menu   In Lotus 1-2-3, the row of commands appearing below the Menu bar consisting of File, Edit, View, Style, Tools, Range, Window, and Help.

mixed cell reference   A cell reference in which only the column reference or only the row reference is fixed. Examples: A$1, $A1.

number (number constant)   Numbers are constant numeric values (such as 3 or -1.9) and are a basic type of cell entry.

number format   The method used to punctuate numbers. Lotus 1-2-3 has several number formats, including U.S. Currency ($10.00), Comma (1,000), Percent (10.3%), and several date number formats.

point (measurement unit)   The basic unit of typographic measurement; a point is 1/72 of an inch. Used to describe the size of printed characters.

point mode   A method of building formulas that reduces the need to keep track of literal cell references and instead allows you to use the mouse or arrow keys to point to the cells or ranges that are to be referred to in the formula.

portrait orientation   The orientation of a page with the long edge positioned vertically.

precedent   The order in which mathematical calculations are performed. For example, mathematical operators such as multiplication and division have higher precedence than addition and subtraction. The formula 1 + 2*3 equals 7 (not 9), because the multiplication is performed before the addition.

precedent   See formula precedent.

protect   A method of preventing cells from being overwritten by unauthorized users of a worksheet. Initially all cells are protected, but the file must be sealed before the protection is activated. Individual cells may be selectively unprotected before the worksheet is sealed to allow those cells to be changed.

range   A rectangular block of cells identified by any two of its diagonal corner cells. A range can be as small as one cell or as large as the entire worksheet. Example: the rectangle of cells whose upper-left corner is A3 and whose lower-right corner is D5 is called A3..D5.

range name   A user-created name that refers to a cell or a range of cells. Range names can make formulas and macros easier to read and understand.

record (database)   A row of information in a database. A record is composed of fields.

relative cell reference   Within a formula, a cell reference that can change if the formula is copied. This is the default (standard) kind of cell reference in Lotus 1-2-3 formulas and is most often what will work best if a formula is copied. Contrast with absolute cell reference.

row   The horizontal subdivision of a worksheet. Rows are labeled with numbers.

Selection indicator   Located at the left of the Edit line, the Selection indicator displays the current cell address or range.

SmartIcon   Provides a shortcut for a 1-2-3 command. The menu bar displays the task a SmartIcon will perform if the right mouse button is pressed while the pointer is positioned over a SmartIcon.

sort   To rearrange information according to some ordering rule. Usually sorting is applied to 1-2-3 range names.

spreadsheet   *See* worksheet.

status bar   The bottom portion of the Lotus 1-2-3 window, the status bar displays characteristics of the active cell (such as number format, number of decimal places, font, and point size). The status bar also provides various worksheet mode indicators and shows the current date and time.

text constant   Data, usually consisting of words, that serves to identify parts of the worksheet or store non-numeric information.

value   A number constant or a formula that produces a numeric result. Values can be used in arithmetic calculations.

worksheet (spreadsheet)   A table consisting of rows and columns of information, ideal for setting up calculations for a wide variety of applications. Originally implemented manually on green columnar paper, worksheets can now be manipulated electronically with programs such as Lotus 1-2-3.

worksheet window   The window in which the worksheet is displayed. Several worksheet windows may be active at one time, and one worksheet window may contain several worksheets. The worksheet window usually is maximized within the application window.

wrapping text   To break a long line of text into two or more lines.

X-axis   The horizontal axis (usually the bottom edge) of a chart. The X-axis is often broken into the various chart categories.

Y-axis   The vertical axis (usually the left edge) of a chart. The Y-axis is often a numerical scale.

Index